PREVENTING TEEN VIOLENCE

**Recent Titles in
Contemporary Psychology**

Resilience for Today: Gaining Strength from Adversity
Edith Henderson Grotberg, editor

The Destructive Power of Religion: Violence in Judaism, Christianity, and
Islam, Volumes I-IV
J. Harold Ellens, editor

Helping Children Cope with the Death of a Parent: A Guide for the First Year
Paddy Greenwall Lewis and Jessica G. Lippman

Martyrdom: The Psychology, Theology, and Politics of Self-Sacrifice
*Rona M. Fields, with Contributions from Cóilin Owens, Valérie Rosoux,
Michael Berenbaum, and Reuven Firestone*

Redressing the Emperor: Improving Our Children's Public Mental Health System
John S. Lyons

Havens: Stories of True Community Healing
Leonard Jason and Martin Perdoux

Psychology of Terrorism, Condensed Edition: Coping with the
Continuing Threat
Chris E. Stout, editor

Handbook of International Disaster Psychology, Volumes I-IV
Gilbert Reyes and Gerard A. Jacobs, editors

The Psychology of Resolving Global Conflicts: From War to Peace,
Volumes 1-3
Mari Fitzduff and Chris E. Stout, editors

The Myth of Depression as Disease: Limitations and Alternatives
to Drug Treatment
Allan M. Leventhal and Christopher R. Martell

Preventing Teen Violence

A Guide for Parents and Professionals

Sherri N. McCarthy
and
Claudio Simon Hutz

Contemporary Psychology
Chris E. Stout, Series Editor

Westport, Connecticut
London

Library of Congress Cataloging-in-Publication Data

Preventing teen violence : a guide for parents and professionals/edited by
Sherri N. McCarthy and Claudio Simon Hutz.
  p. cm. — (Contemporary psychology, ISSN 1546–668X)
Includes bibliographical references and index.
ISBN 0–275–98246–7
  1. Juvenile delinquency. 2. Juvenile delinquency—Prevention. 3. Violent
crimes—Prevention. 4. Violence in children. I. McCarthy, Sherri N. II. Hutz,
Claudio Simon. III. Contemporary psychology (Praeger Publishers)
HV9069.P74 2006
364.36—dc22   2005026907

British Library Cataloguing in Publication Data is available.

Library of Congress Catalog Card Number: 2005026907
ISBN: 0–275–98246–7
ISSN: 1546–668X

First published in 2006

Praeger Publishers, 88 Post Road West, Westport, CT 06881
An imprint of Greenwood Publishing Group, Inc.
www.praeger.com

Printed in the United States of America

The paper used in this book complies with the
Permanent Paper Standard issued by the National
Information Standards Organization (Z39.48–1984).

10 9 8 7 6 5 4 3 2 1

Contents

Preface

The idea for this book was born a few years ago, after the tragedy of September 11, 2001. I was asked to write a chapter for *The Psychology of Terrorism* (Stout, 2002). While writing that chapter it occurred to me that attitudes toward violence and levels of aggression were key factors in determining whether a person—particularly an adolescent—is likely to engage in an act of terrorism. Thus, that chapter became the seed for this book and has been expanded and refocused on factors responsible for adolescents' acts of aggression.

More important than understanding the factors responsible, however, is taking a proactive stance toward preventing senseless violence among adolescents and constructively refocusing aggression. Thus, even more than examining causes of aggression, this book seeks to offer suggestions for societal solutions and provide specific strategies and techniques for working with adolescents.

The current reality for adolescents in many parts of the world is a violent one. War—whether gang warfare within neighborhoods, civil war, or socially sanctioned warfare between countries—is an experience faced by many of our youth. School shootings and beatings are increasingly common, and the more subtle forms of violence such as bullying and sexual abuse continue. Anyone who interacts with adolescents, whether as a psychologist, teacher, probation officer, counselor, parent, relative, or neighbor, can benefit by a better understanding of aggressive behavior. What are the potential causes? How can such behavior be constructively channeled? These are the questions we seek to answer in this book.

I knew from the beginning that I could not answer these questions alone. I asked my coauthor, Dr. Claudio S. Hutz, then Dean of the School of Psychology at the Federal University of Rio Grande do Sul, Brazil, and an expert in adolescent psychology who has worked with youth in several countries, to undertake this somewhat daunting task with me. This, I hope, provides a broader, more international perspective to the questions addressed here. I also asked several colleagues responsible for important research in this area of adolescent psychology to assist. Most notably, Dr. Edith Grotberg, whose work on resilience in adolescents is internationally respected, contributed text and ideas that are interwoven throughout the book. Dr. Ludwig Lowenstein, who has long been involved in working with troubled adolescents in the United Kingdom, provided valuable information on sex offenders and victims of sexual abuse. Dr. William Kolodinsky and Dr. Vincent Schroeder, both of whom have worked with sex offenders in Florida, also contributed. Dr. Augustus L. Little, former president of the American Middle School Association and long-time veteran of school violence through his work as a teacher and administrator in public schools in New York City and Florida, as well as university teacher preparation, offered his expertise. So did his wife Suzanne, a teacher, school psychologist, and mother of six. Dr. Thomas Franklin Waters of Northern Arizona University shared his efforts with adolescent substance abusers. Dr. Elza Dutra of Federal University do Rio Grande do Norte, Brazil, shared her expertise on teen suicide. Dr. Carlo Prandini of Italy and Frank Hollingsworth, former president of Teachers of Psychology in Secondary Schools (TOPSS), developed one of the valuable teaching ideas shared here.

Some of my brilliant graduate students, not so long out of adolescence and their own experiences with anger and adolescent violence themselves, offered valuable insight, too. Andrew Gold's information on anger management, Michall Moore's contributions to Dr. Kolodinsky's section on sex offenders, and Diana Estrada's summary of statistical information and insights on teen violence are all recounted here. Dr. Jas Jafar, of the University of Malaysia, offered insight on teen development in the Muslim world. My Russian colleagues Dr. Natalia Parnyuk, Dr. Valerie Sitnikov, Dr. Victor Karandashev, Dr. Olga Yamashkiva, and Dr. Veronika Artemeyeva were invaluable, both in guiding my experiences with adolescents in Russia during my Fulbright Scholarship there in 2003–2004 and in sharing their own research on Russian adolescents. Elaine Schenkel, my special Brazilian guardian angel, shared her knowledge of public schools and helped familiarize me with the many aspects of culture relevant to adolescent development in Brazil. Christine and Peter Gaylarde, my "Brazilian parents from England," not only helped with relevant research from psychobiology but provided a wonderful environment for me in which to write.

Debra Carvalko, who initially believed in this project, and Elizabeth Potenza, my patient editor at Praeger, who reassured me through computer crashes and international communication problems, willingly extended my deadline and allowed the evolution of this book, also deserve credit. So does Rene Pinto, my traveling companion and shipmate across time and space, for help with last-minute translations and for keeping me sane during the stress of deadlines.

This book is dedicated to my grandson, Leif Janes, who I hope will have a safer world to grow up in, and to my children, Colin Tucker and Chrysallis Janes, and their many friends with whom I interacted as they traversed the dangerous passage of modern adolescence. All are now safely through that passage and sail on the calmer seas of young adulthood. But there were many times when I, as a parent trying to guide those young ships, feared they would crash on rocky shores and sink. My experiences as a parent, as much as my professional experiences as a teacher and psychologist working with adolescents, are responsible for my interest in this topic.

The first two chapters of this book provide a general overview of adolescence and adolescent aggression. These are followed by chapters directed toward specific issues such as school violence, sexual aggression, substance abuse, and suicide. The content includes specific applications for parents, counselors, teachers, psychologists, probation officers, and others who work with teens. Though this book is based on research and written by experts in adolescent psychology, it is written to be easily comprehended, engaging, and useful to all who interact with youth. Thus, though important references to original studies are provided for those who wish to delve further into technical research in this area, the book is designed for a general audience. We hope all who read it will find it useful and that it will, in some small way, contribute to a safer, saner, and more peaceful future world.

Sherri N. McCarthy

CHAPTER 1

DEFINING ADOLESCENCE AND EXAMINING ADOLESCENT AGGRESSION

Some of the information in this chapter originally appeared in Sherri McCarthy's contribution to The Psychology of Terrorism, *Chapter 8, Volume 4, edited by Chris E. Stout and published by Greenwood/Praeger in 2002. We would like to thank Dr. Edith Grotberg for her valuable contributions to this chapter. We would also like to recognize Andrew Gold's contributions to the information on anger management training recounted here.*

What Is Adolescence?

In the psychological literature, adolescence is generally defined as the transitional period between childhood and adulthood. Adolescence begins when the physical capability to reproduce is present and ends when a role implying adult status has been achieved (Muss, 1996). The age boundaries are not exact; they vary somewhat from culture to culture. Some societies, in fact, may not even include a period of adolescence (Schlegel & Barry, 1991), but it can be assumed that adolescence begins around the age of 12 years and ends around the age of 25 years, with some individual variation, in most industrialized countries today. These are rough estimates, of course, and individual variation exists within every culture. Sometimes, "rites of passage," either formally or informally created, determine entry into adulthood (McCarthy, Prandini, & Hollingsworth, 2001). Bat mitzvah or cincinera, a debutante ball or receiving a driver's license, voting or military service, graduation from secondary school or university, supporting oneself financially or getting married, becoming a parent or becoming fully legally responsible for one's actions—all of these events may, to some degree, determine the end of adolescence and entry to adulthood.

A protracted period of adolescence is seen primarily in highly industrialized nations where advanced education is required to enter the workplace and economic independence from parents is seen as a "right of passage" into the adult world, but even this varies greatly. "Street kids" responsible for their own survival both physically and economically from a very early age also coexist in these countries along with their more advantaged peers (Hutz, da Silva, & McCarthy, 2004; Sitnikov & Parnyuk, 2004).

During adolescence, which occurs primarily during high school and early college years for the majority of youth in industrialized nations, many critical attitudes and behaviors are solidified. Erickson (1968) postulated that adolescence was a period of pivotal importance, when one's identity was formed. Adolescents wrestle with such important issues as "What do I stand for?" "Who am I?" and "What do I want to do with my life?" The answers to these questions derived during adolescence allow individuals to commit not only to an occupational direction but also to a value system (Marcia, 1991). This value system is naturally an important factor in determining the types of behavior seen as acceptable.

The struggle for identity and development of a cohesive and satisfactory value system may be an ongoing process throughout each of our lives, but it is particularly intense during adolescence. The advent of formal operational thought, as explained by Piaget (Inhelder & Piaget, 1958), promotes self-reflection and can even express as a particular form of egocentrism (Elkind, 1985) in which adolescents assume they are the central focus of others' attention. The physical changes of puberty, including the increased levels of adrenaline that fuel the growth spurt and the advent of hormonal changes, heighten perceptions and intensify feelings. Experiences seem more vivid. Memories become more deeply rehearsed and processed.

For these reasons, attitudes formed during the stage of identity formation that occurs during adolescence are likely to be long lasting, even permanent, and to exert a great influence on behavior. One's self-concept, as determined initially during adolescence, is critical to regulating behavior in the future. One's sense of possible selves (Markus & Nurius, 1986), based on experiences, modeling, and information acquired during this period, can influence the likelihood of engaging in or refraining from violent activities. The attitudes toward others established during adolescence can lead either toward or away from a tendency to stereotype members of groups (religious, ethnic, economic, or cultural) to which one does not belong. This can result in hate and prejudice. Hate crimes, racial conflict, and gang warfare are built on these stereotypes, and experiences during adolescence will either exacerbate or prevent development of these attitudes.

Note that these attitudes are *formed* during adolescence; however, they are not in place during that period of life. They are not inborn traits, although particular tendencies that are likely to be triggered by certain types of socialization may be inborn, and they are not irreversible. The violence engaged in by adolescents may be viewed as a sort of experimental interaction with the environment. Both the extent to which adolescents experiment with violent behavior and the ways in which they experiment are socially determined and constrained by the environment (both physical and social) within which they mature.

Although many of us seem to expect adolescents to behave as adults, suffer the consequences of their own behavior as adults (this is especially true in the U.S. criminal justice and public education systems at present), and reason as adults, it is important to remember that, despite a physical appearance that may suggest otherwise and their own attitudes to the contrary, this is not a reasonable expectation. Adolescents do not function as adults. They are experimenting with adult behaviors and attitudes by their actions just as an infant experiments by continually dropping objects to the floor to learn about cause and effect. Results of this experimentation may be as messy, in a different way, as the infant's full cereal bowl continually tossed from the high chair to the kitchen tiles. In fact, when it comes to violent behavior, it is even messier, sometimes having deadly consequences. But it is still just experimentation. The infant will throw down the objects that are readily available, and the results of the experimentation with these objects will be critically important in the development of cognitive reasoning skills and intelligence. The adolescent will experiment with behaviors that are readily observed and available, and the result of this experimentation will be the values that govern future behaviors. Thus, the period of adolescence is a critical window for constructively channeling aggression. Educational strategies aimed at the prevention of developing attitudes that lead to violence and hate crimes are especially useful during this time of development.

What Is Adolescent Aggression?

According to the *Oxford Pocket Dictionary*, the term *aggression* means "an unprovoked attack." An *aggressor* is one who is likely to make an unprovoked attack or start a quarrel. *Roget's Thesaurus* lists several synonyms for the term *aggression* including attack, offense, invasion, irruption, siege, bombardment, air raid, combat, and dispute. Synonyms for *aggressor* are soldier, warrior, combatant, troops, and other terms depicting military forces. This brief foray into common definitions is telling.

Society as a whole, at least modern U.S. society, tends to condemn adolescent aggression and view it as inappropriate while condoning military action and warfare. Yet, at their roots, both are identical—at least in a semantic sense. Keeping in mind that adolescents still frequently encode literal messages, as do children, and have difficulty with ambiguities and fine distinctions, it is no surprise that adolescents raised in a cultural milieu that condones warfare and military action view violence and acts of aggression as acceptable parts of daily life. Yet, from the point of view of parents, teachers, counselors, police, and the adult world in general, unprovoked violence by teens—and even provoked violence, when the provocation is not viewed as credible from the mainstream adult social perspective—is definitely unacceptable. Distinctions are made between firing unprovoked on one's classmates and firing on "the enemy," whoever that enemy might be and for whatever reasons that group might be defined as an enemy. But such distinctions can be difficult for adolescents—and perhaps even many adults—to make, especially when it comes to defining the enemy who deserves to be shot.

Is aggression ultimately wrong? If one espouses a pacifistic viewpoint, perhaps it is; yet it may still serve some long-range evolutionary value, because it has been a part of human behavior for so long. Current research in both genetics and psychopharmacology is even defining genes, chemicals, and hormones responsible for aggressive impulses (Brown, Goodwin, Ballenger, Goyen, & Major, 1979; Cocorro, 1987; Vergnes, Depaulo, & Boehrer, 1986). If aggressiveness is a part of human biochemical make-up, it is likely there for some ultimate creative purpose. Our purpose here is not to judge aggression, but simply to define it. We note that acts of adolescent aggression are problematic in our current society and hope to find ways of remedying this problem. Adolescent aggression for our purposes is defined as socially unacceptable acts resulting in harm to oneself, others, or the property of others, often involving physical violence and force. It includes obvious acts resulting in physical harm and death such as drive-by shootings, school shootings, and violent rape. It also includes less obvious acts such as bullying, intimidation, hazing, and destruction of property through vandalism or arson. Threats to others and misuse of authority are acts of aggression. Mutilating or harming animals is included in the definition. So is suicide and intentionally harming oneself through substance abuse, vomiting/bulimia, cutting, and other forms of self-harm, albeit these forms of aggression are directed only at the self.

What Factors Are Responsible for Adolescent Aggression?

As noted previously, recent research has indicated that our genetic make-up and our brain chemistry can contribute to acts of aggression (Cocorro, 1987). Genes and biochemistry should not become a scapegoat for acts of aggression, however. Pop culture seems to be in danger of replacing the old "Devil made me do it" clichéd blame for antisocial acts to "Genes and brain chemicals made me do it," or made *them* do it, as one of the more bizarre arguments from the discipline of criminology for imprisoning large numbers of adolescents, discussed more in future chapters, asserts. Genes and brain chemicals alone are not responsible. The interaction between genes and environment is dynamic. Environmental factors that trigger the genetic potential for aggression or that influence brain chemistry to result in more of a propensity for violence are required, too. And even when both genetic or biochemical potential and environmental triggers exist, violence and aggression often do not occur. Individual will and self-control, morals, and events all exert inhibitory influences. Thus, we cannot just "blame it on the genes" and label a violent child a "bad seed." Nor can we limit all of our attempts at solutions to modifying brain chemistry through psychopharmacology. We need to identify and control environmental triggers that lead to violence and aggression among teens, and we also need to identify ways of developing the internal emotional control that inhibits violence. As Edith Grotberg (2003) so aptly notes, we need to make teens resilient against behaving aggressively. She writes:

Genetic variations affect how people respond to stress, with some being vulnerable to depression and others being resilient. The conclusion is that the environment makes the difference (Insel, 2003). And it is the environment that makes possible the promotion of resilience, a universal human capacity. New findings strengthen the importance of resilience and the role of the environment in promoting resilience. This includes awareness that the genetic make-up of individuals may influence which resiliency factors are most effective. For example, self-confidence and optimism are more likely to benefit youth with the tendency to become depressed when adversities loom. Management of impulses, responsibility, respect, empathy, and caring for others are more likely to benefit youth who have a tendency to become violent. The task, however, is made more difficult in light of the attractiveness of violence in our society.

We revisit research on resilience later in the book and also look at moral development and strategies for developing self-control. Here we summarize a few environmental triggers that lead to adolescent aggression.

Stress

There is no doubt that we live in a world that is stressful. Not all types of stress are harmful, of course. Making choices induces stress. Attaining goals and high achievements induce stress. There appears to be an "optimum level" of stress for each person, and a total lack of stress in a physical sense is death. Separation and bereavement also induce stress, though, as does the hectic pace at which most of us must live our daily lives. This hectic pace is increasingly transmitted to our children, who are overscheduled from early childhood and given little time for the real business of children—discovery through free play. Longer school days, more days of school each year, day care, summer camps with organized and structured activities, dance and music lessons, youth groups, and part-time jobs increasingly characterize our youth. This, combined with other truly stressful situations, such as the media focus on fear—terrorism, crime, violence, and war—has likely created the most "stressed out" generation we have yet seen.

High mobility also creates stress. Most children in the United States today have moved more than three times before even reaching adolescence; this constant separation from home, friends, and extended family induces grief (often unresolved) and separation anxiety. Divorce rates continue to climb, and separation from parents, even if only briefly, also introduces stress even in the most civil of arrangements. It may well be that the radical increase in attention deficit disorders we have seen in the last generation, especially in the United States, is nothing more than a natural biochemical adaptation to increased stress. This hypothesis has certainly been entertained in the psychological literature, and there is even some evidence in support of it.

Without a doubt, the current generation experiences more stress, and of a different and more on-going nature, than any generation before. It is no longer just children in war zones, famine zones, and areas of major environmental disaster and plague zones who experience posttraumatic stress syndrome. All children are at risk. As the stress is ongoing, it cannot even be viewed as a posttraumatic condition.

Extreme stress triggers a flight-or-fight syndrome by releasing the neurochemicals and hormones responsible for this response, such as adrenaline, cortisone, and others. These neurochemicals and hormones also trigger aggression (Brown et al., 1979; Fanselow, 1991; Flannely, Murroko, Blanchard, & Blanchard, 1985; Vergnes et al., 1986). This is true for people of all ages, but particularly salient for adolescents, where vulnerability to fear, anxiety, trauma, and stress is heightened as a result of physiological and psychological development. The same factors that make adolescents particularly vulnerable to the psychological impact of stress also make them particularly susceptible to developing attitudes and "scripts" that will lead to violent activities.

Social Expectations and Cognitive Attributions

A second important environmental factor that can lead to violence and aggression is social expectations as governed by attributions. Social psychology, in studies focused on person perception, causal attribution, and attitude formation, has provided us with much insight regarding how stereotypes form and how this can lead to prejudice, discrimination, and acts of violence toward others. Much of this is rooted in attribution theory. Attributions are inferences that people draw about the causes of their own behavior, the behavior of others, and events. In some cases, because of faulty logical processes, negative modeling, unsavory media influence, and other methods that lend themselves to propaganda, attributions may occur based on appearance alone. Physical features, combined with one's beliefs about what such features imply, are one of the most common ways impressions of others are formed (Bull & Rumsey, 1988).

Attributions contribute to perceiver expectancies. These expectancies then influence behavior toward others. This confirmation bias has been evidenced in many studies (Cohen, 1981; Fiske & Taylor, 1991; Fiske, 1993; Snyder, Tanke, & Berscheid, 1977) and seems related to stereotype formation and prejudice. When individuals encounter groups they view with prejudice, they are likely to see what they expect (Stephan, 1989). Behavior toward others can, in turn, influence the behavior of others. This is the self-fulfilling prophecy phenomenon described by Merton in 1948 and since documented empirically (Rosenthal, 1985). Adolescents are especially susceptible to this phenomenon because they are still unsure of their identities. As Swann and Ely (1984) demonstrated, self-fulfilling prophecy is most likely to occur when target persons are uncertain about their self-views.

Other common errors of attribution are also worth noting. Defensive attribution (Lerner & Miller, 1978) is the tendency to blame victims for their own misfortune. Several studies (Kristiansen & Giuletti, 1990; Salminen, 1992; Thornton, 1992) have illustrated this error. The fundamental attribution error (Ross, 1977) is the tendency to explain the negative behavior of others as connected to personal rather than situational factors, whereas one's own negative behavior is viewed as situationally determined. The reverse pattern characterizes positive acts—that is, situational for others and personal for self.

Other cognitive distortions related to the formation of attitudes that may lead to aggression and violence against members of particular groups include categorization and stereotyping. Individuals perceive those like themselves (on dimensions such as appearance, age, race, gender, religion, occupation, nationality, or some other salient dimension) as an "ingroup." Those who are not similar are perceived as an "outgroup." People usually have less favorable attitudes toward members of the outgroup (Meindl & Lerner, 1984). This is certainly a factor in adolescent gang violence and hate crimes based on race, gender, or sexual orientation.

Group categorization is likely a feature of the human brain "hardwired in." Efficiency of processing is dependent on categorization. Basic logical processes rely on it. Even safety and survival are rooted in the ability to quickly distinguish a predator from a nonpredator. Meta-cognitive awareness of this process, and how it functions, is essential to prevent stereotyping and prejudice. Stereotypes are widely held beliefs that membership in a certain group automatically bestows certain characteristics. The most prevalent stereotypes seem to be based on physical appearance, gender, age, and ethnicity (Eagly,

Ashmore, Makhijani, & Longo, 1991; Fiske, 1993). Stereotyping, in turn, leads to prejudice—the formation of a negative attitude toward all members of a particular group.

In addition to faulty attributions, categorization, and stereotyping, two other avenues that researchers have demonstrated lead to prejudice are competition for resources and threats to social identity. As the economy shifts to an increasingly capitalistic, global base, and Western society continues to encroach on other cultures, it becomes apparent that these two avenues are increasingly likely to be driven. More than half a century ago, Sherif's experiments (Sherif, Harvey, White, Hood, & Sherif, 1988) clearly demonstrated that competition led not only to prejudice against members of competing groups, but to violence against those members. Simple competition for resources is certainly not the only cause for striking out against others who are perceived as different, however. If individuals perceive that their group is being threatened, they often look for scapegoats in other groups (Pettigrew, 1978) and strike out against these groups. A perceived threat to the group is often seen as even more devastating than a personal threat (Bobo, 1988). These findings seem to provide a strikingly clear explanation for the rise of gang violence in the United States and even to wars. The ongoing struggle between northern Ireland and England, racial turbulence, and aversive racism (Dovidio & Gaertner, 1998) in South Africa and the United States, and tribal and religious warfare throughout the world can be explained in these terms. These world events are then transmitted to adolescents through direct or indirect experiences and media and become a major part of the behavioral repertoire they develop. These conflicts are viewed as acceptable, and violence is seen as a means of resolving conflicts. When perceived literally, in the black-and-white reasoning that bridges from adolescence to adulthood, this is encoded as a sanction for acts of aggression. Aggression becomes an acceptable behavior.

Media Influence

Evidence of the role media has on the attitudes and behavior of children and adolescents is well documented (Murray, 1980). Research over the last four decades (Bandura, 1968; Bandura, Ross, & Ross, 1963; Banks, 1971) has established that television plays a role in developing attitudes toward members of groups and influences actions. The vicarious modeling that occurs influences behavior among adolescent viewers and influences identity development. The roles Web-based entertainment, videogames, and music play are certainly similar. If young viewers are not educated to think critically about what they see, to question it, and to actively separate entertainment from reality, they are not likely to do so.

It is important to stress that media are best used as a tool in preventing violence, however, rather than as a scapegoat for its occurrence. Any movie, series, game, or song that presents members of other religious, racial, or geographic groups as enemies or subhuman must share in the blame for creating a mindset which leads to bullying, aggression, and intergroup conflict. Concerned citizens around the world should actively boycott and prevent such uses of media. Our present challenge is to use the media to provide programming, experiences, and models to youth that illustrate the fallacy of assuming that those who believe, look, think, or act differently should be attacked, discredited, or otherwise discounted. Using this powerful tool to stress human similarities across cultures and to highlight that individual differences are positive rather than negative is essential if we are to prevent youth from engaging in violence against members of other groups, other human beings, and other forms of life.

Peer Influence

The peer group becomes increasingly important during adolescence. In the United States, adolescents are likely to spend well over 50 percent of their time with age-mates (Csikszentmihalyi & Larson, 1984). Obviously, all of the time in school occurs with age-mates, but American teenagers also average more than 20 hours per week outside the classroom with peers, compared with 2 to 3 hours reported in Japan and Russia (Savin-Williams & Berndht, 1990). Peer relations can be either positive or negative, depending on what occurs. At best, such unsupervised interaction with peers can result in a bridge into adult social roles and an opportunity to develop friendships and social skills, and also to gain emotional support. At worst, they can reinforce the ingroup/outgroup dynamics that lead to prejudice and hate, antisocial behavior, and lack of attachment to society at large. What makes the difference?

Diversity versus homogeneity of the group with which an adolescent primarily associates is one important variable. An adolescent who interacts positively with peers from a variety of backgrounds (socioeconomic, cultural, geographical, and religious) is more likely to develop an acceptance of individual differences and a wariness of stereotyping; an adolescent who interacts only with peers who are similar is more likely to develop a mistrust of other groups. Such experiences during youth may even affect physiological responses of the amygdala and result in differential processing of emotional cues based on race or group (Hetherton, 2002; Phelps, O'Connor, Cunningham, Funayama, Gatenby, & Banaji, 2000) later in life. It is important to engage adolescents in positive, prosocial activities with diverse groups 'of friends. The tendency of adolescents to gravitate toward "rival gangs" based on race, economic factors, or attitudes should be counteracted to avoid the development of the mindset that leads to the ability to engage in terrorist belief systems and activities.

Role Models and Social Learning

The powerful role of social learning, based on identification with and imitation of others perceived as "high status" members of the community, has been well established for decades (Bandura, 1962, 1965, 1969, 1971). Adolescents look up to sports figures, political leaders, actors, and musicians, as well as family members and peers, to find "models." They use these models to help determine their own potential beliefs and actions—their "possible selves." The more consistent the modeling, especially among those with whom adolescents interact on a daily basis, the more powerful it is. If the models available to youth espouse values and attitudes that lead to prejudice, hate, mistrust of other groups, violent resolutions to problems, and aggression, then adolescents act aggressively. If, instead, the models espouse acceptance of diversity, nonviolent problem-solving strategies, and humanitarian values, then violence and aggression among adolescents are less likely to occur. Educational and societal interventions need to provide nonviolent models to adolescents.

Social Identity

Threat to one's social identity is another avenue that leads to prejudice and acts of violence. This may be relevant to the U.S. school shootings in Colorado, California, Arkansas, and elsewhere. Although no real "profile" for adolescents likely to engage in such acts has emerged from the efforts of U.S. criminal justice agencies, the one commonality that seems to characterize most cases is that of a rather isolated Caucasian male. In an educational environment increasingly tuned into diversity and cultural differences, it may be this group that has the least social identity and perceives the most threat. According to social identity theory (Tajfel, 1982; Turner, 1987), self-esteem is determined in part by the "collective self," which is tied to group membership. Salient groups include nationality, gender, religion, occupation, and so forth. Threats to both individual and group identity lower self-esteem and motivate individuals to engage in acts designed to restore it. Threats to group or social identity are most likely to provoke responses that foster prejudice, discrimination, or violence (Crocker & Luhtanen, 1990). A common way to deal with threats to one's social identity is through outgroup derogation—insulting, discounting, and otherwise harming others who are perceived as threatening (Branscombe & Wann, 1994). Social isolation and lack of a cohesive ingroup are likely to make such behavior even more likely.

Because of the heightened sensitivity and the struggle for identity that adolescence spurs, teens and young adults are even more likely to be susceptible to these reactions than adults. This is one situation where "knowledge is power," however, and Socrates's admonition to "Know thyself" can be a useful tool for understanding and regulating such behavior. Interventions that encourage self-examination and critical thinking are likely to be beneficial.

What Strategies Are Useful for Constructively Refocusing Adolescent Aggression?

The rest of this book is devoted to answering this question, but a brief overview of some of the strategies that will be referred to in subsequent chapters is offered here. If, as may well be the case, aggression has survived because it has some long-range purpose or evolutionary value to humankind, regulating and refocusing adolescent aggression seem more logical goals than attempting to punish and eradicate it. Several activities, such as individual and group sports and other forms of competition which may be useful for this, are discussed later. Martial arts training and various forms of relaxation training and biofeedback may also be useful and warrant further exploration.

Providing young adults with an understanding of the human tendencies to categorize described in the preceding section seems crucial, however, and a secondary school curriculum seems to be a natural place to include this content. A curriculum that not only points out such important information about human tendencies but that also breaks down barriers between groups and brings students into positive interactions with members of the "outgroups" they are threatened by is an even more powerful tool. Applying systematic interventions to reduce fear and prejudice while increasing self-understanding and critical thinking skills among youth seems to be our wisest course in combating senseless acts of violence by adolescents.

Interventions for Reducing Prejudice

Integrating strategies to prevent the formation of stereotypes that lead to prejudice and hate into high school and college curricula is critical if we wish to prevent violence and constructively redirect adolescent aggression. As previously alluded to, making individuals mindful of the ways in which stereotypes are formed and prejudice results is a powerful cognitive tool for diminishing aggression. Siegler (1991) has shown that providing adolescents with information that addresses specific flaws in their reasoning encourages them to use more advanced rules. Incorporating instruction in contextualized logic into the curriculum (McCarthy, 1999a), and focusing this instruction on disconfirmation of stereotypes and prejudice is a promising strategy. Devine's (1989) strategy of shifting from automatic to controlled processing or Langer's (Langer, Bashner, & Chanowitz, 1985) recommendation of incorporating "mindful" rather than "mindless" processing might be achieved in this way.

An even more powerful strategy for reducing prejudice is through controlled intergroup contact. As Fazio and others have demonstrated (Dovidio, 2002), the best predictor of reduced prejudice as measured by indirect, spontaneous measures is the amount of contact with other groups that has occurred early in life. Aronson (2001) has demonstrated for decades how use of cooperative learning in schools using heterogeneous grouping not only benefits student learning but also reduces contention among groups. His classic work on "jigsaw classrooms" (Aronson, Stephan, Sikes, Blaney, & Snapp, 1978) is relevant for reducing school violence against individuals perceived as "outgroup" members. Simply bringing members of potentially hostile groups into contact, however, is not sufficient. If not appropriately directed, such contact may actually exacerbate hostility and prejudice. Instead, the contact needs to be controlled to allow for positive interaction.

Brewer and Brown (1997) demonstrated several requisites for designing intergroup contact that reduces stereotypes and prejudice: (1) individuals from several groups must work together toward a common goal, (2) there must be a successful outcome or product from the cooperative efforts, (3) group members must have the opportunity to establish meaningful connections with one another that have the potential to develop into long-term friendships, and (4) the contact must be structured so that each individual is perceived as of equal status to the project. If these guidelines are followed, prejudice is reduced and acts of hate toward members of the group previously perceived as hostile are diminished. Given the research summarized previously, it seems clear that assignments that meet these criteria should be incorporated in classrooms around the world if we wish to reduce the likelihood of violent acts among our youth and citizens of tomorrow. More specific strategies for doing so are addressed in future chapters.

Channeling Anger Constructively

Anger seems to be a common emotional state for many adolescents. Whether anger is created by fear, insecurity, dissatisfaction, frustration, or a combination of these feelings, many adolescents experience it. Anger expresses itself in many different ways. It may be directed inward, resulting in substance abuse, eating disorders, self-mutilation, or even suicide. It may be directed outward, resulting in violent and antisocial acts toward others such as bullying, delinquency, gang violence, school shootings, or rape. Anger among youth seems to be on the rise, and constructive forms of dealing with this anger are lacking. It may be that anger is simply a form of energy to fuel action, and destructive acts are simply evidence that individuals have not been provided, through education and life experiences, with the tools for more creative or artistic expression of this energy (McCarthy & Gold, 2002). Some adolescents see only destructive acts in their environment and, lacking other options, social learning results in their participation in these observed destructive acts to release emotion. As a result, shootings at school are becoming frighteningly commonplace. Juvenile arrests for violent or aggressive acts have increased dramatically in recent years. In 1975, 1,273 juveniles were arrested for murder in the United States (Goldstein & Glick, 1987). By 1993, the number had nearly tripled, to 3,284, and it continues to rise. Juvenile courts, originally designed to deal with problems such as truancy and shoplifting, have been handling more than 1,500,000 cases per year since 1992 and the number is currently over 2,500,000. Of every 10 murders prosecuted in the United States currently, 1 was committed by someone under 18 years of age. If the definition of adolescence, as noted earlier, rather than the legal definition of adulthood, nearly half of the murders committed fall in that category. Violent acts committed by juveniles have risen in number proportionally far more rapidly than the number of juveniles in the population (Schatz & Eddington, 1995). Gang violence continues to increase. Aggression is another expression of inappropriately expressed anger directed at society.

Viable treatments to curb the aggressive behavior of adolescents need to be incorporated not only into offender rehabilitation but also into mainstream education (McCarthy & Gold, 2002; McCarthy, 2003). A major challenge facing counselors and educators is designing interventions that reduce violence and aggression. Psychology has devoted a considerable amount of study to the emotion of anger. From definitions and speculations on cause that date back to the work of William James in the last century and the James-Lange theory of emotion to current cross-cultural research into facial expression and bodily responses, psychology has explored and attempted to define the emotion of anger. A vast literature base on causes, correlates, and definitions of anger exists. In addition to definitions, psychology has provided several methods for measuring individual differences in anger, aggression, and hostility (Tagnney et al., 1996). Observational techniques such as event sampling, tallying and observer rating scales are common. Many tests have also been developed to predict likelihood of aggressive acts and to assess perceived levels of aggression (McCarthy, Gold, & Garcia, 1999).

Research indicates that improvements gained by traditional behavior modification programs decrease when the program is withdrawn (Marriott & Iwata, 1984). Barfield and Hutchinson (1989) noted that a group setting using a variety of teaching and experiential modalities offered helpful alternatives to habitual maladaptive expressions of anger by adolescent boys in residential treatment and tended to have lasting impact after release. LeCroy (1988) found that clients in residential treatment centers who received anger management training reduced the frequency of angry outbursts. In addition to decreasing observed aggressive behaviors, the training also resulted in clients reporting other positive benefits, such as an increased ability to relax.

Bistline and Friederick (1984) found long-term and stable reduction of perceived anger and observed aggressive acts resulting from implementing cognitive-behavioral techniques of stress inoculation to control anger. Kellner and Tutin (1995) developed an anger management training strategy that aimed to teach adolescents more about the physiology, consequences, and triggers of anger, as well as to help them develop coping strategies to manage their feelings and reduce aggressive acts. This strategy also incorporated cognitive-behavioral techniques such as assertiveness training, communication skill building, guided relaxation, self-talk, thought-stopping, and mediation. In addition, it used gestalt techniques of role-playing, primal screams, art therapy, and the empty chair. In a study on use of anger management training with 12 adolescents in residential treatment, Dangel, Deschner, and Rasp (1989) found that observed aggressive acts were reduced. Wilcox and Dowrick (1992) also reported progress beyond that expected from the regular treatment program when anger management training was used. They recommended that adaptations of their methods for use with adolescents might prove beneficial. Anger management training appears to be a helpful strategy for providing coping skills to incarcerated adolescents with a history of violent crimes and aggressive behaviors. It is likely that such training would be even more beneficial if available to all, so that appropriate coping skills could be developed *before* antisocial acts result from unmanageable and/or unacknowledged anger.

Summary

In light of the research summarized in this chapter, five major areas need to be addressed in the education and socialization of youth if we wish to constructively channel adolescent aggression. First, education needs to provide adolescents and young adults throughout the world with tools for understanding, acknowledging, managing, and constructively expressing anger and for thinking critically about their actions. Second, positive role models and mentors who display appropriate social skills, express anger constructively, and do not engage in acts of hate against others need to replace dysfunctional family and media role models. Third, the curriculum needs to include information and learning activities that develop meta-cognitive awareness in students so that categorization, stereotyping, and prejudice are understood and counteracted in daily thought processes. Fourth, cooperative learning strategies that provide the opportunity to work with individuals from divergent backgrounds in order to successfully accomplish common goals need to characterize education. And last, the members of these divergent groups need to come not just from a particular community but from the global community. Students need to interact and learn with youth from a variety of countries, cultures, belief systems, lifestyles, and backgrounds. Education needs to become not just a regional or even a national enterprise, but a global endeavor.

The educational system alone, even though it is often the most popular scapegoat for youth problems in the political arena, cannot turn the tide of adolescent aggression. Parents, social service agencies, criminal justice agencies, and society as a whole are all critical agents in this process. Still, the educational system is a good place to start and to integrate the other entities, from family to police to social service agencies, within. This can turn the tide. For that reason, we next address school violence and look at strategies for dealing with adolescent aggression in public schools.

CHAPTER 2

School Violence: An Overview

We would like to thank Dr. Edith Grotberg, Dr. Augustus Little, and Diana Estrada, M. Ed., for their valuable contributions to this chapter.

World attention has been drawn to scenes of violence in the U.S. school system over the past few years. We were horrified when we received the dreadful news that 18-year-old Eric Harrison and 17-year-old Dylan Klebold had launched a violent assault against their classmates, killing 13 and wounding 20, before taking their own lives on April 20, 1999. This happened not at an inner-city school replete with poverty, gang violence, and crime, but at respectable Columbine High School in Littleton, Colorado. This school, in an upper-middle-class suburban area, was recognized for its academic and athletic success. The Columbine tragedy and similar events that followed in junior highs and high schools from Arkansas to California shocked the American public and led us to ask ourselves certain questions. "Why did this happen?" "What could make a child or adolescent so angry that it would lead him to take a gun and shoot a fellow classmate?" "What can our school system do to ensure that our children and our youth are safe?" The film *Bowling for Columbine* by director Michael Moore even won awards for attempting to answer these questions when it was released two years later by suggesting that lack of gun control and the social milieu in U.S. society was to blame. But is the level of violence in society and lack of gun control really a way to answer these questions?

In the United States, at least, Central and South American countries are also perceived as violent societies with easy access to guns. Whether or not this perception is accurate is open to question, but school violence, at least of the level of the Columbine shootings and other such incidents, has not been as common in Central and South America.

In Russia, also currently perceived as a violent culture in the United States, school shootings of teachers and other students by students seem unimaginable. School violence is not unknown there, however, as the terrorist siege of the school in Beslin during 2004 demonstrates. Still, availability of guns, level of violence accepted in society, and whether or not wars are an ongoing part of the cultural mindset in a given country do not fully explain violence in schools. These are part of the answer, but the issue of school violence is much more complex. Family structure and dynamics, school policies, respect for educators, and societal perception of consequences are all aspects. Attitudes toward authority and levels of anger, isolation, and hopelessness among adolescents are also important factors. Before we can even attempt to answer the questions about why school violence occurs, however, we must define the term *school violence* and identify the types of violence that exist.

Defining School Violence

The term *school violence* has evolved over the last 10 years. It first surfaced in 1992 to describe criminal acts and aggression in schools that harmed the educational environment. Since 1992, a vast amount of literature has been written on the subject. Researchers have become concerned with increasing school violence rates and have attempted to understand the growing phenomenon, so as to find a feasible solution. School violence is a term that brings fear and concern to communities throughout the world. It reflects societal values that schools should be a safe haven, a place of learning and nurturing—not a battleground where children are harmed and lives are often lost. Because school violence is a multidimensional construct, there is not a definitive statement that appropriately specifies its dimensions. We will, however, attempt to understand what is currently known about school violence and provide some possible solutions for diminishing it in the future.

Researchers have identified three major types of violence that happen within schools: student-to-student violence, student-to-teacher violence, and teacher-to-student violence. A fourth type, perpetrated by family or community members against students or teachers, also occurs. Acts of terrorism directed against students and teachers by outside groups, such as the Russian crisis in 2004, must now be included, as well.

Student-to-Student Violence

When acts of violence surface on school grounds, the major instigators are most often students harming other students. There are several reasons why a student may decide to harm his or her peers. Factors such as neglect, medical issues, trauma, societal devaluation, racism, dysfunctional conditions within the home, an excessive exposure to violent television, social alienation, bullying by peers, and the overall social milieu in which the adolescent lives must all be considered. Understanding causal trajectories is important for future prevention and is discussed more in other chapters when we focus on how best to remedy existing violence in the school setting.

In the United States, Joan L. Curcio and Patricia F. First (1993) developed different categories and degrees of student-to-student violence that can be observed on school campuses. The list is not fully inclusive and some items have been modified or added, but it offers a structure for examining student-to-student violence in school settings. The list is divided by intensity of violence and is composed of:

1. Extreme acts of violence, including

   Murder

   Rape

   Drive-by shootings on or near school property

   Firing a weapon in a crowded school hallway

   Lethally stabbing a peer

   Possession of firearms on school property with intention to harm a peer

   Possession of knives or other sharp objects on school property with intention to harm

   Hate crimes

2. Serious acts of violence, including

   Sexually assaulting a peer

   Racial and ethnic group conflict

   Drug abuse and drug dealing with intent to harm self or others

   Threatening the life of a peer

3. Potentially serious acts of violence, including

   Fist fighting on campus

Taunting and intimidating peers

Bullying peers

Gang membership and activities involving violence

Wearing gang identification and symbols

Teasing and harassing the opposite sex

Group hazing

Theft of property

According to recent statistics, one of four students in the United States will be victimized by one or more of the types of school violence on this list. More than 16 percent of eighth graders, 14 percent of tenth graders, and 12 percent of twelfth graders fear for their safety in school and often find themselves staying home out of fear of getting involved in violent confrontation with peers. Increasing absentee rates in American high schools are frequently associated with students' fear of the school environment. Phobia of attending school is often a condition that requires psychological treatment for adolescents in the United States. Many students do not finish school because of this phobia, as attendance policies prevent them from earning credit if they are frequently absent. The increase in home schooling in the United States seen in recent years is also likely associated with increasing fear of attending school because of perceived danger on the part of both students and parents.

At least 1 in 10 American schools will experience some sort of violent crime (i.e., murder, rape, sexual battery, suicide, physical attack, fights with weapons, and robbery). Furthermore, one of six students is aware of someone who has died in a violent incident.

Student-to-Teacher Violence

No teacher is ever free from potential physical harm brought on by students on school campuses, and this is not a particularly recent problem. In 1978, a study sponsored by the Department of Health, Education and Welfare on safe schools revealed that approximately 12 percent of U.S. high school teachers reported being threatened with physical harm every month. They admitted not knowing the appropriate procedures for confronting disruptive students and therefore were reluctant to do so. A similar study was repeated 20 years later with Chicago teachers and students. Even more teachers were reporting being threatened and/or assaulted by students than in the original study. Many students admitted to assaulting a teacher at least once or even twice during the school year. A significantly larger percentage of teachers reported that their personal property had been vandalized or stolen at school. What is even more shocking is that 9 of 10 school incidents were never reported to police agencies or the public. School administrators who do not want to draw unfavorable attention to their campuses or risk civil lawsuits are the most likely explanation for this lack of reporting. However, denying and hiding the problem does not solve it; instead, this denial exacerbates it.

When violent acts occur, action needs to be taken. Specific state laws protect school employees from assault. Attackers can and should be prosecuted. When an attack on a teacher occurs, the police should be contacted immediately and the battered teacher needs to seek the immediate advice of an attorney. Many teachers are emotionally invested in their students, however, and protective of them. They are hesitant to feel responsible for potentially harming their future by involving them with criminal justice agencies, and in light of the increasing lifelong consequences for adolescents who acquire police records in the United States, this concern is justified.

Schools are generally ready to take disciplinary action against students who violate school rules; however, victimized teachers also need to be supported emotionally. The tendency to "blame the victim," a natural human tendency that many experiments in social psychology have substantiated, is certainly likely to occur in schools. Teachers who have been assaulted are viewed by their peers as incapable of classroom management, poor teachers, or in other negative ways. This also makes teachers less willing to report threats and assaults. Teachers should not be blamed for these incidents unless a careful subsequent examination of facts justifies such blame. They should instead be referred to counseling programs specifically designed to address victimization and trauma.

Why do administrators allow teachers who are assaulted to be placed in this uncomfortable role, and why do they seek to hide problems within their schools? One major reason may be a lack of training. Administrators lack the conflict resolution skills needed to diffuse violent incidents. Many U.S. states do not even require public school administrators to have experience as teachers. This is not the case in many other countries, where teaching experience is required and administrators are elected by staff and faculty; but, even in these countries, administrators are unlikely to be trained in counseling or conflict resolution. The educational system and programs may also be held responsible for contributing. They share in the responsibility of producing administrators who have not yet learned the skills needed to confront and diffuse physical attacks. Perhaps such training should extend to teachers, as well. Here is an example of what may be required of a young teacher, as told by Dr. Augustus L. "Skip" Little. Little is an internationally known researcher, author, and presenter, who is active in the American Middle School Association and the Coalition to Prevent School Violence. He is a former New York City middle school teacher, as well as a former school counselor, principal, and school superintendent. He has also been a professor of educational psychology at Valdosta Sate University and Northern Arizona University, specializing in middle grades education and adolescence. Here is Little's story, which clearly illustrates an example of student-to-teacher violence as experienced by a beginning teacher:

Fresh out of a local university, I stood before my first students in a turbulent junior high school in the inner city of New York. I knew my content and how to write a good lesson plan, but I was never prepared for what I faced in my first teaching position.

I remember my interview to this very day. I was called by the central district office to show up at the school on a certain day and time. As I drove there from my suburban home, my hands began to sweat holding the steering wheel of my car. The roads became more and more littered with uncollected garbage and then burned-out cars. Eventually, burned-out or abandoned four- and five-story dwellings lined the streets. I finally found the address on my note paper, parked my car, and approached the school. I walked past four young men playing some sort of dice game on the hot concrete with a pile of money lying on the ground between them.

The school was a stately three story building built in the early 1900s and was encircled by a six foot iron fence. I approached the 10-foot steel front door of the school and began to pound my fist on the door since there was no bell. Then a small, bald elderly man emerged. It was like the wizard who appears behind the curtain in The Wizard of Oz. *He was the man who would set my entire life on a new course. It was my first principal! I extended my hand and introduced myself, and he responded, "You're hired." I was in shock. What about the interview I practiced for so hard in my college courses? What about reviewing my resumé or my portfolio? The warm late summer New York sun reflected off his perspiring brow when he said, "If a prospective teacher drives to this place, gets out of the car, and knocks on this door, that's enough for me." Little did I know that I had embarked on a journey that set the direction of my professional life forever.*

About a month into the school year, I was preparing to take my seventh grade language arts class on our first visit to the school library. The library existed within this fortress much more like an oasis in this jail called a school. The principal had motorcycle chains and locks placed on the emergency exits so that students would not open the school's unprotected doors to the community. I had practiced how to exit the classroom, how to walk in the hall, and what to do and not do in the library with my students. As I went down the hallways, 30 something children of poverty followed me like baby ducks following their mother. As I walked faster, so did they; when I stopped, so did they. They followed me down the stairs like a brook flowing over rocks. The line swayed left and right as the students jumped one or two steps at a time. Then we arrived on the ground level and set our course for the library. As I turned the corner with my followers right behind me, I was confronted by a young man who was obviously too old to be one of our students. Perhaps it was an alumnus visiting his former teachers?

The young man immediately pulled an ice pick from his pocket and said, "I am going to kill you." Every lecture I had in my education courses ran through my head at the speed of light. I could not find any information on how to react to this. Perhaps I missed the day they taught us that. Anyway, I immediately reacted with a natural instinct. I began speaking to the youth while slowly circling around him causing him to turn to follow me as I moved. Now I had my students to his back. I knew that had to be step one. I then continued to talk to him while I slowly walked backwards toward the front office about 50 yards away. I remember as I backed into the office, that the secretaries all had a look on their face indicating that I should be a lot more scared than I was at the time. The principal's secretary motioned me to continue into the inner office and into the principal's office.

As we entered the principal's office, life went into light speed. Within a second or two, our uniformed and armed school resource officer came barging through the door and instantly apprehended the youth, handcuffing him to a radiator pipe in the corner of the room. At the same time, we could see a crowd of community members gathering outside the window demanding the youth to be released.

Soon, I was surrounded by six New York City policemen who ushered me out of the building past the crowd and into a police car, whisking me off to the local police station to complete a report. Months passed, and I was subpoenaed to appear at the trial of the youth who confronted me. It was my first visit to an actual trial and again something that the university never prepared me for. At the trial, the young man's mother pleaded with the judge to lock her son up. Through an interpreter, she said that the young man was crazy and that she could not sleep at night because he had threatened to kill her and her younger children while they slept. The recently graduated public defender argued that she should take the child home with her and he should not be incarcerated. Then with a frown and a falling gavel, the judge released him on community service. I was shocked! The prosecuting attorney then explained to me that the judge had just four vacancies for that day in juvenile detention and had 23 cases. Therefore, he had to incarcerate the "worst" four of the day.

Such was my induction into the world of school violence. Since then I have dedicated my professional life to make schools a better place for both students and the adults who work there. At that time in my professional career, I was not even aware of what I should be looking for in a school where I chose to teach or how as a teacher in a school I could make it a less violent place for students and their teachers. Further, my undergraduate teacher education program had not prepared me for the vast change in student behaviors demonstrated in schools in Table 2.1.

As Little's experience and the information here shows, student-to-teacher violence is a major problem in U.S. schools. Little was able to deal with the situation calmly and effectively as, fortunately, most teachers probably are. An interesting statistic is that within the United States, the job in which one is most likely to be assaulted while at work is that of night-shift convenience store worker, and the second most likely job is that of public school teacher. When teachers themselves are afraid, this can exacerbate aggression and violence. Just as animals sense fear and react to it, so do adolescents. Fear combined with a hard-line authoritarian attitude can create rebellion and reactions to authority among unstable adolescents.

Teacher-to-Student Violence

Teachers and administrators often forget that they are entrusted to care for students on campus and they violate their students. There are two abusive actions that define when school administrators have physically violated students. One is physical abuse and the other is sexual harassment. Other behaviors may be just as destructive toward students emotionally.

Although in many places corporal punishment is against state law, some states continue to uphold the right to use corporal punishment as a means of exerting control to maintain school discipline. That punishment often becomes a form of abuse. There have been instances where teachers have beaten students without having a motive, often

Table 2.1
National Center for the Study of Corporal Punishment and
Alternatives Uniform Discipline Reporting System (Offense Details)

1940	1990
	06–Physical sexual harassment, molestation
Defiance	07–Sexual assault, including attempted and completed rape
01–Failure to follow specific instructions by a person in authority	08–Assault with a gun
02–Arguing beyond acceptable limits	09–Assault with knife
03–Raising of voice beyond acceptable limits	
04–Use of profane language	10–Assault with weapon other than gun or knife
05–Display of an obscene gesture	11–Other
06–Refusal to follow a school rule	*Fighting between Students*
07–Dishonesty in dealing with another person	01–Hitting, punching, kicking, choking, etc.
08–Creating a disturbance	02–Making verbal or gestural threats
09–Leaving the classroom without permission	03–Verbal taunting
Defacing School Property	04–Slapping, poking, pushing
01–Littering	05–Other
02–Creating graffiti	*Activities Interfering with School Performance*
03–Throwing books	01–Not completing assignment, homework, etc.
04–Purposely destroying school property	02–Excessive talking in class
05–Accidentally destroying school property	03–Inattentiveness in class
06–Throwing other objects	04–Not prepared for activity
07–Pulling fire alarm	05–Failure to return to/from parent
08–Setting a fire	06–Creation of disturbance
09–Other	07–Leaving classroom without permission
Illegal Activities	08–Carrying a beeper
01–Stealing	09–Other
02–Trespassing	

(Continued)

Table 2.1
National Center for the Study of Corporal Punishment and
Alternatives Uniform Discipline Reporting System (Offense Details)

1940	1990
	Breaking Miscellaneous School Rules
03–Possession of weapon	01–Smoking
04–Extortion	02–Leaving school grounds without permission
05–Gambling	03–Making excessive noise
06–Possession or use of drug	04–Tardiness
07–Selling drugs	05–Truancy
08–Other	06–Cutting class
Assault or Abuse	07–Loitering
01–Hitting, punching, or kicking	08–Use of profane language
02–Making verbal or gestural threats	09–Use of obscene gesture
03–Reckless endangerment (e.g., shooting gun in public, speeding on school grounds, setting off firecrackers)	10–Dishonesty in dealing with another person
04–Unnecessary use of force	11–Other
05–Verbal sexual harassment	

Source: Thomas Toch, Ted Gest, and Monika Guttman, "Violence in schools,"
U.S. News & World Report, vol. 115, no. 18 (November 8, 1993), p. 30, citing data
from Congressional Quarterly Researcher.

injuring them seriously. Some students have received lesions from
excessive discipline. In one instance described in an article published
in the *Law Report* titled "The use of force by public school teachers
as a defense against threatened harm," a 230-pound teacher picked up
a 14-year-old student and dropped him on the ground, fracturing his
arm. The student weighed half as much as the teacher. Some of these
teachers have been reported as child abusers when excessive physical
force is confirmed. Cases of student sexual assault in which school
personnel molest elementary children as young as 5 years old are also
a matter of public record. School employees have also been reported
to intimidate or threaten students. Unfortunately, this is a violent
behavior that is most often concealed. Community members are in
denial or too ashamed to admit that violence or sexual abuse may be
occurring on school grounds. This encourages the illegitimate use of
power. A conspiracy of silence results. The best thing that can be done

Table 2.2
Types Of Violence: Victims and Perpetrators

	% of Student Victims	% of Student Perpetrators	Perpetrators' Gender	
			Male	Female
Verbal insults	60	50	60	40
Threats	26	23	34	12
Pushing, shoving, grabbing, slapping	43	42	54	30
Kicking, biting, hitting with a fist	24	26	37	15
Threats with a knife or gun	4	5	8	3
Using a knife or firing a gun	2	3	6	1
Theft	43	1	2	1
Other	2	14	18	9

Source: *The Metropolitan Life Survey of the American Teacher: Violence in America's Public Schools* (1993), conducted for Metropolitan Life Insurance Company by Louis Harris and Associates, Inc., pp. 71–72.

to prevent the use of excessive corporal punishment is to expose the truth when it is confirmed (Table 2.2).

Other Acts of Violence

Acts from outside the school directed at students, teachers, and administrators are also becoming increasingly common. The event in Russia in 2004, where an entire school was held hostage, is a frightening extreme example. Other situations are more common. Custody battles often result in violence in schools. An emotionally unstable father in Arizona who had lost custody recently entered his child's classroom and threatened the teacher and class for attempting to stop his abduction of the child. The event ended with the father killing both himself and the child in front of the class. Although such events are often hidden from media attention, they are becoming increasingly common. Witnessing violence in an elementary classroom perpetrated by a parent certainly has potentially long-lasting psychological effects on all of the children who witness it. School bus hijackings are also becoming more common. Less dramatic but also common are events such as bus accidents where many adolescents are killed. These, too, are perceived as violent deaths by those affected. Now that we have defined and discussed school violence, we next examine some of the more common explanations offered for its occurrence.

Biopsychosocial Factors

Biological factors affect the level of violent behaviors. Experiments on mice reveal that the number of attacks by mice against other mice correlated to the level of testosterone induced by researchers. It is difficult to measure the effects of testosterone in humans; however, studies reveal that high levels of circulating testosterone have led to an increased aggressive response to provocation and intimidation. Steroids and asthma medications have been linked to increased aggression in humans. Serotonin deregulation has also been linked to violent behavior, as have changes in levels of certain neurotransmitters, especially norepinephrine, often induced by medications. Violent or suicidal behavior has been linked in some instances to reactions to medications that modify brain chemistry, including Prozac and Ritilin, both frequently prescribed for adolescents who are depressed, hyperactive, or have attention deficit disorder. As noted in the previous chapter, though, biological and biochemical factors alone do not explain aggressive behavior among adolescents.

Violent behavior is a complex phenomenon that cannot be explained on the basis of only one set of variables. According to Paul Kettle, author of *Biological and Social Causes of School Violence* (2001), "Violence is a complex behavior, an interaction of psychological, biological, and social factors that can lead a human being to a violent act that we may then witness on our television" (p. 53).

Developmental psychologists frequently refer to biopsychosocial factors. This term accounts for the various complex interactions between biology and environment among psychological, social, and biological factors. To show a clear example of how this combination of factors can explain teen violence, Edith Grotberg notes:

As this chapter is written, new scientific information makes a powerful case for promoting resilience in children and youth. For years, scientists traced the roots of the mental disorder, depression, to a specific interaction of genes and the environment—the nature-nurture issue. The prevailing belief was a genetic cause for mental illness. But, when some subjects of the study who had the gene for depression were found not to become depressed as a result of traumatic experiences in life, it was concluded that the interaction of the gene with the environment determined the outcome. In other words, nature and nurture interact to determine what happens to individuals. Environment provides cues that cushion from or cause specific behaviors. Because violence is widespread in our society at present, social causes are at least as influential as biological causes of aggression.

Not only teens enjoy viewing acts of violence; so do adults. Our culture is replete with movies, TV shows, video games, and books that have violence as a major theme. This focus is usually justified by the "good guys" defeating the "bad guys," and increasingly, the "good gals" defeating the "bad gals" or "guys." Violence is seen as an appropriate response to threats ranging from feared attacks to retaliation for actual attacks. Violence has behind it aggression and aggression behind it has assertiveness, and assertiveness has behind it self-confidence, and self-confidence has behind it "We will survive!" Our cars reflect this pattern. We like big cars because we feel more powerful and ads like, "Get out of my way or I'll kick your butt!" describe the aggressiveness. More recently, we see Hummers on the road—an imitation of the military vehicle, the Humvee. We are aggressive; don't get in our way; we will not be afraid. We will survive. This is the mantra of our current society in the United States.

Fear is behind reactions of aggression and violence. But we must be clear: We enjoy feelings of fear. Even as children, we enjoyed playing hide and seek, waiting for someone to jump out screaming and scaring the searcher as the race to the goal was made. Halloween is a guaranteed fear rouser, as well as one of the most popular holidays among U.S. youth. Children dress to scare; they go to parties that have all kinds of scary pictures and activities intended to get a fear response.

More people are interested in the news when scary things are happening and Neilsen ratings rise. Fear sells advertising for the media. Fear is roused because the event might happen to you or members of your family. You feel the fear vicariously and want to watch the path of the scary events. Those who lived with the sniper experience in the metropolitan Washington, D.C. area which lasted three weeks in October 2002 watched TV news reports, read the papers, and talked with friends and fellow workers every day. Once that danger was over, however, people returned to indifference to the news. When things are going well, when things are calm, when we feel safe, we can easily become bored. Some people tolerate boredom better than others, and this may in part be genetic and/or biochemical. Regardless, in the United States, we do not like to be bored! Replacing boredom with fear seems to be the current trend.

What are the limits of exposing children and youth to fear-related violence? Remember the fairy tale about Hansel and Gretel? Most children in the United States know that one well by the time they enter school. Hansel and Gretel, as a result of their fear, burn the witch to death. What about Little Red Riding Hood, another well-known children's story character? As a result of her fear, a man kills the wolf. Now, those are acts of aggression, acts of violence. There is a more recent competitor for responses to fear than fairytales and cartoons, even though indirectly. We develop video games that are intended to threaten the player and that encourage violent responses. And more, these games don't stop at acts of violence against the bad guys; they also include the good guys:

> *A teenage boy is playing a video game and within a few minutes he kills six police officers, shooting them in the stomach; he stabs two people with a stake; he participates in a drive-by shooting; he breaks the necks of four officers. He spends almost four hours engaged in this game and comes out with a very high score for acts of violence.*

There is no attempt to make violence justifiable because bad things were done; violence is a pleasure and its own end. And we don't even wait until children reach the teen years to begin this social conditioning. We start them much younger.

> *A boy of about 7 years was seen standing at a machine game on a boardwalk of a resort area. In the game five crocodile heads and part of their bodies appeared at different intervals on a platform. The object of the game was for the boy, who held a large, thick, stick, to wham the crocodile heads as they appeared. The heads would then withdraw to come out again. The parents were standing behind the boy, cheering him on, praising him each time he smashed a crocodile and urging him to get the next one.*

We know enough about the development of the mind to realize that the line between fiction and reality is very thin among children and youth. What they are doing in video games and in other games of violence—while supposedly fiction—is easily seen later as a form of reality. Further, when something is presented and sold as acceptable for use by children and youth, and parents do nothing to intervene, the children and youth are sent a message that violence is OK if you feel fear or if you are challenged to protect yourself or others. Of course, the viewers are assumed to identify with the one being threatened—they have a right, indeed, an obligation, to respond. They accept and adapt to violent responses.

Gender may be considered a biological factor responsible for aggression. There is no question that boys are seen as more violent than girls, but to what extent this is a social phenomenon and to what extent it is a biological one is unknown. As more and more girls adopt violent behavior in correlation with social changes and more violent media representations among females, the social aspects of the phenomenon are strengthened. Still, at present in the

United Sates, boys generally form the gangs that engage in acts of violence, boys play more video games involving violence, and boys engage in more physical solutions to problems and aggravations. Society has different expectations for boys than it does for girls, especially in terms of feelings and behavior. In many ways, boys are encouraged to be aggressive, even engage in violence, as an appropriate response to feelings of fear or vulnerability; but society is not in tune with the reality of what boys really feel and want to do. Interviews with boys identified some of the expectations society had for boys that do not apply to girls and, indeed, are contrary to what boys want. This information came from interviews recounted in Canadian Boys: Untold Stories *(2002):*

1. *They were not given much support from parents and teachers and yet were expected to deal with the adversities of life on their own because that's what is expected of males.*

2. *They have a harder time growing up than girls because they are expected to be tough, participate in sports, and constantly prove themselves. If they are highly intelligent and don't engage in masculine activities, they are called "nerds." (The overwhelming success of the Harry Potter books, where Harry is clearly a "nerd," gives some idea of how much children and youth want and need more than tough males as a role model). They feel parents protect girls more than boys and that boys are left alone to engage in more risk-taking behavior. And they feel that parents punish boys for not living up to the conventional standards of masculinity.*

3. *They feel boys are expected to fight when challenged and are discouraged from showing their feelings, except feelings that express anger in the form of aggression. The astounding fact is that when feelings are not identified and labeled, all the emotions converge into anger!*

4. *Boys want more understanding so that they can be themselves and not try to be what parents, girls, or other guys expect them to be. (pp. 2–5)*

Research conducted in the United States suggests that males raised by females in single-parent homes are even more prone to feelings such as these, as well as to violence. Because they do not have a male role model with whom to interact on a daily basis, they determine what it means to be a male based on exaggerated media images. Is society ready to assume some responsibility for the outcomes of these messages to youth? The psychological influence is profound and certainly accounts for at least some of the increase in aggression and school violence we are witnessing.

Psychological influences are important factors leading to acts of violence. One of the most important factors influencing these psychological responses seems to be personal experience with violence and the amount and type of violence present in a person's environment. If one has experienced violence firsthand or witnessed it while growing up, then one is at a greater risk for behaving violently.

Violence in the Home and Community

Early experiences within the family setting provide the foundation for a child's learning. Observing violence within the family structure can provide the foundation for the child's violent behavior. Initial causes of violence within the family have been traced to weak family communication, maternal bonding or lack thereof, ineffective monitoring, parental indifference, negligence, and values that support the use of violence. Early childhood experiences have been correlated with the future development of violent behavior, especially during adolescence. Children as young as one year who were physically abused at home were more than twice as likely to become physically abusive during adolescence (Elliot, Hamburg, & Williams, 1998, p. 44). Statistics provided by JoAnn Guernsey (1993), author of *Youth Violence*, reveal that 70 percent of all juvenile violent offenders come from single-parent homes. One in 10 U.S. elementary school students goes home to an empty household. One in four females and one in six males are sexually assaulted before age 18 years.

Exposure to violence within the community plays an influential role in young people's attitudes toward violence. Poverty, discrimination, and a lack of education have been identified as potential risk factors for interpersonal violence. The media tend to portray more violent behavior among ethnic minorities, particularly African Americans and Hispanics, but in the United States, many low-income neighborhoods are composed of members of ethnic minority groups. Research shows that poverty and residing in a low-income neighborhood are stronger predictors of violence than ethnicity. Although gang behavior is generally associated with race, leading to the false impression of a genetic or biological connection, it is the environment that appears to be ultimately responsible.

In addition to poverty, lack of education and discrimination, ineffective social organization, and lack of social controls within certain communities have been associated with the presence of gangs, drug distribution, violent role models, and violence itself. Lack of employment and isolation or deficiency of social resources contribute to the shaping of children's attitudes toward violence.

Violence among Peers

Children who have been significantly affected by violence may not know how to interact appropriately and positively with peers in the school setting. They may lack the communication and interpersonal skills needed to interact positively with others. This may be because they have never felt a sense of belonging, acceptance, or nurturing within the home setting. They have formed no attachment to society. For these insecurely attached children, being in the school setting, though designed to provide a positive atmosphere, may create conflict, aggravation, and ultimately, violence toward peers. Statistically, 15 percent of gun violence at school erupts over long-standing arguments, 12 percent over romantic disagreements, and 10 percent in disputes over possessions. Children may also react with violent responses when they have failed to achieve peer approval, academic success, self-efficacy, or positive and satisfying relationships within the school setting. According to Delbert et al. (1998):

> Research suggests that much school-related violence is linked to competition for status and status-related conformations among peers. The peers with whom children choose to associate help to determine what behaviors he or she will model and adopt; the choice of friends is often influenced by early exposure to violence, problematic family and internal controls, and aggressive behavior patterns developed earlier in childhood. (p. 45)

Presence of gangs in schools is also associated with an increase in school violence. Both gang members and nonmembers are equally susceptible to violent attacks when gangs roam the schoolyard. Often, nongang member students who attend schools with gangs and gang activity are more likely to carry a weapon to school out of fear of being attacked.

Media: A Culture of Violence

Since 1994, the number of teens arrested for serious violent crimes (i.e., murder, rape, robbery) has actually decreased in the United States, from 500 arrests per 100,000 teens to fewer than 350 arrests per 100,000 by 1999. More than 100,000 teens under the age of 18, however, were arrested for violent crimes in 1999, and an increase in school violence has been reported as well. Psychologists continue searching for the roots of violent behavior. We have discovered that media violence does exert a lasting impact. Leonard Eron, senior scientist at the

University of Michigan's Institute for Social Research, tracked 856 people, beginning at the age of 8 years. He gathered statistical data and recorded their aggression levels as rated by their peers, as well as police records when relevant, and correlated this to the amount and types of television programs they watched throughout childhood and adolescence. Statistical data were recorded when they were ages 8, 20, 29, and 30 years old. Evidence showed that the more violence on television they watched as children, the more aggressive they became. Those who watched the greatest amount of television violence were also more prone to developing antisocial attitudes and using abusive language.

The average U.S. household has three televisions in the home. Television brings stories and messages into the living room. Individuals watch seven hours per day of television on average. Children from age two onward generally watch more than three hours per day. The effects of television stem not only from its content, but also from its great presence in the daily lives of children. The time spent watching television removes the child from social, intellectual, and physical growth through play, creative work, reading, and sports. Whereas in some cultures, such as Russia and Brazil, television is more likely to be a shared family activity, discussed afterward and placed in social perspective according to family values, in the United States, children are more likely to engage in viewing alone or only with siblings and peers.

Debates about the content of television and appropriateness or inappropriateness of media control still rage, but it is clear that the content of television is not benign. According to Paul Kettle, MD, (2001), "By the time a child graduates from elementary school, he or she will have witnessed more than 100,00 acts of violence and 8,000 entertainment murders from his or her living room" (p. 62). The American Psychiatric Association (1993), American Academy of Pediatrics (1990), National Institute of Mental Health (1982), and Surgeon General's Scientific Advisory Committee (1972) have all come to the same conclusion. Experiencing violence on television can lead to violent behavior in today's youth. Combined with a violent media influence and daily experiences with violence throughout childhood, readily available guns and weapons become more of a concern, as do lowered inhibitions from experimentation with drugs and alcohol.

Interpersonal disputes between students and between students and teachers have increasingly resulted in aggravated assault and the use of lethal weapons. This is indisputably correlated to the easy access of handguns. Gunshot wounds are the leading cause of death among teenage boys in America. The homicide rate in the United States is 10 per 100,000 people and is now the most common cause of death among adolescent males. Firearm deaths and injuries have become an epidemic. It is impossible to examine social cases of violence without looking at the prevalence of guns in today's society. Approximately 135,000 U.S. students bring handguns to school everyday, according to some estimates.

Not only do adolescents have easy access to weapons, they also apparently have easy access to alcohol and drugs. Experimenting with altered states has characterized adolescence in many societies throughout history, sometimes in formalized rites. It has certainly become an informal rite of passage in modern-day societies, as well. Whether done to emulate adult behavior, to fit in with the peer group, or simply out of the heightened curiosity that characterizes adolescents, using alcohol and illegal drugs is a commonly reported activity among adolescents. It is also an activity that can lead to increases in violent behavior. We discuss the influence of drugs and alcohol on adolescent aggression in Chapter 4 and look at some potential solutions. It certainly is a problem in school settings as well as elsewhere. For now, though, we turn our attention to strategies for remedying violence in public schools.

CHAPTER 3

STRATEGIES FOR EDUCATORS TO PREVENT YOUTH VIOLENCE

Some of the information recounted in this chapter first appeared in articles by Sherri McCarthy in The School Discipline Adviser *in 2003. We would like to thank Edith Grotberg, Augustus and Suzanne Little, Elaine Schenkel, and Diana Estrada for their contributions.*

Metal detectors at inner city public high schools through which students must pass when entering are not uncommon. Many U.S. public schools have used this technology to screen for knives and guns for decades. A visible police presence on campus is also not unusual, as gang-related violence on or near school grounds is not particularly uncommon. Such measures may be necessary even though extreme. Nearly all U.S. public high schools and junior highs have one or more police officers assigned to work with violence management and prevention.

School violence prevention strategies typically fall into three categories: (1) behavior management (that is, related to discipline and punishment), (2) measures related to environmental modification (for instance, video cameras, security guards, and uniforms), and (3) educational and curriculum-based measures (for instance, conflict-resolution and gang-prevention programs). All methods have their advantages and disadvantages; however, all three should be combined to provide safe, orderly schools.

It is important to stress the necessity for a cohesive community effort to diminish and prevent school violence. The current trend seems to be to expect school personnel to be entirely responsible when problems occur. Schools and teachers are often used as scapegoats for problems. This practice makes achieving solutions more difficult. Although part of maintaining a safe environment is certainly the responsibility of school personnel, it is a shared responsibility. Parents, community members, police, and social service agencies are equally responsible. Without a cohesive, community-based effort, establishing and maintaining safe schools is impossible. Efforts to connect all responsible members through neighborhood coalitions are necessary. Schools cannot accomplish the task alone.

Resources for Creating Safe Schools

There is no "one size fits all" solution to school violence. Each school's staff, students, building, community, and resources are unique, and so are the things that work or do not work in each school setting. There is no rubric or map to follow for every school setting, as each school differs too greatly in terms of students, personnel, community resources, finances, curriculum and other issues. Therefore, it is the responsibility of each school's parents, administrators, students, teachers, and community members to define a successful antiviolence strategy for the particular school with which they are connected. Many resources are available and, to save long hours searching for the gems among the sand on the Internet, useful sources compiled by Augustus Little, who shared his own experiences with school violence in the last chapter, appear at the end of this chapter. Of course, Web addresses and sites may change from time to time, but as of 2004, this list was current and useful. Share this information with the schools in your area and encourage the use of the strategies suggested later in this chapter, whether or not you work in a school setting or have children attending public school.

In addition to providing this useful list of resources, Little and his wife Suzanne also offered their assistance and insight for the remainder of this chapter. The following information describes research-based practices for creating and maintaining safe schools.

Effective Practices

Safe schools do not necessarily build their discipline programs on unusual or innovative practices. They include a number of school management procedures that have been used through the years.

Well-disciplined schools include award assemblies, parent involvement events, and the sending home of "Happy Grams" to acknowledge and reward good behavior. If teens are recognized for positive behavior, they are less likely to engage in negative behavior to attract attention. Negative behaviors of adolescents are often attempts to be recognized. If attention from adults and peers is craved, whether that attention is positive or negative often becomes secondary in importance to adolescents. By providing acknowledgment and attention to all teens for positive behaviors, these behaviors are encouraged. It is important to note that providing recognition must go beyond traditional practices such as honor roll and awards for athletic achievement. Not all teens are scholars or good in sports, but all teens do need positive acknowledgment, praise, and regard. Effective schools find something for which each student can be praised and acknowledge each student for individual strengths. In well-disciplined schools, faculty seek out the potential problem areas that may create the misbehavior and remove them. They understand that students misbehave for a reason, so discipline includes changing the potential for a student acting unacceptably by rearranging the environment.

An often forgotten part of a good discipline program is an emphasis on the encouragement of positive behavior through the use of rewards. Well-disciplined schools have programs that include award assemblies, the sending of positive messages to parents, praise for positive behavior, and privileges earned for positive behavior. Few well-disciplined schools report that their programs are based totally on some particular well-publicized discipline system. Most claim they use some form of well-publicized discipline system, but with modifications to meet their seemingly unique situations. Consistent with the findings of Little and Little (2001), a common theme among well-disciplined schools is the key role played by the principal. If the principal is enthusiastic, supportive, and encouraging, with a strong belief that things will work out, then discipline problems can be effectively handled. What characterizes a good principal? Perhaps the following interview with a successful principal will offer some insight. These suggestions for improving classroom management are offered by Elaine Schenkel, a former Fulbright Scholar to the United States and a principal and teacher in Brazilian public and private schools.

Sherri (S)
    McCarthy: Elaine, I know you have more than 25 years experience in public education in Brazil, both as a teacher and as

a principal in elementary and high schools. You've also spent time in the United States as a Fulbright Scholar and when your own children were in elementary school. Based on this experience, what differences have you noticed between U.S. and Brazilian schools that have implications for improving classroom discipline?

Elaine (E) Schenkel: I've seen many differences, most of them related to rules and student behavior. For example, I noticed that early elementary classes in the United States tend to be very quiet compared to those in Brazil. In Brazil, there is much more verbal communication among students, and rules such as "raise your hand" don't exist. More active learning seems to occur in Brazil. The U.S. schools were even quieter than Brazilian hospitals!

S: Do you see this as positive for student learning?

E: At first, compared to Brazilian schools, where there is often so much noise and activity among young students that it is difficult to learn, I thought it was. It is definitely better for the teacher! But it is not necessarily better for the students. Activity and communication are how students learn best. In the United States , there are more rules but there are also more problems. The best learning environment is probably somewhere in the center of the two systems. Too many rules and too little noise can be as detrimental to the learning environment as too much noise and too few rules.

S: It seems as if you are recommending that teachers should have fewer rules. Clear, useful rules such as "Show respect for others when they are speaking" might replace the more structured "Raise your hand" or "Don't talk during work time" that characterize many classrooms. Is this the case?

E: Yes. Students need guidelines and structure more related to learning and not focused only on behavior. When my own children attended school in the United States, they went to a magnet school in Houston. One positive example of teaching I saw was that students were oriented very well to the scientific method. Even very young students successfully completed science projects following specific steps or guidelines provided by the teachers. This is the case in reading instruction, too. It was very systematic. In the United States, students learn separate skills of decoding, comprehension, note taking, and so forth. In Brazil, there is less structured instruction.

The best way to keep students well behaved is probably through providing developmentally appropriate, well-structured learning tasks. Students who are enjoying what they do and not feeling frustrated do not cause behavior problems. So, in an ideal classroom, not too many behavior-oriented rules are needed because the structure is in the teaching itself. On the other hand, a classroom where students are frustrated and not learning from the teacher will have students who appear difficult to control no matter how many rules there are. Good teachers don't need to rely on rules to keep their classrooms running smoothly; they need to rely on effective, well-organized teaching activities, empathy, and sensitivity to student needs.

S: Sensitivity to student needs. As an educational psychologist, I agree that this is very important. But it is often difficult to achieve for teachers in a multicultural society where students come to the classrooms with very different values, experiences, expectations, and even languages. Your own children were an example of this. Did they speak any English when you first arrived in Houston?

E: No, absolutely not. My daughter entered first grade speaking only Portuguese. I requested that she be placed in kindergarten instead, because it was impossible for her to follow the lessons in first grade in a foreign language. The teachers were not at all familiar with Portuguese. An example that illustrates my points about both too many rules and lack of sensitivity comes from her experience. Students in her classroom were allowed to use the restroom only at specific times. This was never the case in Brazil. Just from a physical standpoint, this rule seems silly. Students have different body clocks. They do not all need to use the restroom on the same schedule and often they cannot. This arbitrary rule can undermine learning. Students who are uncomfortable physically will not learn as well.

Another problem for my daughter was created in this situation because of insensitivity to language. The teacher apparently assumed my daughter spoke Spanish rather than Portuguese and would say in Spanish that it was time for her to use the restroom. My daughter would refuse because the Spanish word for "using the restroom" means, in Portuguese, "taking a bath." My daughter could not accept the idea of bathing in a toilet! So she naturally refused. Because of this, the teacher viewed my daughter as a behavior problem, and I was called to school to fix the situation! Once my daughter understood that she was not being asked to bathe in a toilet and the teacher understood that my daughter did not speak Spanish, the problem was solved. This is an example of how arbitrary rules and misunderstanding of language and expectations can *create* behavior problems in the eyes of teachers and principals rather than prevent them. It is also an example, though, of the importance of involving parents in school situations when they arise. It is very important for teachers and administrators to work with parents.

S: This story does make a very important point about student behavior! You illustrate how understanding student needs and providing good instruction will prevent problems. The reverse will cause them. As a principal in Brazil, what advice did you give teachers who had problems with students in their classes?

E: I always advised them to approach each student as an individual, with very different personalities and needs, and to try to understand the reasons, from the student's perspective, for the behaviors that were creating a problem. But this again relies on clear communication between teacher and student. Language is part of this; so is an understanding of family dynamics. Teachers in Brazil naturally seem more attuned to differences in students based on background, though. In the United States, the emphasis seemed to be on treating every student exactly the same way. This doesn't necessarily work because students are not all the same. There may be advantages in some situations to this, and disadvantages in others. Both Brazilian and U.S. schools deal with very diverse students—culturally diverse, linguistically diverse, and economically diverse. This is a challenge for teachers. But understanding and valuing the diversity, even though it makes it a little more difficult in the classroom at times, probably are better for long-term reduction of behavior problems than expecting every student to behave and learn exactly the same way.

One area that naturally allows for expressing diverse talents and styles is art and music education. At the time I was in Houston, at that specific school, I found an emphasis on the importance of helping students develop abilities in music and in art. I thought that was excellent for the students. Providing acceptable means of expressing different feelings and views through art, music, literature, and theatre is very important! Here in Brazil, I noticed after I came back that our system had improved in this area of learning, but I understand many schools in the United States have since cut back on art and music education.

I also perceived in the United States how students were engaged in sports or outdoor activities. In Brazil, physical education was once treated as a compulsory subject. Nowadays it is considered an important means of individual development. Sports can be a useful outlet for aggression.

S: So, to summarize, from your perspective as a parent, teacher, and administrator who is familiar with schools in both the United States and Brazil, important points to improve classroom behavior include:

1. Sensitivity to student needs and differences

2. Developmentally appropriate and well-structured lessons

3. A few necessary, well-justified guidelines for behavior

4. Parent involvement when possible

5. Allowing students to express their feelings through art, music, and sports

Is there anything else you would like to share with our readers?

E: I think one problem U.S. teachers face to a greater extent than Brazilian teachers is related to how society perceives their authority. In Brazil, parents, students, and society in general accept that the teacher is in authority during school activities. That authority is rarely if ever challenged. In the United States, nearly everyone questions the authority of teachers and is likely to blame every problem in society on the schools. Neither extreme is ideal. If teachers are competent and caring, it is best that their authority not be questioned. But there needs to be a way to make sure they are always working for the best interests of their students. I think it would be easier for U.S. teachers if society were more supportive and respectful of their authority. This would probably reduce behavior problems. Raising the status of teaching as a profession in the eyes of students, parents, and society as a whole would minimize discipline problems. On the other hand, I think it would be better for Brazilian teachers if parents were more involved in the educational process. Sometimes it is good for teachers to be questioned and held to task. And interaction between home and school can be very valuable for students.

S: I agree. Teachers as professionals should be viewed with respect, and I am hopeful that we will continue to make progress in that direction. Thank you for sharing your insight!

Perhaps this brief interview will provide a sense of what an effective principal considers important for maintaining a safe school. Along with a competent principal, well-disciplined schools typically have at least one staff member who is enthusiastic and supportive of the principal in setting up and carrying out selected discipline procedures. Many principals attribute the success of their discipline program to getting the staff to believe in the school and the programs. They note that supportive staff has a contagious effect on getting students to be more positive about programs.

In well-disciplined schools, the authority and responsibility for handling most discipline problems are placed in the hands of classroom teachers. Discipline problems as a whole are apparently not handled any more effectively by making the school office the center of discipline control. The principal and counselors may be available to handle exceptionally difficult discipline problems, but the teacher should have the authority to deal with most discipline situations.

In addition, most well-disciplined schools have an open-review policy that enables parents and other members of the community to provide input about the school's programs and policies. These schools do not necessarily accept all the advice they receive, but they do listen and consider it when evaluating and modifying school policies.

Student-Orientated Schools and the Role of School Psychologists

Suzanne Little points out that well-disciplined schools typically focus their operation around the care of students. Programs are instituted, with the main priority being those things that benefit students rather than what works easiest for the school staff. One key person in maintaining a student-oriented approach is the school psychologist. What does an effective school psychologist do to maintain a safe school environment? Suzanne Little answers that question as follows:

There have been many descriptions of the role of the school psychologist. However, the consensus is that a school psychologist uses training to assist adolescents in developing the capacity to be capable, productive citizens who exceed all expectations held by others. School psychologists may use different approaches to achieve this goal, but most provide these three core services: assessment, consultation, and intervention/prevention.

A school psychologist is highly trained in a variety of assessment techniques including the assessment of intelligence, achievement, personality, social skills, behavior, and learning styles. In addition, a large portion of our time is spent assisting schools by determining eligibility for special education services.

A school psychologist is also trained in the area of consultation, which includes having knowledge of behavioral modification and classroom management techniques. We spend a considerable amount of time giving alternative strategies to school personnel (teachers, parents, administrators) in regard to student learning, behavior, and child development. In addition, a school psychologist is often a liaison between mental health agencies, community services, and parents.

Intervention and prevention are both important parts of a school psychologist's daily responsibility. They often work one-on-one with parents and families to help solve conflicts. Social skills training, behavioral modification, counseling (individual and group), and other strategies all work toward preventing learning and behavioral problems within the school setting (Fagan & Wise, 2000).

Because the majority of school psychologists are not trained teachers, they bring a unique perspective to the field of education with regard to research and planning. They can assist in evaluating the effectiveness of academic programs, as well as classroom or school-wide behavior and learning approaches.

Although school psychologists are often thought of in their assessment role as a "tester," their ability to be a proactive force against youth violence is one of their strongest assets. By using intervention and prevention skills, they have a wide variety of information, services, and expertise to share with parents, school officials, and community representatives (for example, police, court personnel, and so forth). In cooperation with these individuals, the school psychologist can be the center of a proactive program that attempts to diminish the possibilities of youth violence. Unfortunately, in many settings schools' demands on and expectations of their school psychologist lie only in the area of assessment. This approach often does not leave the school psychologist the time or resources to be available in a proactive intervention and prevention program. Assessment demands and expectations often prevent school psychologists from using their consultative role with parents, teachers, school administrators, and personnel to prevent and deal with youth violence. It is important to have appropriate staff to handle the amount of work associated with the demands of identifying and testing students for special education, but it is also important to use the skills of the psychologists in a broader sense to improve the school environment. School administrators should be encouraged to acknowledge the potential contributions of school psychologists to improve the school environment. Psychologists can be a significant factor in decreasing youth violence and maintaining well-disciplined schools.

Well-disciplined schools do not base their discipline program on one or two isolated practices. Several procedures need to be a constant part of the school environment. Sending home newsletters to inform parents and students of school activities is important for establishing a sense of connection between school and home. Adolescents often perceive that there is little interaction between home and school, and this can lead to problems. On the other hand, often even when schools make an effort to inform parents of activities, there is little interaction between home and classroom. Some parents are simply too busy with their own lives, often out of economic necessity, to devote attention to school issues. Other parents may be intimidated by interactions with school personnel because of their own lack of education. They prefer to let the schools manage their teens alone, without input.

Offering workshops on topics of use to the community are ways schools can engender more support and encourage interaction between parents and school personnel. In high-poverty areas, workshops on job-interview skills and writing resumes, for example, can be provided for students, parents, and other community members. Integrating social services into the schools in these neighborhoods also builds ties with parents and community. One of the most successful inner-city schools with which I have worked in Arizona, for example, housed a Department of Economic Security office, a free daycare center, and a charity warehouse, which provided clothing and other goods to those in need on the campus. The warehouse required recipients of goods to "pay" for what they received by donating time in the classroom or in other ways helping teachers with school-related duties, attending parenting workshops, accompanying their adolescents to counseling sessions, or otherwise spending time with their teens. The nature of the contribution required was determined on an individual basis to most benefit the students, school, and family. This arrangement was highly successful.

Highlighting student achievements, as noted previously, is also important. Allowing students to assist in the "thrift shops" and at community workshops is a good strategy to achieve this goal. Using the workshops and bulletin boards in the warehouse to highlight efforts and successes is a natural way to positively acknowledge students.

Another effective practice is to develop discipline codes with students and parents so that there is a perceived "buy-in" to the rules and the rules are not seen as arbitrary and authoritarian. Many schools currently deal with discipline problems and attendance problems by suspending or expelling the students from school. This is not an effective practice. It may end up placing adolescents who already have problems in situations where they are likely to develop and create more problems. Developing in-school suspension systems that continue to provide education to troubled teens rather than barring problem students from receiving an education and putting them on the streets where they are likely to create more problems is necessary. Many public schools need to be forced to revise and rethink their current policies on attendance, suspension, and expulsion. Developing work-study curricula for students who must work and providing flexible scheduling and night classes for students who must support themselves or assist their families is essential. Schedules can affect school discipline. Making school schedules match community needs is necessary, and this is one area in which Brazil has a better model than the United States. After many years of teaching in U.S. schools and teacher preparation programs, it has been enriching to interact with teachers and students who have been trained and work in completely different educational systems in Brazil and Russia.

It is even more interesting to realize that teachers, schools, and students in Russia and Brazil are not really very different from their U.S. counterparts. Learning styles of the students in those countries mirror those of U.S. students. Teaching strategies used by effective teachers are the same. In fact, there is some evidence that the characteristics of good teachers as perceived by students are similar across cultures.

Effective school principals in all countries also have similar characteristics and priorities and share the same concerns. Limited budgets, lack of parental support, and student conduct are high on the list. The inner-city public high schools in all three countries look and feel very much like the inner-city public high schools in the United States I've worked and done research in, complete with graffiti, although the graffiti in Russian schools tends to be short-lived, as the students are responsible for repainting whenever it appears. The Russians have had restorative justice down to an art ever since they required German soldiers to rebuild their cities after the Great Patriotic War (World War II). Looking on as an observer, though, one feature of the public high schools in Brazil—the scheduling of courses—immediately caught my attention. At first, it may seem that a schedule couldn't possibly be related to student behavior. From the perspective of an educational psychologist, however, that isn't true. As Bronfenbrenner (1994) pointed out, there are several interactive social environments influencing each person, from the individual to the immediate family and neighborhood to the overall social milieu. When dealing with student discipline, we tend to focus on the individual and, perhaps, on the family or neighborhood, but we overlook other issues in the greater social milieu that can be just as critical to influencing student behavior. These are issues such as resources and social conditions, and how well scheduling and content of classes match those conditions.

Maslow's (1968) concept of the hierarchy of human needs leading to self-actualization is also relevant. For self-actualization to occur, several other basic needs must first be met. These include physiological needs such as eliminating hunger and thirst, safety and security needs, needs for affiliation and acceptance, needs for esteem through achievement and recognition, and cognitive and aesthetic needs. For learning to occur, everything else must be in place. We seem to do a good job in U.S. education addressing these needs. We provide free or reduced-cost meals; we constantly focus on issues of safety, security, and discipline; and we work to build rapport with students and improve classroom climates to meet needs for love and affiliation. Teachers have been educated to build self-esteem in students. We have standards and lots of knowledge to share for cognitive needs. Cuts to art and music programs combined with the often drab and dismal aesthetic conditions of many schools may not address aesthetic needs too well, so students turn to Hollywood and music to fill that gap—but five out of six isn't bad, right? And how does this possibly relate to scheduling? Actually, all of the first four needs—physiological, security, affiliation, and esteem needs—are directly related to scheduling in Brazil. I suspect they are in much of the United States, too. We just have not noticed yet. Let me explain.

For many Brazilian students, working to help support the family is an economic necessity that must begin as early as possible. The average family income here is less than $300 per month. The contribution of each family member, including children, to support basic needs is important to family stability and security. Contributing to family income is tied to needs for affiliation, love, and esteem. Working as early as possible is a reality, not an option, for many students. Considering this fact of life, it is amazing that some cities in Brazil—Porto Alegre, for example—have a 97 percent literacy rate and a quality of life better than that of many U.S. large cities as measured by infant mortality, environmental quality, absence of homelessness, and other indices. School scheduling may be a major contributor to this achievement. Schools offer classes continuously from 8 A.M. to 10 P.M., Monday through Friday and even on Saturdays. Students can select the schedule that best fits with their work requirements. They can go to classes in the morning, afternoon, or evening. Students who work during the day can attend school during the evening. If they have a night job, they can go to school during the day. Teachers, too, have a flexible schedule. Each teacher instructs five courses or so but selects the times most conducive for family and personal needs. Several of my associates, for example, like to have afternoons free and prefer a morning/evening combination schedule. This sometimes requires teachers to offer classes at more than one school, but it works. More important, it works for the students.

Although it is likely that there are many students in the United States in economic circumstances and with family expectations similar to those described previously, these students do not have the ability to successfully combine education and work. They drop out or else they are suspended for poor attendance because they choose to meet physiological, security, affiliation, and esteem needs in a manner acceptable to their families and neighborhoods. Or else, they attend school grudgingly—perhaps even at the insistence of parents who want them to have a better life. This frustration may result, unwittingly, in a variety of problem behaviors. Suspension, after all, is one way to resolve the internal dilemma, so students may act out or not attend school in order to be suspended. Thus, scheduling does influence behavior. Modifying school schedules to match the social milieu to allow students to meet basic needs in whatever life circumstances they find themselves may prevent many discipline problems and would certainly reduce the high school drop-out rate.

It seems fitting that schools with banners quoting Paulo Friere on the importance of providing public education for *all* would develop a schedule that promotes attendance for all students. Several charter schools in Arizona and other areas in the United States that are successful with inner-city, high-risk youth have adopted similar models. It is certainly a practice that more schools should consider, and it may take community outcry to cause this to happen. This simple change could go a long way toward improving the school environment.

Improving School Environment

Principals of well-disciplined schools point out how important it is for both students and teachers to feel they are in an environment where accomplishing positive results is possible. The ideal environment of a school is one that encourages good communication, mutual trust, and success in reaching positive goals. This environment is compatible with Edith Grotberg's emphasis on creating resiliency. She writes the following about school environments:

School is where children and youth develop their social skills, as well as their academic skills. School is where children and youth must learn to deal with issues of peer pressure, bullying, relationships with teachers, and other authority figures. It is where they learn to become members of a larger society. It is where they become more independent of the home as the primary social group. Schools have expectations of certain behaviors and values among their students, including:

1. a sense of responsibility

2. self-control

3. achievement and mastery of skills and subject matter

4. appropriate group behavior and team work

5. *acceptance by peers*

6. *respect for oneself and others*

7. *taking turns*

8. *listening to the teacher*

9. *obeying rules*

10. *accepting authority*

Both home and school require a sense of responsibility and sharing. But some of the other expectations are different, such as feeling empathy and caring for people. In some cases, home promotes this. Many schools do not. A youth who expects or displays empathy and caring in the school may be rebuffed or even teased for being such a "softie."

Another difference concerns relationships with people of different ages. At home, the relationships are across ages, with children and youth relating to a range of age groups. At school, the relationships are with same-age peers. As a matter of fact, youth in different grades tend to relate primarily with those in the same grade. And, often, children who are older than their class-mates are shunned. This peer organization of the schools may be a necessary adaptation to the limits of funds and the teaching of specific subjects, but is not organized for broad social development.

This is an interesting observation. Several studies in educational psychology support the use of cross-age classrooms and cooperative learning strategies as the best means of mastering not only content but also appropriate social skills. The old "one-room schoolhouse" model common in much of the United States until the last half of the twentieth century naturally lent itself to this type of an educational model. Perhaps the long-touted decline in U.S. public education is due to a change from this model to an age-graded system, which is more rigid and does not allow for individual pacing and cross-age collaboration, both of which are more compatible means of learning from a social developmental perspective.

The older system developed thinking skills, social skills, and elements of resilience based on an inherent structure allowing older students to nurture and care for younger students in a way more similar to family dynamics. The age-graded system results in students competing with each other aggressively and viewing students of different ages and grades as members of an outgroup instead of part of an extended family. Peer relationships are important, but many that develop in the age-graded system have destructive elements. Because of this, it is necessary to incorporate additional strategies to build resilience and nurture positive social development. Edith Grotberg is currently involved in training teachers toward these ends. Here are more of her comments regarding training teachers to foster resilience and nurture positive social development among their students:

Perhaps too many adults think peers can only be a negative influence. Evidence suggests that peers can influence each other in positive ways, as well. They do this by modeling what is better behavior or by making it clear that they disapprove of unkind or aggressive behavior. But the fact is, peers tend to hang out with those who have similar values and behaviors. It is difficult to break up cliques or gangs; they clearly need each other as they are.

Many teachers, concerned about peer pressure and other problems youth present to them, express interest in learning more about the promotion of resilience as a way to help youth deal with the experiences of adversity they have in the schools. Resilience is the human capacity to face, overcome, be strengthened by, and even transformed by experiences of adversity. The resilience factors that can be promoted and used in dynamic interaction in dealing with adversity consist of external supports, labeled by the author as I Have; *inner strengths, labeled* I Am; *and interpersonal and problem-solving skills, labeled* I Can *(Grotberg, 1995). Each factor can be promoted separately or in combination.*

I have conducted workshops with teachers for Continuing Education (American Psychological Association) credit to help them to foster resilience among their students. The following goals were set for teachers:

1. *Use the language of resilience*
2. *Apply resilience promoting responses to situations of adversity*
3. *Give examples of the dynamics of promoting resilience*
4. *Report situations of adversity accurately*
5. *Describe ways in which resilience may be promoted or used and ways it is not promoted, or is destroyed*

As a result of the workshops, the following changes were reported by teachers and supported through empirical data collection. Teachers were more able to:

1. *Find role models for their students to demonstrate how to deal with the problem*
2. *Feel more empathy in a common adversity, and relay this to students*
3. *Talk to others, sharing thoughts and feelings and encourage students to do so*
4. *Help students to manage behavior when considering doing something unacceptable or out of anger*
5. *Seek help from those who are trusted*

These changes suggest that teachers before the training focused on subject matter more than on interpersonal relationships, but the training refocused their priorities. A follow-up study conducted six months later indicated that they were continuing to promote resilience in their students and in themselves by maintaining these improvements.

Other workshops, including both elementary and middle-school students, made quite clear that the line for empathetic interaction seems to be drawn at sixth grade. Up to that level, teachers are very involved with the interpersonal relationships of the children, but from sixth grade and higher, teachers focus on subject matter. The concern about students is more on expecting good behavior than on interpersonal relationships. This is ironic, for when students enter adolescence, they need increased social support and empathy. It may be that part of the problem we currently see with adolescent aggression is the result of a school system that is not developmentally attuned to student needs. With the emphasis in school on subject matter combined with increased freedom and distance from support at home, youth are left to create their own interpersonal behaviors, unless teachers begin to understand the importance of the promotion of resilience as part of their interaction with their students. If teachers do not empathize with the increased sensitivity to peers inherent in adolescent development, many students may drop out of school. Here is an example:

A teenager is dropping out of school. Here is his reasoning: I don't like school. I don't like my teacher because he is always scolding me for not getting my homework in. I don't like to do the homework because I don't understand how to do the problems and I don't want to admit I can't do them. That makes me look stupid and I don't like to look stupid. I am failing and so I might as well drop out.

Teachers often play a critical role in the lives of students, especially when students have serious problems at home. They are not only role models of behavior, but they are often the only supports some students have that help them deal with their adversities. Ruth Simmons, the President of Brown University, was brought up in poverty, and her family could provide her with little help as she showed a great interest in reading. Some teachers recognized her intelligence and ability and were especially supportive of her when her mother died. She was encouraged to continue in her studies and was helped in finding financial support to pursue advanced studies. This is just one of many examples. Empathy and understanding are necessary traits for teachers of adolescents to foster resilience.

Changes that seem to be made with workshops suggest that there is receptiveness to the promotion of resilience that should be tapped; however, it is important not to see resilience as something separate from the general curriculum. This is especially true for adolescents who come from communities that put them at risk. Schools are part of the community, to be sure, but the community is larger than families and schools. The community is the broad ecological setting for families and schools, providing health and social services, as well as security. It is the I Have part of resilience. A community must be responsible for roads and buildings and have laws that provide guidance to the individuals who live within its bounds. The community also is made up of political structures that determine what kinds of values are used to make decisions and take actions. A study of resilient communities (Suarez-Ojeda, 2001) identified four major factors that characterize resilient communities:

1. *Collective self-esteem: The community is proud of itself in terms of cleanliness, provision of services, and caring for its citizens*

2. *Cultural identity: The members of the community identify themselves with the community even through change*

3. *Social Humor: The community does not take itself too seriously and is able to joke and recognize the humor of life*

4. *Collective honesty: The community demands that all its institutions be honest*

In contrast, Suarez-Ojeda (2001) described communities he studied that did not foster resilience as having these qualities:

1. *Lack of cultural identity: Many people do not identify with their community; rather they continue to identify with the community they came from and see themselves as temporary and disengaged residents in their current place of residence*

2. *Fatalism: When people believe they can do nothing about what happens to them and that all is predetermined, they become passive and easy targets for those who wish to dominate and control*

3. *Authoritarianism: When there is a vacuum of cultural identity combined with fatalism, it is inevitable that authoritarian governments will take over*

4. *Corruption: When no one cares about the community; when one's sense of identity exists elsewhere, or when there is passive acceptance of conditions, the community will be taken over by the corrupt, the greedy, and the unsavory.*

Well-disciplined schools tend to make strong efforts to get parents and community agencies involved in the school program. Such schools go beyond programs such as newsletters and activity calendars sent to parents to keep them informed of school activities. Teachers in these schools are more prone to call and interact with their students' parents. Community leaders are brought in to give lectures and assist in selecting scholarship winners, science fair winners, and the like. Organizations are established in cooperation with other agencies to solicit involvement, build the resilience factors noted previously, and diminish the factors that destroy resilience. One example of such an organization is a community justice alliance developed in southwestern

Arizona to combat problems with gang-related crime. The alliance, initially organized and funded through the county attorney's office, began meeting more than three years ago in the local school. Gradually, more and more concerned community members began to participate. Since its inception, the group has completely changed the dynamics of what was once a very rundown, unsafe area. New streetlights, wider streets, improved housing, better public services, and a renewed interest in school, resulting in fewer discipline problems and a lowered drop-out rate, are just a few of the accomplishments. The major accomplishment is that community members have learned they *can* make a difference and the community has become resilient. Such interagency cooperative efforts housed in schools are essential to decreasing school violence, especially in high-risk areas where gangs and drugs add to the problem. The next chapter provides more in-depth information on the role of substance abuse in teen violence, as well as some constructive solutions.

Resources Compiled by Augustus Little

In an attempt to assist schools Mitchell (2000) compiled a sample of the many resources devoted to school safety and violence prevention. Canter (1998) compiled relevant sources for school psychologists to use when dealing with adolescent violence. These are included here along with others I find helpful. With the use of the resources mentioned here, it is hoped that you will be better prepared than I was to face the challenges that exist in our schools. It has been a long journey for me, but I realized a long time ago that the road to success is always under construction. Here are some resources to help as you travel that road.

Organizations

Center for the Prevention of School Violence	www.ncsu.edu/cpsv
Center for the Prevention of Violence	www.colorado.edu/cspv
Children's Safety Network	www.edc.org/HHD/csn/ index.html
Conflict Resolution Education Network (CREnet)	www.crenet.org
Girls Incorporated National Headquarters	www.girlsinc.org

Institute on Violence and Destructive Behavior	http://interact.uoregon.edu/ivdb/ivdb.html
National Criminal Justice References Services	www.ncjrs.org
National Resource Center for Safe Schools (NCRCSS)	www.safetyzone.org
National School Safety Center (NCSS)	www.nsscl.org
National Youth Gang Center (NYGC)	www.iir.com/nygc
Office of Juvenile Justice & Delinquency Prevention	http://ojjpdp.ncjrs.org
Safe and Drug-Free Schools Program (SDFSP)	www.ed.gov/offices/OESE/SDFS

Online Publications

Creating Safe, Drug-Free Schools: An Action Plan	www.ed.gov/offices/OESE/SDFS/actguid/index.html
How To Combat Truancy	www.ed.gov/pubs/Truancy
ERIC Clearinghouse on Educational Management	http://www.uncg.edu/edu/ericcass
ERIC Clearinghouse for Counseling	http://www.uncg.edu/edu/ericass
Partnership Against Violence Network	www.pavnet.org
ERIC Clearinghouse Virtual Library	www.uncg.edu/edu/ericass/lihome.htm

Many Web sites are available to educators and parents. Some of the most informative ones include:

National School Safety Center	www.nsscl.org/
OJJDP—School Violence Resources	www.ojjdp.ncjrs.org/resources/school.html
Center for the Prevention of School Violence	www.ncsu.edu/cpsv

CDC Media facts: Youth and Violence	www.cdc.gov/od/oc/media/fact/violence.htm
The School Violence Watch Network	www.cybersnitch.net/school violencewatch.htm
Guide for Preventing and Responding to School Violence	www.theiacp.org/pubinfo/pubs/pslc/svindex.htm
Center for Mental Health School Violence Prevention	www.mentalhealth.org/school violence/
Federal Activities Addressing Violence in Schools	www.cdc.gov/nccdphp/dash/violence/index.htm
Electronic Government Information on School Violence	www.lib.umd.edu/GOV/el-schviol.html
Criminal Justice Resources: School Violence	www.lib.msu.edu/harris23/crimjust/school.htm
Safety Zone	www.safetyzone.org/
National School Safety and Security Services	www.schoolsecurity.org/
APA HelpCenter: Warning Signs of Teen Violence	www.helping.apa.org/warningsigns/index.html
School Violence Virtual Library	www.riccass.uncg.edu/virtuallib/violence/violencebook.html
Urban Education Web	www.eric-web.tc.columbia.edu/
OJJDP—Gang Resources	www.ojjdp.ncjrs.org/resources/gangs.html
Violent Kids Information Site: School Violence	www.violentkids.com/articles/violence_article_4.html

Here is a list of helpful printed information worth studying. I hope these resources will assist you in establishing safe schools in your community. I offer these resources to my students who are preparing to be teachers, counselors, and administrators in public schools.

Books and Journals

Anderson, B. (Ed.). (1995). *Taking back tomorrow: A school leader's guide to violence, security and safeguarding our school children.* Alexandria, VA: National School Boards Association.

Brock, S. E., Sandoval, J., & Lewis, S. (1996). *Preparing for crises in the schools: A manual for building school crisis response teams.* New York: Wiley.

Brooks, B. & Siegel, P. (1996). *The scared child. Helping kids overcome traumatic events.* New York: Wiley.

Canter, A. & Carroll, S. (Eds.). (1998). *Helping children at home and school: Handouts from your school psychologist. (Section 8: Safety and Crisis).* Bethesda, MD: National Association of School Psychologists.

Centers for Disease Control. (1992). *Suicide prevention programs: A resource guide.* Atlanta: Author

Duhon-Sells, R. (1995). *Dealing with youth violence: What schools and communities need to know.* Bloomington, IN: National Educational Service.

Dwyer, K., Osher, D., & Warger, C. (1998). *Early warning, timely response: A guide to safe schools.* Washington, DC: U.S. Department of Education. (Available at www.naspweb.org/center. html)

Garrity, C., Jens, K., Porter, W., Sager, N., & Short-Camilli, C. (1994). *Bully-proofing your school.* Longmont, CO: Sopris West.

Poland, S. (1998). *School violence: Lessons learned.* Longmont, CO: Sopris West.

Ross, D. (1996). *Childhood bullying and teasing: What school personnel, other professional, and parents can do.* Washington, DC: American Counseling Association.

Walker, H. M., & Gresham, F. M. (1997). Making schools safer and violence free. *Intervention in School and Clinic, 32* (4), 199–204.

Young, M. A. (1998). *Community crisis response team training manual* (2nd ed.). Washington, DC: National Organization for Victim Assistance.

This next list summarizes materials for teachers to use in the classroom to prevent violence.

Goldstein, A., Palumbo, J., Striepling, S., & Voutsinas, A. (1995). *Break it up: A teachers' guide to managing student aggression.* Champaign, IL: Research Press (phone: 217-352-3273).

    Step-by-step procedures to a team approach to handling student disruption and aggression; also available on video.

Kreidler, W. J. (1994). *Conflict resolution in the middle school: A curriculum and teaching guide.* Boston: Boston Area Educators for Social Responsibilities (phone: 617-492-8820).

    More than 150 activities to help students deal effectively with conflict in grades 6–8. (Companion curriculum for elementary students also available. Creative conflict resolution: More than 200 activities for keeping peace in the classroom.)

National Crime Prevention Council (1992). *Special focus—Preventing violence: Program ideas and examples.* Washington, DC: Author (phone: 202–466–6272).

    A cross section of antiviolence programs.

Peace Grows, Inc. (1992). *Alternatives to violence.* Akron, OH: Author (phone: 216-864-5442).

    Curriculum materials designed to reduce violence through mediation and other peaceful strategies for high school students. Includes material for training workshops of 4 to 40 hours.

Prothrow-Stith, D. (1987). *Violence prevention: Curriculum for adolescents.* Newton, MA: Education Development Center, Inc. (55 Chapel St, Newton, MA 02160).

    Sample lessons, exercises, projects, and handouts to help students become aware of positive ways to deal with anger and conflict.

Shure, M. B. (1994, 1995, 1996). *Raising a thinking child.* Henry Holt & Company, Inc. (book, workbook); Bantam Doubleday Dell (audiotape).

    Multimedia program to teach problem-solving skills.

Violence prevention: Totally awesome strategies for safe and drug-free schools. (1995). Blacklick, OH: Meeks-Heit Publishing Co. (phone: 800-682-6882).

    Resources, curriculum, annotated bibliography, teaching strategies. Meeks-Heit also publishes a series of Violence Prevention Student Handbooks.

Agencies

American Association of Suicidology, 2459 S. Ash, Denver CO 80222; (phone: 303-692-0285).

Federal Emergency Management Agency (FEMA) PO Box 70274, Washington, DC 20024; (phone: 202-646-3484).

National Crime Prevention Council, 1700 K St NW, Second Floor, Washington, DC 20006; (phone: 202-393-7141).

National School Safety Center, 4165 Thousand Oaks Blvd, Suite 290, Westlake Village, CA 91362; (phone: 805-373-9977).

National Organization for Victim Assistance (NOVA), 1757 Park Rd. NW, Washington, DC 20010; (phone: 800-TRY-NOVA).

CHAPTER 4

AGGRESSION DIRECTED INWARD: SUBSTANCE ABUSE, SUICIDE, AND SELF-HARM

Some of the information recounted here first appeared in a chapter by Sherri McCarthy and Thomas Waters in Handbook of Practice-Based Research *(Oxford, 2003) and in a chapter on adolescent suicide by Elza Dutra published in Portuguese in* Children and Adolescents at Risk: Theoretical Aspects and Strategies for Intervention *(Casa do Psicólogo, 2002) edited by Claudio S. Hutz and translated for use here by Rene Pinto and Sherri McCarthy.*

Adolescence has been viewed historically as a difficult time, fraught with "storm and stress." G. Stanley Hall (1904) viewed adolescence as when "the wisdom and advice of parents and teachers is overtopped, and may be met by blank contradiction" (p. 79). Taking historical and theoretical views in combination with contemporary research, the core of the "storm and stress" view seems to hinge on the idea that adolescence is more difficult than other periods of life, both for adolescents and for the people around them. Conflict with parents and society, depression, mood disruptions, and risky behavior seem to characterize adolescence as described by both historical and contemporary scholars, including G. Stanley Hall (1904), Margaret Mead (1928), Anna Freud (1958, 1969), Eccles et al. (1993), Steinberg and Levine (1997), and others. Even Shakespeare, in *A Winter's Tale*, covers this view in a soliloquy delivered by an old man near the beginning of the play:

> I would there were no age between 10 and 23, or that youth would sleep out the rest, for there is nothing in between but getting wenches with child, wronging the ancientry, stealing and fighting.

Hall concurs, describing "a period of semicriminality" as "normal for healthy adolescent boys." Research confirms that in the United States and other Western countries, the teens and early twenties are years of highest prevalence for a variety of behaviors that carry the risk of harm to self and others. Risky behavior, including substance abuse, risky sexual behavior, and criminal acts, peaks in late adolescence (Arnett, 2000). If Hall's assessment that "semicriminality is normal" is accepted, then criminalizing adolescents through heightened contact with police and jails may be counterproductive, but that is the trend in the United States regardless, especially for crimes related to substance abuse. One theory seems to be that removing people who perform an act deemed illegal from society by locking them up in a cell, regardless of circumstances, is the best way to make society safe. Given what we know of adolescent development, this is obviously absurd, but it seems to be a theory accepted by many in the United States, although this is less so in other countries. In Brazil, for example, adolescents are rarely incarcerated for substance use. Family, group, and individual counseling are certainly better strategies for addressing adolescent drug addiction, but in the United States, many adolescents are jailed for crimes related to casual drug use.

Substance Abuse Treatment Strategies in Criminal Justice Settings

In 2001, the number of juvenile arrests in the United States had risen to more than 2,300,000 and it continues to escalate. The majority of arrests are for drugs and drug paraphernalia. Some (though certainly not all) illegal drugs and alcohol are correlated with aggressive, violent behavior and, from that standpoint, may be problematic. Certainly, substance abuse of a serious nature is a form of aggression—it is aggression directed inward. Anger, depression, pain, and other negative emotions are dealt with through attempts to self-medicate. Rather than acting out to release the emotions that cannot be accepted, drug addicts direct the aggression against themselves. Suicide and other forms of self-harm are also examples of inwardly directed aggression.

Rather than arresting and jailing adolescents who express their inwardly directed aggression through substance abuse—a strategy that, in the long run, is likely to either transform their anger to outwardly expressed acts of aggression or exacerbate the problems responsible for drug use in the first place—it makes far more sense to provide adolescents who are arrested for substance use with counseling and treatment. One way to accomplish this within the legal structure currently in place is through drug courts.

Drug courts are becoming increasingly common. They are effective models for delivering treatment to adolescents arrested for offenses related to substance abuse in the United States, as they prove to be efficient, effective, and less costly than incarceration. More than a decade has passed since the first drug court model in the United States was established. Dade County, Florida, implemented the model in 1989 as a diversionary program for offenders facing charges of simple drug possession.

Several states have begun to legally mandate treatment as part of sentencing for drug-related cases, but this procedure often differs from drug court models. The mandated treatment is often not funded or overseen by the court. Offenders may be unable to afford treatment and must rely on whatever managed care system is available through state welfare indigent care coverage, if any. From both a cost and treatment perspective, this is not optimal, especially in rural areas where there is a severe shortage of psychologists, substance abuse counselors, and detoxification units. The current national average stay for substance abuse treatment through managed care is 3.8 days for detoxification, followed by 10 daily sessions and 16 follow-up sessions. For those in rural areas, the detoxification and treatment generally occur in another city, offering high costs but little in the way of assistance to offenders when they return to their homes and to the conditions that trigger and exacerbate their problems. Treatment through a drug court model allows for continuing long-term counseling in the community, generally one or more years, and assistance with the triggers and issues that are responsible for abuse. The cost is lower and benefits are higher, as success is often correlated with time in treatment and with cultural and contextual factors in the therapeutic milieu. This is clearly a preferable model.

A drug court is a special judicial body given the responsibility to handle cases involving drug-using offenders through an extensive supervision and treatment program. Drug court uses a case management team approach. The team is typically composed of the presiding judge, the prosecutor, the defense counsel, a psychologist and/or substance abuse treatment specialist, a vocational counselor, a probation officer, education specialists, and community leaders (Belenko, 1996). Drug courts attempt to motivate offenders to overcome their substance-abuse problems and reconnect to the community as productive citizens. In addition, these courts are intended to ensure consistency in judicial decision making, enhance the coordination of community agencies and resources and increase the cost-effectiveness of sentencing, and maintenance for those convicted of minor drug-related crimes. Since the implementation of the first U.S. drug court, more than 150,000 offenders have participated in or are currently involved with treatment in similar programs. The current number of active drug courts in the United States exceeds 400, with more than 200 more in various stages of implementation and development. More than 100,000 participants have graduated from drug court programs (Hora, Schma, & Rosenthal, 1999; Robinson, 2001). Such courts have expanded recently into the juvenile justice system.

Although many psychologists view forced, or coerced, treatment as less than optimal, research suggests that, in the case of substance abuse offenders, there may be benefits. For example, beyond a 90-day threshold, treatment outcomes appear to improve in direct relationship to the time spent in treatment, with one year generally found to be the minimum effective duration for treatment. More than 60 percent of those who enter treatment through drug court models are still in treatment after one year (Belenko, 1998) compared to only 10 percent of those who voluntarily participate in substance abuse treatment programs. Clients who remain in treatment for extended periods apparently overcome much of the initial resistance coercion creates, as research on the outcomes of many U.S. drug courts shows success despite initial perceptions of coercion on the part of participants. This is especially true when continued individual and group counseling is mandated in the treatment program (Satel, 2001). Thus, from a psychological perspective, drug court models that keep clients in treatment with qualified clinicians for more than one year, whether or not the initial entry is viewed as coerced, are likely to show success. Cognitive-behavioral therapy appears to be an especially useful approach with recovering addicts (Spurgeon, McCarthy & Waters, 1999) and is often the treatment of choice in drug court programs.

Assisting recovered addicts in dealing with cues to prevent relapse is also critical from a psychological perspective (Foxhall, 2001). Therefore, a drug court model that includes extensive focus on a relapse prevention plan is likely to assist in client success. Because "triggers," or people, places, things, and events that have become associated with drug use through classical conditioning (Spurgeon, McCarthy, & Waters, 1999) can also lead to relapse, long-term programs that establish new habits, social networks, and living arrangements are likely to demonstrate more success. Goal-setting and the increased self-efficacy and sense of personal control that arises from meeting goals are also likely to be important to treatment success. Certainly there is evidence that a variety of variables, including (1) drug history, (2) history of physical or social abuse, (3) family of origin alcohol or substance abuse, (4) length of abstinence, (5) employment status, (6) social support system/access to services, (7) religious affiliation, and (8) cultural cohort variables related to age and ethnicity impact success rates. Type of treatment (group or individual, cognitive-behavioral, or psychodynamic) and length of treatment are also related to success rates.

Long-term individual therapy using a cognitive-behavioral approach seems to show evidence of being the most effective treatment strategy overall, especially when combined with goal-setting and social support, which leads to improved self-efficacy. Education, job satisfaction, economic improvement, stable family relationships, and friendships are also correlated with success. An effective drug court model should combine all of these forms of support for optimum success. Psychologists should have an important role in designing and delivering services for criminal justice agencies and courts that develop drug courts. By the very nature of the relationship that ensues, practice-based research and research-based practice go hand in hand in such collaborations.

When developing a drug court treatment model, it is important to focus on the unique characteristics and needs of the area, and the agencies and clients the court will serve. There is not, unfortunately, one "best" decision tree for all courts. Each must be approached as a unique entity, and on-going research must influence treatment and operations. There are several important questions to consider in planning effective drug court treatment programs. Questions focused on potential clients include these:

1. What are the characteristics of the population to be treated?
2. What languages and cultural orientations are most common?
3. What is the average age of clients?
4. What is the average socioeconomic status?
5. What types of use patterns are most frequent?
6. Which substances are generally abused?
7. What types of assessment tools are most appropriate?

Other questions may also be important, and it may be that common patterns may not be evident among clients in some areas. In our experience, however, this is not the case. When drug courts are integrated into communities, the clients they serve often have common characteristics, problems, and use patterns.

Questions focused on planning and implementation include these:

1. What types and sources of funding are available to hire staff, administer treatment, and collect data?

2. What is the level of training of the staff in the agency who works directly with clients?

3. What is the common organizational philosophy toward clients? Is punishment or rehabilitation favored?

4. What types of training, resources, and services for staff will facilitate effective psychological treatment?

5. How can available community resources and services best be coordinated to serve in substance abuse treatment?

6. How will decisions be made, in an ongoing and systematic way, to improve treatment? Who will be responsible for these decisions, that is, a community board, the judge, the interdisciplinary team?

7. How can the community best be apprised of and involved with treatment?

It may be necessary to collect preliminary data and conduct focus groups to address these questions. It is also necessary to address how data will continue to be collected throughout the program. Questions focused on continuous data collection and reporting include these:

1. Who will be the audience for the data?

2. Who will analyze the data and determine results?

3. What types of evidence will the local voters understand and prefer to see?

4. What criteria do the funding agencies involved demand?

5. What mechanisms are already in place to provide data?

6. Will the data that are routinely collected be reliable and valid?

7. What types of issues related to confidentiality (or, in the case of minors, parent and family rights) may influence how data are collected?

All of these questions must be answered before initiating a treatment program. Because the answers are likely to differ depending on location and agencies involved, psychologists working in such programs need to be true research-practitioners and may be well advised to use a phenomenological approach, tempered by careful examination of quantitative data from other, similar programs, during the planning stages. Be aware that each program will function somewhat differently and require unique procedures. Use available data to make decisions concerning which treatment modalities and data collection procedures are most appropriate. An example follows that is based on our experience for use by those involved in developing, working in, and evaluating drug court programs. This example is based on a plan devised for a drug court implemented within a juvenile probation agency in the southwestern United States. The process began by setting specific goals in collaboration with judges and agency directors. A research model with several data-generating activities was then planned. The overall goal was to determine the effectiveness of juvenile drug court from three different perspectives: (1) implementation, (2) process, and (3) outcomes.

Overall, the evaluation plan sought to determine whether program objectives were met by determining the impact of participation on the target population. This was to be accomplished by assessing whether graduation from drug court had any long-term (beyond one year) effect on participants' use of drugs and criminal activities and by determining if differences in other, related dimensions existed between graduates of drug court treatment programs and other youth who had been arrested for possession and/or use of illegal substances assigned to the same agency who had not participated in drug court treatment.

A relatively simple quasi-experimental design could assess to what extent, if any, substance abuse counseling caused the desired changes in participants, but this traditional assessment model was not considered optimal for several reasons. Implementation, process, and outcome are all important segments to examine from a phenomenological perspective. Key questions need to be answered even before determining and delivering treatment. These questions address characteristics of the target population. Who are the youth in the agency's charge? What were they arrested for? What is the common family structure they experience, including socioeconomic considerations, parent education, culture, and language? What are their prior arrest records like? What is the level of severity of substance abuse among members of this group?

Once these questions are answered, a treatment strategy that will reach this target population needs to be developed and implemented. Implementation must then be assessed. The primary objective of assessing implementation and process is to determine the extent to which the operationalized version of drug court treatment within a particular agency compares to the original design and intent. Gathering data about the common attitudes and practices of staff, organizational philosophy, and climate is important to this dimension of assessment. Also, when problems are identified and changes are introduced, such as staff training or policy revisions, do such changes achieve the desired effect? This must also be determined, and as it is an ongoing process to improve treatment, it also will affect results.

Process must be addressed. Because of the multiple influences, regulations, and procedures in effect in criminal justice agencies, it is impossible to implement a "clean" comparative experimental design. Instead, each agency program must be studied as an individual entity. Questions addressing process for the particular agency presented here as an example included:

1. How many juveniles were screened for the program? How many were accepted? How many were declined? What patterns or reasons influenced this selection of subjects?

2. What types of treatment services are routinely provided for participants with specific characteristics, such as mental health issues and drug use? What is the average length the services are provided? What is the level of family involvement?

3. What ancillary services, if any, are provided to participants or their families?

4. What is the frequency of drug testing during each phase? Are drug tests given on a random basis? For what types of drugs are the participants being tested? What are the results?

5. Who is graduating from the program? Are there common characteristics of participants who successfully complete the program compared to those who do not? If so, what are these?

6. Who is being terminated from the program? What are the reasons for termination? During what phase of the program are participants generally terminated?

7. What sanctions are being given to the participants? What are the reasons for the sanctions? What are the incentives being given to the participants? What are the percentages of incentive versus sanctions being given to the participants?

8. Does school attendance and progress improve during the program? If so, what programs or services provided by schools may also be influencing the outcome? Are learning disabilities or problems identified and addressed during the program?

9. What is the level of judicial supervision? How many court hearings does the participant attend?

10. Is information communicated effectively among the team members?

11. What fees are assessed to the participants? What fees did the participants pay?

12. How does the drug court process compare with historical methods of
treating juvenile substance abusers? What is the cost of the program
in comparison to other methods?

Process evaluation should answer questions such as these and provide
important data for interpreting results. It should also indicate any gaps
in the treatment program. These gaps might include additional treatment services needed, cultural diversity issues, gender issues, political
or community issues surrounding the drug court team, and parental
or peer concerns. Evaluation should also indicate the strengths of the
program and identify which participants with specific characteristics
benefit most from the program. Process evaluation is used throughout
planning and implementation as a learning tool to guide and refine
the program in a direction that will increase its effectiveness. Process
evaluation incorporates both qualitative and quantitative tools, strategies and reports, which include summaries of:

1. Referrals/screening to program

2. Declines to program

3. Participant demographics

4. Community demographics

5. Participant offense history, adjudication, and hearing data

5. Activity hours and program levels/phases

6. Treatment completed

7. Sanctions completed

8. Adjudications in the program

9. Detention days served by participants in the program

10. Drug type testing of participants

11. Completion/expulsion rates

12. Re-arrest history and detention days served by graduates and non-
graduates from the program.

This list was compiled based on accessible records and existing
agency reports that provided relevant information. Another consideration of process evaluation is how to define, measure, and establish
program success. Setting outcomes objectives that are in line with the
expectations of local constituents of the agency, political climate, and

realistic treatment success rates are necessary. The following outcome objectives were identified as indicators of success for the drug court treatment program within this agency:

1. The juvenile drug court program will reduce commitments and out-of-home placements of substance abusing juveniles by 20 percent over two years.

2. Juvenile drug court graduates will show a 60 percent improvement in school attendance and academic performance as measured by passing grades.

3. Seventy-five percent of the participants will successfully complete the drug court program.

4. Seventy-five percent of the juvenile drug court graduates will remain drug and crime free for more than one year after graduation.

5. Seventy-five percent of graduates' families will report improved family relations.

6. Seventy-five percent of graduates' parents/guardian will report improved awareness of parenting skills and substance abuse issues.

7. Graduates will report a 30 percent increase in vocational readiness according to interviews.

Data to assess these outcomes were generated in several ways. Observations were used extensively. To assess program activities, pre- and post-interviews of program staff, participants, and family members of participants were recorded and reviewed. Data on drug testing, attendance at counseling sessions, school records, use of referral services, program compliance, and use of sanctions for all youth within the jurisdiction of the agency were collected and reviewed. The impact of drug court treatment on agency resources, such as costs, jail space, human resources, and time, was also assessed and compared to previous years. To compare outcomes for adolescents who completed drug court treatment to those of other defendants, local, state, and federal criminal justice databases were used. In addition, follow-up interviews were conducted with all participants at six-month and one-year intervals after completion of drug court. Participation in follow-up community support groups for all drug participants for one year after completion of treatment was also tracked.

A matrix identifying the major data elements needed for the evaluation, where the data were located, and the person responsible for the data was developed and implemented by the agency. Information and data were reviewed quarterly. The quarterly reports were reviewed with the Drug Court Advisory Board, which made recommendation for alterations to the program. Annual reports were compiled and shared with the public.

Before beginning treatment and data collection, focus group meetings with members of the target population and/or their advocates to obtain input into the design and implementation of the evaluation plan were conducted. The strategy presented here for measuring the overall effectiveness of cognitive-behavioral substance abuse treatment with adolescents provided information to enhance drug court operations and contributed to the growing body of knowledge concerning the effectiveness of drug courts and of cognitive-behavioral treatments within substance abuse counseling. The planning related to developing, implementing, and evaluating this juvenile drug court is presented here to consider as a model for others conducting and assessing such programs, and we strongly recommend that such programs be implemented.

Treatment for substance abuse delivered within drug court models appears to have promising results, despite initial concerns about coercive treatment. The extended length of treatment and the influence of behavioral control on developing new habit patterns exercised within this environment seem to enhance success rates, provided treatment programs are overseen by psychologists who integrate practice-based research and evaluation into practice. A phenomenological approach to combining qualitative and quantitative data, as described here, is among the best methods to incorporate (Gomes, De Souza, & McCarthy, 2005) in the practice-based research that ideally characterizes effective drug court treatment programs. As more psychologists become involved and gather data on success rates, identify useful practices for specific populations, develop screening and assessment tools, and train probation officers and other agency personnel in effective cognitive behavioral techniques, it is likely that the benefit of drug court treatment programs for adolescents, from both societal and cost/benefit perspectives, will continue to be recognized.

Addressing substance abuse among adolescence through treatment rather than punishment is an appropriate avenue. If used properly, the inherent controls and limits that are a part of the criminal justice system can be beneficial, replacing the lack of consistency in parenting many of these adolescents may have experienced. Though no substitute for appropriate, authoritative parenting, it is certainly a better remedy than incarceration. Another appropriate remedy is anger management training, which is described later in the book.

Suicide Prevention

A more extreme form of self-harm than substance abuse is suicide. The subject has been taboo for many years and still is in some cultures. Suicide is surrounded with prejudice and myth. Suicides are often unreported for a variety of reasons, from issues regarding insurance payment to lack of awareness on the part of medical professionals (Dutra, 2000). For all of these reasons, it is often difficult to find accurate information about suicide. Statistics are often not entirely accurate regarding suicides and research on intervention strategies is difficult to conduct, in part because surviving family members often feel shame or guilt admitting that a child or spouse committed suicide. The topic is still fraught with moral and religious overtones, and the debate about whether or not one has the right to end one's own life continues. Philosopher Albert Camus (1952) addressed suicide, pointing out the moral dilemmas surrounding the topic, and his work may have reduced some social taboos, but talking about suicide and suicide attempts is still an uncomfortable topic for many.

In the United States and Canada, about 25 of every 100,000 adolescents commit suicide. In the former Soviet States and Russia, rates are much higher, around 75 in 100,000. In Brazil, rates are lower, but part of this may be a function of the reporting system. Part of it is also because suicide, for religious reasons, is still more taboo than in other parts of the world. Males are more likely than females to commit suicide in most parts of the world, whereas females are more likely to attempt suicide. India and China are exceptions, where the trend is the reverse, (Bathia, Kahn, Mediratta, & Sharma, 1987; Zhao-Xiong & Lester, 1998). Among adults, those who are married are less likely to commit suicide than those who are single, and the age group most at risk for suicide is over 65 years. Among this group, suicide may often be a form of self-selected euthanasia.

The second most likely age group to commit suicide is adolescents. In Brazil, approximately 30 percent of reported suicides are committed by adolescents between 15 and 24 years old (Cassorla, 1991a). In the United States, suicide is the third leading cause of death in this age group, after homicide and accidents.

Identifying adolescents at risk for suicide is challenging, but schools, community organizations, and criminal justice agencies all should be prepared to work with adolescents at risk. Clinical depression, low affect and apathy, continuing sadness, isolation, and threats of suicide should all be treated as potential warning signs (Dutra, 2002). Adolescents who have been physically or sexually abused and those who come from families where drug and alcohol abuse is problematic, where families are cold and rejecting toward each other and the children, and where one or more members have committed suicide are also at greater risk (Brent, 1989; Cassorla, 1987). These adolescents are also more likely to abuse drugs and alcohol themselves and to be sexually promiscuous, antisocial, and disobedient. Thus, it is not surprising that, in both the United States and the United Kingdom, adolescents who are jailed are also at increased risk for suicide. Current suicide prevention programs within most adolescent correctional facilities are inadequate (Fenn, McCarthy, Trent, & Hutz, 2004).

Cassorla (1987) notes that depression in adolescents also often results in aggression, hostility, fights, irritability, and antisocial behavior. This seems to substantiate that suicide and self-harm are simply other forms of aggression that are, for a variety of personality, social, and environmental factors, directed inward instead of outward. It is also worth noting that, compared with children who have not reached puberty and adults, depression rates tend to be higher among adolescents (Brent, 1989; Rutter, Izard, & Read, 1987).

Timing of puberty is another factor in suicide risk among adolescents. In fact, timing of puberty—whether early, before age 12, during the middle of the teen years, or late in the teens—has been demonstrated to correlate to several psychiatric disorders. Garber, Lewinsohn, Seeley, & Brooks-Gunn (1997) demonstrated that major depression, substance abuse, addiction, disruptive behavior disorders, anxiety, eating disorders, and suicide attempts were all correlated to the rate of maturation. In an extensive study of nearly 2,000 adolescents in the United States, early-maturing females showed significantly elevated rates of depression and behavior disorders. They also had lower self-esteem, poorer coping skills, less support from family, and greater frequency of suicide attempts than other adolescents. Adolescents who are in contact with the criminal justice system and early maturing females are at the greatest risk for suicide; however, other adolescents are also at risk.

For each successful suicide, there are at least 8 to 10 more attempted suicides. Among adolescents, this proportion is much higher. Various researchers report that between 15 and 120 attempted suicides occur among adolescents for every actual suicide (Cassorla, 1985, 1987). Brazilian adolescents who are likely to attempt suicide are more likely to be from lower socioeconomic classes and to have experienced poor and negligent parenting throughout childhood. Physical and sexual abuse, difficulty in school, problems with substance abuse, and difficulty getting along with others also characterizes these adolescents (Dutra, 2000; Kotila & Lonnequist, 1987; Botego et al., 1995; Cassorla, 1984; Mioto, 1994).

In addition, such adolescents often feel as if they are different from others. They consider themselves weak, incompetent, and unattractive. They feel they cannot meet the expectations of parents, teachers, friends, or themselves and may be perfectionists. They feel misunderstood and perceive that they will be heavily judged and punished for each error they make. They feel vulnerable, as if no one can help them; they are pessimistic; and they feel rejected (Rutter et al., 1987; Hutz, Koller, & Bandiera, 1996). They may have experienced many changes of residence and family and lack resilience. Finding ways to build resilience among this group, using many of the strategies provided elsewhere in this book, is very important.

To identify adolescents who may be at risk for suicide, Dutra (2002) suggests the following:

1. If you notice that an adolescent seems to be seeking attention, pay attention!

2. If an adolescent is discussing suicide or threatening self-harm, take this seriously and try to intervene.

3. If an adolescent seems to be discarding or giving away valued objects and personal effects of great emotional value, this can be a sign of trouble.

4. If personal hygiene and self-care suddenly become unimportant, this signals depression and possible suicidal thoughts.

5. Alcohol and drug abuse and other forms of self-harm may be precursors to suicide attempts.

6. Taking unreasonable risks consistently is a trouble sign.

7. Sexual promiscuity; attempts to escape from, rather than constructively solve, problems; and general hopelessness are all warning signs of potential suicide.

8. Expressed feelings of desperation, hopelessness, and guilt indicate potential problem behaviors and suicide.

Specific strategies to be used by parents, teachers, counselors, educators, medical professionals, and others when working with troubled adolescents include these (Dutra, 2002):

1. Offer attention in a warm, compassionate way. Show that you care about the well-being of the troubled adolescent.

2. Listen and rephrase what you hear.

3. Encourage the adolescents to talk about their feelings.

4. Make sure adolescents who are potentially suicidal have support and do not live alone.

5. Help adolescents who are troubled to make use of community mental health resources.

Suicide is certainly a form of adolescent aggression that requires attention. It is associated with the same types of difficulties in family and social milieu—exposure to violence, frustration, problems with esteem and identity formation, and lack of appropriate social support. This form of violent self-harm, like other forms of violence among adolescents, needs to be understood and prevented.

Other Forms of Self-harm

Other forms of self-harm include eating disorders, cutting oneself, and self-handicapping behaviors. Research has demonstrated that certain styles of parenting and certain types of homes are more likely to produce self-harming behaviors (Pacheco, 2004). For example, demanding parents who provide little warmth and expect perfection from their children and themselves may place their offspring at greater risk. In the final analysis, though, all forms of self-harm, from these disorders to substance abuse to suicide, are misdirected aggression. Adolescents are unable to handle the emotions they feel, and they are unable to find constructive outlets for these emotions. Adolescents who engage in self-harm do not act out or strike out at others, generally. Instead they direct their anger inward, toward themselves. Providing adolescents with the knowledge and support necessary to accept and understand the emotions they are feeling—emotions that they may consider wrong or unacceptable, —providing a sense of love and belonging, and providing constructive outlets for these emotions are necessary for this group. Anger management strategies, summarized later in this book, may be useful. Offering an accepting family/peer group or a replacement if such a group is absent, as is often the case, is also recommended. Developing constructive hobbies in the areas of sports, music, writing, and the arts to diffuse anger is worthwhile. Biofeedback training, relaxation training, and various forms of martial arts are also helpful. The remainder of this book offers more detailed suggestions for using these forms of positive intervention to reduce aggression, whether that aggression is expressed as violence or substance abuse, self-harm, or suicide.

CHAPTER 5

Sexual Aggression among Adolescents

We thank Dr. Ludwig Lowenstein, Dr. William Kolodinsky, Michall Moore, and Dr. Vincent Schroeder for their extensive contributions to this chapter.

There are many types of aggressive acts, and some are acts of sexual aggression. This chapter specifically examines these acts, but first it is worth pointing out the interactive relationship between substance abuse and sexual aggression. In many, though certainly not all, cases of long-term substance abuse by adolescents, there is often an attempt to "self-medicate." In other words, adolescents seek to deal with emotional pain they have experienced by masking it through the altered states induced by alcohol and drug use. One cause of such pain may be that adolescents have experienced early sexual abuse themselves and, in fact, many adolescent offenders who are convicted of aggressive sexual crimes against children were sexually abused themselves. Dr. Ludwig Lowenstein, an expert in working with adolescent offenders, is responsible for most of the material in this chapter. He notes this connection when advising psychologists who work with juvenile sex offenders. He writes:

The possibility that the young sexual abuser has also been abused needs to be unearthed and dealt with through discussion, both on an individual and in a group therapy basis. Three emotional reactions tend to occur: first, a tendency to blame themselves resulting in self-loathing for perhaps not having done enough to stop the abuse on themselves taking place; second, a murderous hatred for the abuser; and third, resentment expressed toward those who failed to protect them from the abuse.

All of these feelings lead to anger and aggressive behavior. Based on experience, the aggression takes the form of sexual aggression against others. It is important to keep in mind, as we look at the material in this chapter, that sexual aggression by adolescents, like all acts of aggression by adolescents, often occurs based on either individual experience with such acts or observing such acts by those perceived as role models. These role models may be community or family members or they may be "virtual" models derived from media and society at large, but acts of sexual aggression do not originate in a vacuum. They are based on experience or observation.

Sexual aggression and sexual abuse are both problems that appear to be increasing throughout the world. According to Dr. Lowenstein:

It is becoming increasingly important to identify adolescents who may sexually abuse children. The purpose of identifying potential and real sex abusers is to protect potential victims and to improve the ongoing life chances of alleged perpetrators (Fyson, Eadie, & Cooke, 2003). Research over the last 20 years indicates that adolescent sex offenders account for a significant number of child sex abuse perpetrators. Studies indicate that this group has a variety of severe family problems, including neglect and physical and sexual abuse suffered by them. They also have educational and behavior problems, various psychopathologies, feelings of social isolation, and hence a tendency toward sex offending (Veneziano & Veneziano, 2002).

LeBlanc and Lapointe (1999) suggest that social and psychological difficulties of the perpetrators and victims of sexual aggression are much more serious than those young offenders and adolescents covered by the Youth Protection Act. Many sex abusers have themselves been victims of sex abuse in the past (Sheerin, 1998). Sexual abuse by adolescents of children constitutes severe damage to victims and the urgent need to treat such juveniles, whether they are victims or perpetrators (Eckert, 1998). Yes, research over the last 20 years indicates that adolescent sex offenders account for a significant number of child sexual abuse perpetrators. A number of researchers have noted the incidents of sexually aggressive adolescents including Burton (2000). More than 46 percent of aggressive adolescents began their deviant behavior before the age of 12 years. Studies by Campbell (2000) in the United States and England indicated that one third of sexual offenses in England and 50 percent of sexual offenses in the United States were committed by adolescents.

It is important to note that not all of these offenses are acts of aggression. Many charges are a result of an age difference between consenting partners; for example, in the United States, if one partner is under the age of 18 years, and the other is over the age of 18 years, this is technically a sexual offense and may often be prosecuted. In the United Kingdom, the offender must be a legal adult *and* the age difference between perpetrator and victim must be at least four years. Still, sexual aggression has been found to be a widespread problem among adolescents. Dr. Lowenstein continues:

This is also true in Germany (Krahe, Scheinberger-Olwig, & Waisenhoefer, 1999). Similar findings in the United States were obtained by Pithers and Gray (1998). They noted that nearly 40 percent of all child sexual abuse is performed by youth less than 20 years old, with 6- to 12-year-old children being the source of 13 to 18 percent of all substantiated child sexual mal-treatment. Another U.S. study by Bennett and Fineran (1998) found that 43 percent of a sample of 463 high school students reported being the victim of either sexual violence or severe physical violence by peers in the past year. Perpetrators were more likely to be known rather than unknown to the victim; 70 percent of those who experienced violence by peers were girls.

Two comprehensive U.S. studies by Ryan, Miyoshi, Metzner, Krugman, and Fryer (1996) and Ryan (1998) studied 1,660 juveniles who were referred for evaluation; 22 percent had themselves suffered from sexual abuse and the per-petrators of this abuse were, in some cases, females. Pithers and Gray (1998) found that child sexual abuse has reached epidemic proportions in the United States despite efforts to control this behavior. Failure to treat adolescents who commit such offenses is likely to lead to their becoming sexually assaulting adults (Sheerin, 1998).

According to studies, juvenile sex offenders are a heterogeneous population with diverse characteristics and treatment needs. A number of typologies have been developed to classify various types of offenders. One study indicated that homeless and runaway adolescents were more likely to be victims of childhood abuse (Tyler & Cauce, 2002). In this study, 372 homeless and runaway ado-lescents aged 13–21 years were interviewed. Approximately half the sample reported being physically abused and almost one third experienced sexual abuse. Females experienced significantly higher rates of sexual abuse compared to males, and homosexuals experienced significantly higher rates of physical and sexual abuse compared to heterosexual youth. Sexual abusers were rated as extremely violent by more than half of those who were abused. Biological parents were the majority of perpetrators for physical abuse, whereas nonfa-mily members were more likely to perpetrate sexual abuse. The average age of the perpetrator was late twenties to early thirties, and the majority were male for both types of abuse. The pattern of exploitation and victimization within the family was thought to have serious and cumulative developmental consequences for these youth as they enter the street environment. Early inter-vention programs are needed to break the cycle of exploitation and abuse. Otherwise, these victims become abusers.

When the criminal records of 126 male juveniles arrested for sexual offenses against children or peers were reviewed, there appeared to be more offenses against females who were strangers or acquaintances. Most frequently they had committed their crimes in a public area. Peer/adult offenders were also more likely to commit sex crime in association with other criminal activity, and the evidence points to higher overall levels of aggression and violence. Generally, the aggression of child molesters tends to focus on intimidation rather than physical force. A study by Kaufman, Holmberg, Orts, McCrady, and Rotzien (1998) found that adolescent offenders more frequently used a variety of strategies to gain victim compliance in sexual activities and to maintain victim silence after the onset of abuse, including approaches designed to coerce or manipulate victims.

Hilton, Harris, and Rice (2003) studied perceptions of seriousness for sexual aggression and the influence of gender. Sexual aggression was rated as more serious than nonsexual physical aggression, especially when involving physical force. Girls gave higher seriousness ratings than did boys. Male-to-female aggression was rated as most serious and male-to-male aggression least serious.

There is some evidence that causal relationships connect childhood abuse with adolescent and adult male perpetrators as was noted by Bailey (2001). Similar results were obtained by Veneziano, Veneziano, and Legrand (2000), who indicated that 92 percent of subjects had been sexually abused themselves before committing abuse. Furthermore, male sexual offenders who had been sexually victimized were more likely to select victims and commit sexual behaviors reflective of their own sexual victimization. These findings suggest that sexual abuse of children by some adolescent offenders may be a reenactment of their own sexual abuse.

Wood, Welman, and Netto (2000) studied the profile of young sexual offenders in South Africa. Results showed that half the sample that had committed sexual offenses had a history of consenting sexual interactions and had committed a nonsexual offense and had behavioral problems. Half reported a history of abuse. Typically these individuals had not received any sex education. They were often socially isolated as victims and socially anxious and had a number of friends who they had compared with themselves as having adequate social skills. The home environment was characterized by overcrowding, alcohol abuse, and domestic violence. A male relative was likely to have committed a criminal offense. In the community there was regular violence and sexual activity.

A British study by Manocha and Mezey (1999) confirmed the seriousness of the problem of sexual abuse posed by adolescents and reported a multifactorial etiology, including environmental, familial, interpersonal, and developmental elements. Of particular note was a prior history of abuse and victimization and the lack of protective parenting. Other factors cited as contributing to the potential for being abused are physical abuse, parental separation, and school-related educational and behavioral difficulties. These are more common in sexual abuse perpetrators as well as victims. Another British study of 100 sexually abused male adolescents aged 11–18 indicated that the family and social environment contributed to both the abuser and the abused. Findings were not different from those described in North American literature.

Do you note the pattern here? As with other forms of adolescent aggression, modeling, experiences, family, and societal influences appear to be causal factors. If sex is perceived as a way of dominating or asserting power, a way of winning or of victimizing—if it is viewed as an act of violence or violation and has been visited on the adolescent as such—then the chain is likely to continue and others are likely to be victimized. How can the chain be broken? Dr. Lowenstein writes the following concerning assessment and treatment of adolescent offenders:

Because of the diversity of the population of sex abuse offenders, careful assessment is needed before treatment plans are developed and implemented. Most treatment plans are modeled on those found to be effective with adult sex offenders, but some new programs are aimed more specifically at juveniles. The main approaches currently being used in the assessment of alleged sex abusers who are adolescents is the interview method. This is open to considerable criticism. Interviews are noted for their lack of accuracy unless they are combined with other measures such as history taking and psychological testing. Unfortunately, at the present time there are as yet no highly reliable tests of a psychological nature that can identify with certainty adolescent sex abusers. Lowenstein (1998) attempted such testing by developing a test for alleged perpetrators, alleged victims of abuse, and accusers. Hershkowitz, Lamb, Orbach, and Sternberg (2004) sought to introduce a structured interview protocol designed for investigative interviews of youthful alleged perpetrators of child sexual abuse. All interviews were conducted as part of the investigators regular work and followed the structured interview guide. Older and younger children were questioned similarly, but there were fewer directive questions and option posing prompts to suspects who denied the allegation. Older and younger children appeared to respond similarly. More information was solicited from the perpetrators using invitations rather than suggested or option-posing prompts.

A study by Curwen (2003) investigated the reliability and validity of three scales of the interpersonal reactivity index (iri), emphatic concern (ec), perspective taking (pt), and personal distress (pd) with a clinical sample. These scales were also used to examine the differences in empathy among groups of sex offenders. A total of 123 male adolescent sex offenders ages 12 to 19 completed a battery of psychometric measures that included the (iri) during a sex offender-specific assessment. Moderate internal consistency and convergent validity were established for (iri) scales. Victim empathy was not related to (iri) scales. Justification and acceptance of sexual and interpersonal violence were negatively correlated to (ec) and positively correlated to (pd). Those who committed violent offences reported more (ec) and (pt); however, a generally hostile temperament was negatively related to these scales. Researchers using the (iri) with male adolescent sex offenders should be cautious of the influence of age and socially desirable responding according to Curwen.

A controversial but in some respects favored approach to the assessment of alleged adolescent sex offenders is the use of phallometric testing, (Seto, Lalumiere, & Blanchard, 2000). Results suggest that phallometric testing can identify pedophilic interests among these adolescent sex offenders. Another assessment procedure favored by a number of practitioners is the Achenbach Child Behaviour Check List and the Family Assessment Measure. This test has been used with children who had been sexually victimized by juveniles, (Shaw, Lewis, Loeb, Rosado, & Rodriguez, 2001). The children were given the Family Assessment Measure and Trauma Symptom Checklist for Children. The clinician completed a parental reaction to incest disclosure scale. No differences were found between the younger and older victims of sexual abuse in regards to either penetration or the use of force. Juvenile perpetrators were younger and more likely to be males who were abused in a school setting, home, or home of a relative by a sibling or nonrelated male. Those who were abused by adults tended to be sexually preoccupied and manifested borderline clinically significant symptoms.

Smith and Fischer (1999) used the Abel Assessment for Interest in Paraphilias with juvenile sexual offenders. The mean age of these adolescent sexual offenders was 15.8 years, and they were in seven residential and day treatment centers. The temporal stability, sensitivity, and specificity of the Abel Assessment for Interest in Paraphilias test as used by adolescents in residential and day treatment centers were not supported. The results indicated the need for further refinement of this tool. This was also confirmed by Bonner, Marx, Thompson, and Michaelson (1998) who considered it imperative that further tests that were more accurate were developed with adolescent sexual offenders to indicate risk of reoffending. Becker (1998a, 1998b) also indicated the need for a comprehensive assessment of juvenile sex offenders and their families. It was considered especially important to obtain reports from outside sources; to take a developmental, sexual, family, medical, and psychiatric history; and to assess the family's current attitude toward sexual offenses.

Sexual recidivism among those returning to the community is of great concern to all. When released from incarceration or removal from treatment is being considered, it is vital to predict the likelihood of reoffending in adolescent sexual offenders. According to Murphy, DiLillo, Haynes, and Steere (2001), a number of variables significantly predicted sexual arousal and hence further offending. The most consistent predictors were gender of victim, race, the interaction of race and gender of victim, and, to some extent, the interaction of offender abuse history and gender of the victim. Caucasian subjects tended to show a higher arousal level than African American subjects and thus seemed more likely to reoffend. This had not been reported previously in the literature.

An eight-year comparative analysis of adolescent rapists and adolescent child molesters, as well as other adolescent delinquents in the general population, revealed some interesting results, (Hagan, Gust-Brey, Cho, & Dow, 2001). Of the 150 participants, 50 were adolescent rapists who had perpetrated a sexual assault against a same-age or older peer, 50 were perpetrators of sexual assaults against children, and 50 were delinquents adjudicated for an offense other than sexual assault. Adolescent sexual offenders were significantly more likely to sexually reoffend in the eight-year period after their release from a juvenile correctional facility than were a control group of other adolescent delinquents from the same institution. Juvenile nonsex offenders, child sexual offenders, and adolescent rapists were all significantly more likely to be involved in sexual assaults than was the general male population in the United States.

Sheridan et al. (1998) conducted interviews with clinicians and 22 participants who had completed treatment with North Side Inter-Agency Project (NIAP), a community-based treatment program for adolescent sexual abusers. Clinicians reported that a majority of adolescents completed all steps of the program, and the majority of families had been highly supportive of adolescents' participation in treatment. Difficulties with the management of conflict, the regulation of negative emotions, and cognitive deficits were the principal areas in which clinicians judged these adolescents to have problems in addition to their sexually abusive behavior patterns. Despite having these difficulties, two thirds of the cases were judged by therapists to be at low risk of reoffending after treatment. In just over half the cases, adolescents reported entering into situations after treatment that placed them at risk of reoffending, but in an anonymous questionnaire, none reported sexually reoffending.

Finally Kaufman et al. (1997) examined the predictability of adolescent sexual offenders based on differences in victim, perpetrator, and offense characteristics. Modus operandi denoted the pattern of behavior that perpetrators displayed in the period before, during, and after illicit sexual contact. The study focused primarily on the behavior often labeled "grooming." Results showed that a history of sexual abuse was related to the selection of male victims and younger victims. Furthermore, subgroups of offenders differed significantly in the strategies they used to build victims' trust, gain compliance with illicit sexual activity, and maintain victims' silence after the onset of sexual abuse. To consider the risk of sexual reoffending, it was necessary to investigate these aspects of potential future behavior with perpetrators.

In recent times there has been an increasing amount of research in the area of addressing the therapeutic aspects of young sex offenders. There has been some uncertainty, however, as to the treatment effectiveness for adolescent sex offenders. Different treatment appeared to present different effectiveness levels (Letourneau, 2004). Boswell and Wedge (2003), however, have expressed some optimistic views as to the effectiveness of treating young sex abusers in late adolescence. They undertook a pilot evaluation of a therapeutic community for adolescent male sex abusers. The reconviction rates of both sexual and nonsexual offending were considerably reduced. Subjects were almost unanimously positive about their time at one particular treatment center, and the coping techniques that were developed for them there.

Bentovim (2002) considered the ways of preventing sexual abuse by young people and hence victimizing younger groups into eventually also becoming sex abusers. Bentovim (2002) indicated that sexually abused children often tend to live in violent surroundings, suffer physical abuse, and are exposed to abuse of maternal figures. They also often suffer from disruption and poor quality of care and supervision. Green and Masson (2002) warned against the placement of sex-abusing young people in centers with child victims of sexual abuse. Research suggests that the inadequate ways in which sexual behavior in such centers is perceived and managed serves to compound the problems of both the sexually abusive and nonabusive adolescents placed there.

The research summarized here suggests two things of primary importance if we wish to address the problem of sexual aggression among adolescents. First, family counseling is imperative. Understanding the experiences and dynamics that results in an adolescent sexually attacking a child or another adolescent is requisite for "stopping the chain." Second, the current practice of combining all convicted adolescents in the same facility is likely to exacerbate the problem, not remedy it. Punishment is not the answer. It is part of the problem. Specific treatment programs and placements geared to the offenses of which adolescents are convicted should be the focus of our criminal justice system when it comes to adolescents. Dr. Lowenstein continues:

A chapter by Vizard et al. in Children and the Law (Bull, 2001) discusses definitional issues regarding child and adolescent sex abuse perpetrators and reviews literature on abuser and offense characteristics, theories of etiology, and outcome of treatment programs. Unfortunately many studies had a small number of subjects. They suggested that many factors had not been reported, such as how many individuals needed a repeat of a program offered to them earlier because they failed to complete the program or for other reasons. Vizard et al. sought to differentiate between those labeled as sexually aggressive or sexually abusive.

A study of an Australian adolescent sex offender treatment program by Flanagan and Hayman-White (2000) addressed certain factors related to both victim and perpetrators, such as a history of victimization and self-reported problem behavior as assessed by the Achenbach Youth Self Report Form. Ryan (1999) painted a rather dark picture in relation to the increase in sexually abusing youths despite current diagnostic and therapeutic procedures. This may be partly due to the greater chance of identification of sex abusers and their victims, as well as better professional cooperation.

Vizard and Usiskin (1999) emphasized the role of early trauma in the genesis of abusive behavior and the value of individual psychotherapy with young sex abusers. Such views are psychoanalytic in nature, an approach not currently in vogue. The emphasis today is on cognitive-behavioral approaches. A number of investigators emphasized the importance of multidisciplinary approaches and seeing individuals both through individual therapy and in groups and with families (Erooga & Masson, 1999). They also emphasized the use of a program specifically for working with children under the age of 10 years and with female adolescent abusers.

Brown (1999) emphasized the importance of providing consistent and timely help for those who are perpetrators of sexual abuse because of compulsive tendencies. Brown (1999) also indicated, however, that any treatment should be carried out within the community wherein such children reside. One study from Pittsburgh attempted to evaluate the treatment of juveniles who sexually abused other children and youths. As yet, there has not been any result of such an evaluation indicated. Difficulties may well be due to the fact that young sex abusers suffer from a multidetermined etiology and therefore require a multisystemic therapy (Swenson, Henggeler, Schoenwald, Kaufman, & Randall, 1998).

The importance of involving schools in both the identification and treatment of violent sex offenders is stressed in much of the literature, but thus far there have been little outcome data available concerning this approach. It is encouraging to note that, in one study where youngsters were sent to the Northside Interagency Project (NIAP), all the adolescent sex abusers completed the steps necessary for the program and families also cooperated in the treatment of such youngsters, (Sheridan et al., 1998). Many of these youngsters suffered from conflict in the regulation of their negative emotions and cognitive deficits. These appeared to be associated with sexually abusive behavior patterns. Despite having these difficulties, two thirds of the youngsters were judged by therapists to be at low risk of reoffending after treatment.

This is a valuable observation in light of earlier chapters. It is important to involve the schools, families, and communities in dealing with adolescent aggression. Isolating these aspects of an adolescent's life from each other makes solutions to problem behavior less likely to occur. Placing schools, counselors, criminal justice agencies, and parents in adversarial positions, although a common reality, is not productive if we wish to treat the problem. A united front is necessary. Dr. Lowenstein continues describing research on treatment:

Another study that confirms later research by O'Reilly et al. (1998) showed that youngsters who sexually abused other children tend to have numerous school-related problems and behavioral difficulties in addition to the sex abuse demeanor. The treatment of these conditions would undoubtedly be of value to prevent further sexual abuse. The goal therefore should be early identification and hence treatment of children who are likely to or have already sexually abused other children (Ryan, 1998).

Despite the importance of treatment after identification, it was noted that social and educational problems play a large part in the victimization of children by other children. Treatment often requires the perpetrators in some cases to be placed in special units, and such youngsters are to be treated preferably by cognitive behavioral and psychodynamic approaches (Woods, 1997). There, consideration can also be given to the individual causes of sexually abusive behavior when providing treatment (Ryan, 1997). There also can be individual therapeutic work as well as group therapy (McGarvey & Lenaghan, 1996). It is important to regard adolescent sexual offenders as both victims and perpetrators when dealing with their problems, through the use of cognitive-behavioral and psychodynamic methods (Woods, 1997). As noted, findings suggest that the sexual abuse of children by some adolescent offenders may be a reenactment of their own sexual abuse.

Although numbers of female sex abusers are smaller than of males, it is important to differentiate between male and female abusers. Relatively little is known about adolescent females who commit sexual offenses (Kubik, Hecker, & Righthand, 2002). In a two-part exploratory study, a sample of 11 adolescent females with sexual offense histories was described. Sexually offending females had significantly fewer antisocial behavior problems such as alcohol or drug problems or problems with fighting or difficulties in school. They began their offense behavior at a younger age than their non-sex offending delinquent peers, but few differences emerged with respect to attitudes about offense behavior, such as levels of denial. In a second study, females with sex offense histories were compared with a group of age-matched adolescent males with sex offense histories. The two sex offending groups were remarkably similar. There were a few differences with respect to psychosocial and criminal histories, antisocial behavior, and variables related to clinical presentation and treatment. Likewise, the two groups were remarkably similar with respect to specific sex offense behaviors. The females, however, appeared to have experienced more severe and pervasive abuse compared to the males.

Tardif (2001) studied factors associated with sexual abuse among female adolescents and adults. The subjects studied were 9 female adults, with a mean age of 37.7 years, and 15 female adolescents, with a mean age of 14.7 years. They had been convicted of abuse in France. Data on age, marital status, and family history of abuse, abuse characteristics, abuse victims, sexual problems, psychiatric symptoms, and maternal bonding were obtained by semistructured interview. The results indicated multiple perturbations in family relationships associated with sexual abuse behavior. This included parent abandonment and parent conflict, as well as parent violence. Also more likely to be present were substance abuse, negligence, and physical and sexual abuse, as well as maternal and feminine sexual identity issues.

Miccio-Fonseca (2000) compared 18 female sex offenders with 332 male sex offenders and with 215 females who were not sex offenders on various experiences in their personal histories. Female sex offenders who were the victims of sexual abuse were compared to female sex offenders who were not. The groups were analyzed with regard to psychological, medical, gynecological, urological, drug and law enforcement variables, and homicidal and suicidal histories. Other variables included sexual difficulties and dysfunctions, sexual health, and life stressors. Female and male sex offenders differed significantly on numerous psychological, life stressor, and sexual variables. Female sex offenders differed significantly from females who were not sex offenders on the same set of variables, and they were also significantly younger.

Finally, Mathews, Hunter, and Vuiz (1997) found that female young sex offenders had extensive and pervasive childhood maltreatment experiences. Many of these young girls were exposed to the modeling of interpersonal aggression by females, as well as males. The majority of these juvenile female sexual offenders demonstrated repetitive patterns of sexual offending with multiple victims, suggesting psychosocial disturbances equivalent in severity to the comparison group of males.

As in other areas of aggression research, it appears that females are less likely than males to demonstrate aggressive behavior, but the incidence of female aggression is rising. But then, so too is the modeling of aggressive behavior by females. Females are increasingly engaged in military or police work and video and cartoon characters are frequently violent females. As more aggressive female role models are present, aggression by females also rises. As noted in previous chapters, there may be biological or hormonal factors that make it less likely for females than males to react aggressively, but social acceptance and modeling of behavior, not biology, appear to be the more influential factors.

Regardless of whether aggressive adolescent sex abusers are male or female, though, they require treatment. Several legal and ethical issues are relevant to treatment decisions, however, as noted by Dr. Lowenstein:

Hunter and Lexier (1998) studied ethical and legal issues in the assessment and treatment of juvenile sex offenders. They noted that the evaluation and treatment of juvenile sex offenders represented an area of practice fraught with clinical, ethical, and legal complexity. Other approaches that may be viewed as controversial are the use of phallometric and polygraph assessments. The authors emphasized the importance of establishing ethically sound patterns of clinical practice.

The use of other diagnostic instruments has also been viewed as controversial, for example, personality tests that seek to identify and differentiate sex abusers from nonsex abusers. At present, there are a dearth of assessment procedures that differentiate, with some degree of certainty, when sex abuse has not been admitted. More work needs to be done in this area as attempted by Lowenstein (1998). Such new tools should always be used alongside other personality tests, structured and unstructured interviews, and phallometric approaches. Guilt should never be assumed on the basis of allegations made by alleged victims or those who make allegations on behalf of victims. Treatment, particularly of juveniles, should be considered paramount as opposed to incarceration. The complex history of the known perpetrator should be further studied and considered when treatment procedures are formulated and implemented, with prevention from an early stage being the goal in order to best protect the general public.

Youths who sexually abuse other youths must be provided with psychological and milieu-type treatment, as well as education appropriate to their needs. While distinguishing between sexual curiosity, sexual needs, and sexual needs combined with aggression can be difficult at times, making this distinction helps those who treat this problem.

Sometimes sexual curiosity is loosely associated with strong sexual fantasies. At times, there is an association with aggression and there may be some aggression involved. Being able to identify and diagnose at an early age is likely to make treatment more effective. Rational emotive approaches are likely to be more effective when they are combined with behavioral expectations and monitoring. This requires close observation and a great variety of interactions with others, especially when such youngsters think they are unobserved. One must always be on guard to avoid being lulled into complacency, especially by those youngsters with high psychopathy scores. Words are less important than actions. One must always consider the behavior of children as predominant rather than what they report as to how they feel regarding their rehabilitation. Hence, long-term treatment and monitoring are of great importance. Working with the family of such youngsters is also important when this is possible, as many return to their families for short or long periods. At the completion of their time in treatment, there is still a need for long-term follow-up.

Other signs of maladjustment, which are likely to be linked in some way with sexual abuse of others, must receive attention. Of special importance is low self-esteem resulting from poor educational attainments, a tendency to rely on aggression to achieve goals, poor social skills, and difficulties in controlling impulses. There are also problems with families that require therapeutic intervention.

It does indeed take a village to raise a healthy child. Family, school, social agencies, therapists, criminal justice agencies, community services, and medical care are all intertwined and need to be working together. Unfortunately, this is often not the case at present. Various components of what should be a cooperative and interconnected system often tend to blame each other for the problems rather than actively work together to solve them.

Dr. Lowenstein's reference to problems with self-esteem and self-image is of special interest. Two other psychologists who have worked extensively with adolescent offenders, Dr. William Kolodinsky and Dr. Vincent Schroeder, agree. They write:

The myriad causes of teen sex offending are difficult to circumscribe. Witnessing extreme violence in childhood has been implicated in adolescent sexual offending, as well as in general contact offenses. Among sex offenders, exposure to violence is associated with personalities marked by detachment from emotion and a callous attitude. Prior victimization as a child has been found consistently in the literature on sex offenders (Veneziano & Veneziano, 2002), although measuring the veracity of offenders' self-reports of childhood sexual victimization is challenging.

More recently, research in this area has centered on ways that molestation may inhibit healthy development along cognitive and even psychophysiological lines, or conversely, ways in which children born with deficits might be prone to become molesters. Adolescent sex offenders victimized as children may be reenacting their own abusive history, in line with Bandura's social learning theory (Bandura, 1986). Classical conditioning may be involved, namely, that feelings of sexual arousal from childhood victimization episodes have become strongly linked with violent images or violent fantasies, or with a context of dominator-victim dynamics. These types of constructs—alpha dominance and submission, for instance—are some of the foundations undergirding the evolutionary psychology explanation of sex offending. Other variables beyond abuse and neglect that are linked with this behavior include absence of a healthy family of origin experience, separation from parents, limited social skills, wide varieties of school problems, and psychopathology (Veneziano & Veneziano, 2002).

Adolescent sex offenders also may tend to come from families that are rigid in terms of their adaptability in crises or flexibility in response to developmental changes, emotionally disengaged, and that possess poor overall communication skills. In other words, those whose family attachment is minimal also tend to bond or attach more to deviant peers (Blaske, Borduin, Henggeler, & Mann, 1989), all of which can create a backdrop for sexual assault. Prior victimization and its myriad effects, occurring within a dysfunctional family context, along with poor social skill development and other personality factors such as impulsivity, in the aggregate, become perhaps a blueprint for sexual acting-out behavior as these children progress toward and through puberty.

In support of this, Dr. Kolodinsky notes:

The families I worked with were usually quite extreme along the lines of adaptability, cohesiveness, and communication. Rare was the family who seemed to possess a sense of healthy balance in these three dimensions. In most cases, the absence of a father, or of a strong father figure, was striking. Also, there was a prevalence of mothers who seemed to meet DSM Axis 2 criteria, ranging from Borderline to Dependency and Histrionic personalities. Most mothers seemed to have weak attachments and even the absence of affectionate relationships in general with their adolescent sons, giving the young offenders minimal effective role-modeling at home. Although these families had sons who were in significant amounts of legal trouble, the families were frequently not very well committed to the treatment process, perhaps insufficiently worried that their sons might grow up to be adult sex offenders. Rare was the family who was enmeshed rather than disengaged, or who communicated and problem-solved effectively. Some seemed to want to sweep the problem under the rug and just to move on: one family refused to get additional mental health counseling services for their daughter even after the eldest son, 17, had admitted to sexually abusing his 12-year-old sister for years. Only after Child Protective Services was contacted on two occasions did they finally agree to at least have their daughter assessed, and, even then, they did not get her consistently involved in treatment.

In another case, a 17-year-old adolescent offender had been born and raised until age 8 on the streets of Rio de Janeiro before he and his much younger sister were adopted by a Jewish-American family and brought to live in a large U.S. city. The adoptive parents, well into their forties when this child was brought to the states, were admittedly unaffectionate with this teen and his much younger sister. Although not formally evaluated via Olson's (1987) circumplex model, it was quite evident that there was tremendous emotional disengagement in the family, rigidity with regard to roles and rules, and poor communication skills when it came to resolving conflict, dealing with emotions, and handling emotional and physical affection. One got the sense that this teen was almost chronically thirsting for affection in his life. This, combined with a very insecure attachment style, led him to reach out to his sister for affection and physical comfort, although he eventually (in early adolescence as he reached puberty) began adding sexual activity into the mix.

In my experience, outpatient teen sex offenders escape easy classification. Adolescent offenders seem to come in many shapes and sizes. In most cases though, their limited social skills are quite apparent. In one outpatient treatment group, one consistently unhygienic teen took off his sandals in group and, with great dexterity, proceeded to chew his toenails as if this were commonplace. Only after learning that the group members found his actions "gross" did he even consider reflecting on his behavior. Also, most seemed to feel less confident in relating to their same-age peers than nondelinquents, and it seemed that their affiliation with other same-age offenders, though in itself potentially controversial, was helping them to build relational self-efficacy. Ultimately, making member selection decisions for group work was consistently challenging because of the heterogeneity of psychological functioning, personality type, and sexual offending history.

Part of the key to understanding how to minimize juvenile sex offending is to understand ways in which adolescent sex offenders are alike and dissimilar to other delinquent and nondelinquent adolescents. Many researchers have compared these groups across a wide array of variables. In some cases, these outcomes suggest that sex offenders are perhaps the most pathological or deviant of these groups. They tend to have much lower empathy and to use more extreme types and degrees of cognitive distortion, including per-mission-giving statements to themselves to justify their behavior. In light of the notion that characterological disorders represent a more engrained pathological foundation than neurotic disorders, and to Horner's idea that characterological disorders also likely have their origins in attachment expe-riences in earliest relationship patterns with primary caretakers, a case can be made for sex offenders being a more characterological and thus pathological extension of delinquents. In one study, sex offenders also scored higher on psychopathic deviancy and schizophrenia, two of the more characterologically based MMPI subscales than did other delinquents, who in turn scored higher on the more neurotic MMPI subscales such as Hysteria and Psychasthenia (associated with anxiety).

Other research has found sex offenders to score in normal ranges on some commonly used psychosocial instruments including the Behavioral Assessment of System for Children, although they tended to use a more defensive approach to the test. Irish sex offenders actually scored in more healthy ranges than did normal adolescents on the Child Behavioral Health Checklist and on the Youth Self-Report Form. In addition to these studies, there have been many others beyond the scope of this review in which scores of adolescent sex offend-ers on a variety of psychosocial measures have been similar to those of normal adolescents.

Some of the lack of convergence of research findings may be attributable to the heterogeneity of treatment. Treatment spans a spectrum of orienta-tions and interventions, including insight, cognitive restructuring, values clarification, and covert sensitization, among dozens of others. Various forms of therapy may or may not be carried out by the same therapist. A given regimen may contain any number of the modalities including but not lim-ited to individual, family, group, and multifamily therapy. The theoreti-cal focus of these efforts may involve cognitive-oriented efforts to correct thinking errors and cognitive distortions, family-of-origin psychodynam-ics, a wide array of behavioral techniques, methods to deal with arousal, psychoeducational units on the sexual assault cycle, sexual health, relapse risk and prevention, and victim empathy. When dealing with a disorder that not only causes intrapersonal distress for the offender, but one that creates such destruction in others lives, therapists are often tempted to leave no stone unturned. They feel compelled to throw the kitchen sink at this problem.

In outpatient work, I found that remaining faithful to a holistic protocol in the form of a user-friendly workbook was very helpful in group work. These workbooks typically involved a set of awareness-raising components. Areas covered included:

1. *Acknowledging sexual behavioral history*
2. *Dealing with legal and societal issues and responsibilities*
3. *Gaining awareness of various cyclical patterns of sexual behavior and thinking*
4. *Gaining awareness of relational needs and ways to express them*
5. *Building coping skills*
6. *Gaining empathy for victims*
7. *Making apologies either in person or in role-play or letter writing*

These workbooks provide a structure that offenders find easy to follow. They usually are highly relevant to their participation in group and also offer homework options. Although heavy confrontation might be the first impulse among well-intentioned therapists, as most adolescent sex offenders may struggle with self-esteem and come from families in which there is a paucity of affection, praise, and positive communication, it may also be incumbent on treatment providers to develop activities that boost self-worth.

The definition of this disorder or population is influenced by the legal system; so too is treatment. In particular, treatment programming mirrors judicial processing of these youth, with its emphasis on group or the collective. The most pragmatic and cost-efficient response to the various forces at hand (protection of the victim and treatment of the minor perpetrator) commonly entails placement in residential treatment, for example, removal from family and society to resolve danger to society. Inpatient-based, court-ordered treatment programs consist of adolescent sex offenders living together for several weeks and rely on group therapy modalities.

Unlike any number of mental/behavioral disorders less shaped by legal statute, individual and family counseling tends to be a subcomponent of a more encompassing residential program with an emphasis on group: therapy, milieu therapy, behavioral modification ("level") systems, and psychoeducational classes. The burgeoning literature on modeling a la Albert Bandura casts doubt on this traditional treatment blend, wherein exposure to other sex offenders is a central element. Such exposure may be heightened by the simultaneous removal from the youth's naturalistic context (family, school, community). Research on modeling, however, indicates that normalizing experiences, such as lessons on sexual health and dating, may be preferred. If this finding holds up, we must all confront that normalizing experiences call

for increased (and safe) interaction with "normal" peers. This general senti-
ment is at the foundation of the positive psychology movement. Related ideas
would include membership in heterogeneous membership clubs with themes
such as overcoming adversity, establishment of a mentor, versions of the vision
quest ritual that frame a rite of passage from immaturity and confusion to
maturity and responsibility, pet therapy, and service learning, all of which
help to reverse self-absorption and individualized, naturalistic adaptations
of the sort of structured behavioral modification regimen that exists in resi-
dential treatment. Trends in positive psychology and Bandurian modeling
point to the importance of naturalistic, family, school, and community-based
interventions.

Again, a strong and cohesive community seems to be the key to addressing the problem of adolescent aggression. High mobility, limited interaction with friends, neighbors, and extended family, a sense of fear and isolation—all increasingly common in many societies and certainly characteristic to a great extent of modern U.S. society—undermine healthy socialization. Community groups such as Big Brothers/Big Sisters, Scouts, and other groups that provide for healthy interaction with appropriate adult role models—especially for those youth who do not have such mentors readily available at home—are increasingly important. Building activities into group and school that teach coping skills and thinking skills becomes necessary. Anger management training is one such activity that shows promise for increasing resilience and reducing violence, sexual or otherwise, among aggressive adolescents. The next chapter examines research and techniques for using anger management training with adolescent offenders.

CHAPTER 6

ANGER MANAGEMENT TRAINING STRATEGIES TO REDUCE ADOLESCENT VIOLENCE

We would like to thank Andrew Gold for his extensive contributions to this chapter, some of which also appear in his doctoral dissertation, and his outstanding work in the area of anger management training.

As noted in previous chapters, a variety of situations common in modern, everyday life contribute to the problem of adolescent aggression. A stressful environment; frustration over school, work, or family issues; difficulty with attachment to parents and society; a fear-based society that seemingly values acts of aggression—all of these factors and more increase the likelihood of problem behaviors among today's adolescents. Not only are a variety of environmental agents likely to increase aggression, but few coping strategies or ways of dealing with feelings are likely to be transmitted. The role of the family in educating youth has steadily diminished over the last century, and the school environment is generally focused only on academic content.

One promising avenue for reducing adolescent violence is the introduction of a systematic anger management training curriculum, not only in residential treatment settings for adolescents who have been arrested for their antisocial and aggressive behavior, but also in public schools. Research on anger management training in various settings has supported its usefulness for reducing violent behaviors. This chapter, written in cooperation with Andrew Gold, an expert on the topic, provides a critical review of the literature on anger management training for adolescents. The first section describes a variety of ways in which anger management has been defined and approached in the field of applied psychology. The goal is to offer a critical analysis of the literature describing anger management training with adolescents and offer suggestions on how it may be used to directly or interactively change violent, aggressive behavior. There has undoubtedly been a recent escalation of aggressive behavior in the adolescent population. Anger management training seeks to remedy this problem.

Conflict management, conflict resolution, relaxation training, role-playing, communication skills training, problem solving, assertiveness training, and perspective-taking are all common components of current models of anger management training. Issues related to developing these strategies into a standardized curriculum are discussed, and the chapter not only provides a critical review of empirical research about anger management with adolescents but also offers several concrete ideas and techniques to integrate into school, group counseling, and other settings.

Defining Anger and Anger Management

Tangney, Wagner, Hill-Barlow, Marschall, and Gramzow (1996) described anger as a "universal human emotion," which, in the course of day-to-day life, people of all ages experience (Tangney et al., 1995, p. 797). What is not universal, however, is the way we manage and express our anger. Some of us are inclined to lash out; others tend to hold our anger in. Some of us "stew over perceived injustices"; others orient themselves toward constructive directions, drawing on anger to make changes for the better. Tangney et al. (1995) explored these individual differences in anger management strategies in order to account for constructive versus destructive uses of anger by adolescents.

It is no surprise that high levels of destructive use of anger have been associated with juvenile delinquency (Stern, 1999). What is surprising, however, are the statistics associated with an increasing level of violence and aggression perpetrated by adolescents. Bosworth, Espelage, and DuBay (1998) cited homicide as the second leading cause of death among 15- to 24-year-olds and the third leading cause of death among 10- to 14-year-olds. A 1990 report noted that more than 135,000 students bring a gun to school every day. Clearly, violence and aggression in the adolescent population have become a serious public health problem. Thus, a major challenge facing therapists, parents, and educators, as well as society overall, is the need to create viable programs aimed at the prevention of violence that can be incorporated into the school setting or treatment milieu to improve adolescent skills and abilities in anger management (LeCroy, 1988).

According to Feindler, Marriott, and Iwata (1984), behavior modification programs have attempted, with varying degrees of success, to modify aggressive behavior in adolescents. Although aggressive behavior can be modified through manipulating consequences by various means such as providing positive and negative reinforcements, contracting, response-cost, and time-out procedures, behavioral improvements tend to decrease when the program is withdrawn. Maintenance and transfer of behavior change should be a critical consideration when designing treatment interventions. Feindler calls for the development of self-control training programs, citing a 1979 opinion that adolescent aggression is a nonspecific phenomenon that, lacks instrumentality, existing often as a rapid, unplanned impulsive reaction to provocation. The spontaneous, impulsive nature of adolescent aggression not only makes it difficult to select and use effective reinforcers, but also requires more of an emphasis on self-regulation and self-control training strategies and less reliance on traditional behavioral psychology strategies to be effective.

Bandura and Walters (1963) and Campbell (2000) first integrated the cognitive dimension along with more traditional behavioral techniques. They established that an absence of verbal skills in coping with stress combined with insufficient cognitive mediation led to anger and aggression. Meichenbaum (1977) then extended the work to address the observed cognitive correlates in the development of his stress inoculation treatment. Novaco (1975) applied Meichenbaum's stress inoculation treatment to the area of anger, and the foundational components of current anger management training programs were thus established. Current techniques focus more on providing cognitive strategies, practice with alternatives to aggressive behavior, and insight into feelings and reactions than on environmental manipulation.

Components of Successful Anger Management Training Programs

The first component commonly found in current anger management training programs with adolescents is the process of defining the terms *anger* and *anger management* in a group context. By openly discussing feelings related to aggressive outbursts, adolescents are provided with some of the verbal skills Bandura initially cited as often lacking when angry outbursts result. Labeling and analyzing the feelings related to anger provide a means of reflecting before acting. Allowing adolescents to work to come up with their own definitions and then discuss these to arrive at a group definition is a useful way to model this verbal intervention skill. Group definitions will vary, but a skilled therapist or trainer will ensure that the key aspects of each member's definition are included in the group definition and that it is comprehensive. For example, in McCarthy, Gold, and Garcia (1999) anger was defined behaviorally as "an observed aggressive act resulting in physical contact, or the threat of physical contact toward self, another person, or property with the intent to harm or do damage, or the reported desire to so act." This definition is both concrete—necessary when working with adolescents—and thorough. Bosworth et al. (1998), defined anger management as a cycle, where cognitive, physiological, and emotional triggers are identified followed by a discussion of situations that are likely to engage those triggers and a review of ways to de-escalate anger. Teaching adolescents to identify physiological signs of anger, such as increased pulse rate, tightness in stomach or chest, or change in voice tone, and then label and discuss what seemed to trigger the change is a useful strategy.

Conflict management or conflict resolution training is another common component of anger management training. As outlined by Stern (1999), conflict management skills are conceptualized as self-control skills used by adolescents to reduce stress and avoid escalation of anger. For example, adolescents are asked to keep a daily anger diary where they record patterns of arousal. They are also taught to modify unhelpful internal dialogue and use positive self-statements to reinforce themselves for maintaining self-control.

Another component found in anger management training is the use of relaxation training. Stern (1999), for example, taught adolescents progressive relaxation through the use of deep breathing exercises to address the physiological components of arousal associated with anger. Hierarchies regarding conflict situations that were likely to be encountered were then created, with the situations ordered from least to most upsetting. Guided imagery was then used to practice anger management skills while relaxed, beginning with low arousal situations and proceeding to highly arousing situations. Behavioral role-plays were then practiced in the same hierarchical sequence.

Training in communication skills is another common component of anger management training. As identified by Stern (1999), communication skills involve taking responsibility for thoughts, feelings, and behaviors, through the use of "I" statements. Acknowledging one's own feelings and actions, that is, "I am upset," rather than blaming another for creating these feelings, that is, "You make me mad," enhances self-control.

Problem-solving skills are also a component of anger management training. A typical model, presented in Stern (1999), involves a five-step process where adolescents learn to:

1. Define the problem
2. Brainstorm solutions
3. Evaluate consequences
4. Select an option and develop a plan
5. Monitor and evaluate the plan as it is carried out

Assertiveness training is another component of anger management. Typically a trainer models assertiveness as compared to aggression. Adolescents then role-play ways of acting assertively with group members using previously learned communication skills (McCarthy et al., 1999). Perspective taking is also a common component of anger management as outlined in Bosworth et al. (1998). Considering how others manage anger is also helpful. One program includes a computer-based multimedia component. Adolescents listen to celebrities describing how they resolve conflict and manage stress. They then discuss whether these strategies would be useful in their own situations. This builds on the powerful tool of modeling. Adolescents are likely to imitate the actions of those they perceive as "high status" group members.

All of these strategies are useful with adolescents. Whether used in informal interaction with parents and family members, introduced in school or clubs, or used in treatment settings, all of the skills mentioned here should be developed. There is no doubt that they are useful and beneficial means for minimizing adolescent aggression. In formal studies of anger management training programs, finding ways to assess levels of anger and validate program success is a challenge, however. The next section describes the assessment tools used to measure the various components of anger management training in the empirical studies described here.

Assessment of Anger and Anger Management Training

In her study of parent-adolescent conflict, Stern (1999) used a mea-surement battery to assess communication and problem-solving skills. First, teens and parents were asked to agree or disagree on a 75-item questionnaire regarding perceived conflict over the previ-ous three weeks. The Issues Checklist (IC) followed this Conflict Behavior Questionnaire (CBQ). The checklist is a 5-point scale rat-ing frequency and intensity of discussions at home. After these self-report measures were taken, teens and parents were paired and then asked to have a 10-minute videotaped discussion of an issue that is currently a source of conflict. Four observers using Prinz's (1976) Interaction Behavior Code (IBC) rated these interactions accord-ing to four categories ranging from overall amount of "dyadic insult and friendliness" to overall "effectiveness of problem-solving skills and problem resolution." The dyads were then asked to rate themselves on a 5-point scale regarding the intensity of anger in their discussions and assess how well they solved their problems. This rather comprehensive combination of assessment tools seemed to be a useful means of measuring anger related to family conflict and monitoring its decline as a result of systematic anger manage-ment training focused on communication skills and self-monitoring strategies.

McCarthy et al. (1999) used Novaco's (1995) 42-item Likert-style Provocation Inventory (NOVOCO) and Spielberger's (1988) 80-item State-Trait Anger Expression Inventory (STAXI) to assess self-reported feelings of anger in 20 incarcerated adolescent males. This study used a pretest/posttest design where subjects were pretested on the STAXI and NOVACO, followed by a six-week treatment period during which subjects were taught the components of anger manage-ment in twice –weekly, one-hour training sessions. After the training sessions, the tests were re-administered and a decline in the perceived anger of the adolescents was verified.

Bosworth et al. (1998) used a computer-based, 175-item Teen Conflict Survey to collect both baseline and posttest survey data on a range of attitudes and emotions among 98 seventh-grade students. These included:

1. Attitudes about violent and nonviolent conflict resolution
2. Self-efficacy regarding anger management

3. Intention to use conflict management strategies

4. Self-reported caring

5. Helping behavior

6. Self-esteem

7. Impulsivity

Pretesting was followed by four weeks of violence prevention training, after which posttest data were collected to establish the success of the training among the students.

King, Lancaster, Wynne, Nettleton, and Davis (1999) used the 25-item Coopersmith Self-Esteem Inventory developed by Coopersmith (1981) to assess self-esteem scores for 11 intellectually challenged subjects (ages 17 and older). These authors also used the Anger Inventory-Caregiver Report, which is a 35-item inventory assessing subjects behavior during anger-provoking situations, as well as the 96-item Developmental Behavior Checklist developed by Einfeld and Tonge (1994), to assess overall emotional and behavioral difficulties.

In her study of ideal treatment packages for adolescents with anger disorders, Feindler (1995) used a variety of methods to assess anger and aggression. First, parent and teacher ratings of disruptive behavior by adolescents were gathered using the aggression subscales from the Achenbach Child Behavior Checklist, the Louisville School Behavior Checklist, and the Missouri Children's Behavior Checklist. The 8-item subscale of the Revised Behavior Problem Checklist was also used. To assess perceptions of anger in a variety of potentially anger-provoking situations, Feindler also used the 71-item Likert-type Children's Inventory of Anger by Finch et al. (1987). The 44-item STAXI normed for adolescents on eight subscales (State Anger, Trait Anger, Anger-In, Anger-Out, Anger-Control, Anger-Expression, Angry-Temperament, and Angry-Reaction) was also used. To assess the affective, cognitive, and behavioral responses to frustration, Feindler (1995) also recommends the use of the Children's Anger Response Checklist, which consists of 10 hypothetical conflict situations. To assess the social cognitive processes involved in anger control, a structured interview from the Adolescent Problems Inventory is recommended. Problem-solving skills and deficiencies were assessed via the story completion format of the Adolescent Social Problem Solving Scale, as well as the Problem Solving Measure for Conflict. The final method recommended for measuring individualized self-monitoring of anger by Feindler is the "anger log," referred to in other studies as the "anger diary" or "anger journal." Subjects record daily situations, examples, and experiences of anger for use in the development of role-plays. This comprehensive assessment package is likely to capture a variety of changes in perception, attitudes, and behavior induced by anger management training.

Feindler, Marriott, and Iwata (1984) also used a number of assessment tools in their study of anger control training with junior high school delinquents. They administered the Means-Ends Problem-Solving Inventory, the Locus of Control Scale for Children, the Matching of Familiar Figures Test, and the Self-Control Rating Scale. This was followed by a five-week anger management training course, after which all of the scales were re-administered. These measures assessed level of impulsivity, causal attributions, social cognitions, interpersonal problem-solving abilities, and global perceptions of 36 disruptive junior high school students who, before participating in the training, had been suspended from school multiple times for their aggressive and disruptive behaviors.

Swaffer and Hollin (1997) used the Anger Inventory, the Situations-Reaction Inventory, and the Novaco Anger Scale to gather self-report ratings from 18 adolescents about how angry they would be in various situations. The authors noted, however, that the scales were highly reflective of adult perceptions of anger-provoking events and needed to be adapted to include more relevant anger-provoking situations for adolescents.

Schlichter and Horan (1981) measured the effects of stress inoculation on the anger and aggression management skills of institutionalized juveniles with the Anger Inventory and Imaginal Provocations Test, a Role-Play Provocations Test created by the authors, and the Irrational Beliefs Test. A total of 38 adjudicated male delinquents evidencing verbal and physical aggression participated. All subjects were assessed on each measure at pretreatment and at two-week posttreatment follow-up and showed improvements in anger management.

In a study measuring constructive versus destructive responses to anger, Tagney et al. (1995) looked at the relation of shame and guilt to these responses in 427 adolescents from several public schools in grades 7 through 11. The Test of Self-Conscious Affect was used to assess the tendency to feel shame and guilt. The Anger Response Inventory assessed the range of responses to developmentally appropriate situations likely to elicit anger, and the Self Conscious Affect and Attribution Inventory measured shame and guilt responses to a number of hypothetical situations. It is worth noting here that levels of shame and guilt among incarcerated Brazilian adolescents do not seem to differ significantly from their peers (Hutz, de Silva, & McCarthy, 2004) and this is likely true in the United States as well. In other words, what works in the schools with normal adolescents is also likely to work in prisons with incarcerated adolescents.

Dangel, Deschner, and Rasp (1989) measured success of anger control training with adolescents in a residential setting through the use of a checklist system. First, verbal and physical aggression was operationally defined for subjects and their house-parents. Next, subjects were asked to self-record incidents of aggression throughout the day, and house-parents were asked to keep a record of these checkmarks. Subjects then completed a 25-day anger-control training program. At the end of this program subjects and house-parents completed an evaluation form regarding the effectiveness of the program. Teachers, counselors, and other staff members also completed a questionnaire regarding the subject's behavior both before and after treatment.

As you can see, a variety of tools are available to measure levels of anger, and there have been several empirical studies to support the effectiveness of using anger management training strategies with adolescents. In a meta-analysis of anger management research, Beck and Fernandez (1998) looked at 50 studies incorporating 1,640 subjects over 20 years of research. Of the 50 studies included in the analysis, 15 involved adolescent subjects using either a pretest/posttest or treatment versus control design (Beck & Fernandez, 1998). In the following section, various settings for anger management training programs with adolescents are summarized, including a description of the results from some of these 15 studies.

Settings Where Anger Management Training Is Used

Anger management training with adolescents occurs in a variety of settings. Adolescents receive training in residential treatment settings, community mental health settings, local social service agency settings, and juvenile correctional facilities, as well as in middle schools, junior highs, and high schools.

In their study using stress inoculation to reduce aggression in institutionalized juvenile delinquents, Schlichter and Horan (1981) found active treatment to be superior to no treatment controls, with significant main effects found on residual gains for the Anger Inventory, the Imaginal Provocations Test, and the Role Played Provocations Test.

Wilcox and Dowrick (1992) found a significant reduction in scores on the Anger Inventory and in the State-Trait Anger Expression Inventory in their repeated measures study of anger management training with substance abusing adolescents in a residential setting.

In their study of anger control training with junior high school delinquents, Feindler et al. (1984) found significant differences in pretest/posttest measures on the Self-Control Rating Scale and the Problem-Solving Inventory. They also found an increase in problem solutions to incomplete stories for the experimental group at post-treatment as compared to the control group.

In their pilot study of a computer-based violence prevention program with adolescents in public schools, Bosworth et al. (1998) found increases in students' declarative knowledge about conflict management, self-reported frequency of prosocial behavior, and intentions to use nonviolent strategies. This was accompanied by a decrease in the number of times students reported getting into trouble at home, school, and in the community.

These findings suggest that anger management training with adolescents is an effective strategy for use by educational and counseling personnel toward a reduction in both expressed and perceived aggression by adolescents in a variety of settings. In all settings examined, increases in declarative knowledge occurred regarding the various components of anger management training. This increase served to enhance adolescents' abilities to recognize cognitive, physiological, and emotional precursors of anger and aggression.

Given the self-report nature of many of the measurement techniques used to address the various components of anger management training, it is important for researchers to find ways of separating out social desirability bias (Tagney et al., 1995). Also important is the need for future research to consider the small sample sizes that are inherent when attempting to work with this difficult population. Many studies specifically suggested that results be viewed with caution for this reason. That is, adolescents with significant anger and aggression problems are not typically found in large groups except within the larger correctional or psychiatric facilities. Modern day zero-tolerance policies regarding violence and aggression in the educational setting to some extent rule out anger management training in favor of violence prevention education. There remains, however, a heightened demand for teachers and counselors to create viable programs for use with an ever-increasing population of aggressive adolescents. Zero-tolerance policies, such as suspension and expulsion, are more likely to exacerbate the problem than to solve it. Thus, future research in this area will require educators and clinicians to work more closely with one another to enhance both the predictive nature of assessment and the remedial nature of interventions with angry and aggressive adolescents.

Useful Strategies and Techniques for Anger Management Training

Use of cognitive-behavioral strategies to help adolescents manage anger constructively has proved effective in a variety of settings (Beck & Fernandez, 1998). Making such training available to adolescents is important to avoid increasing acts of aggression and violence. Ideally, counselors and school psychologists should offer anger management groups for all adolescents in public schools. At the very least, teachers should incorporate a few useful strategies into their classrooms to help adolescents recognize and deal with anger. A few promising techniques for classroom use (Gold & McCarthy, 2003, 2005; McCarthy & Gold, 2002, 2003) are:

1. Develop group trust through kinesthetic activities such as the "blind fall" exercise, in which each group member takes a turn at being blindfolded and "falling" from a chair into the arms of other group members. This may be modified by asking the blindfolded member to sit down, trusting that another member will place a chair in the appropriate place at the appropriate time. Trust activities conducted with a group of diverse peers help to overcome the sense of isolation that may later express as anger and acts of violence toward others. Activities such as these help to build group trust and rapport. They can be easily integrated into physical education and social studies classes. Devoting time and attention to building rapport is essential for anyone who works with youth—teachers, counselors, law enforcement officials, and therapists alike.

2. Develop credibility through shared stories, limited self-disclosure, and shared experiences. Acknowledge that anger is not taboo and model your own strategies for dealing with anger. Using stories and poetry as a form of bibliotherapy is also useful. Allowing youth to read about and analyze the actions of others, through literature, can be a powerful tool. Capture the imagination with literature. Have adolescents develop their own metaphors, stories, and poems to express anger. Use journals to record events and feelings, and encourage their shared use with the

group. Use the experiences and actions shared as discussion starters for problem-solving activities. Language arts, writing and literature courses are natural venues for integrating these activities in public schools.

3. Art and music therapies are great tools for developing anger management skills among adolescents. Develop the concept of art, music, and literature as constructive forms of releasing pent-up emotion. Develop team poetry, have students write new lyrics to songs, discuss key scenes from movies, draw cartoons—there are many options. The key is providing many venues and allowing each student to find those that work best. Focus on expression, not technique. Painting a picture, making a movie, composing a song, drawing a cartoon, dancing, writing a poem—any avenue of positive expression should be accepted and encouraged. In a very basic sense, it may be that inability to handle anger is because of a lack of imagination. Rather than going "back to basics" and continuing to cut art and humanities education, providing such education should be seen as a useful part of developing humanity. It is far better to allow adolescents to learn how to express pain with a paintbrush than with a gun.

4. Teach relaxation techniques. Counting, self-hypnosis, meditation, or various exercises from martial arts are all appropriate. Teaching adolescents how to focus on relaxing their bodies provides them with a valuable tool for learning emotional control.

5. Role-play problematic situations. Examples of bullying, misuse of authority, and being treated without respect are common for most adolescents. Acting out situations that can result in anger and practicing various coping strategies develop problem-solving skills. This creates a foundation for positive habits.

6. Reframe passive stressors into active stressors, and help students feel in control of their own lives and reactions. Develop lessons and activities that shift the locus of control to students. Provide for choices in assignments and projects. Build group decision making into all activities. Use physical and experiential exercises whenever possible. Work with guided imagery. Building the imagination and increasing the behavioral repertoire, while modeling proactive, social behavior are the best inoculation you can provide.

Though certainly not a cure-all or panacea, the systematic inclusion of anger-management training, relaxation training, and coping skills/life skills into the curriculum for all adolescents is a potentially valuable strategy to reduce the likelihood of future violence among students.

We have not only worked with adolescents in anger management groups in several settings, but have also been training teachers and psychologists to use anger management training strategies for many years for continuing education credits through the Russian Psychological Association, the International Council of Psychologists, the Coalition for Safe Schools, and other groups. Here is a summary of some of the techniques we use when "training the trainers" to teach conflict management, conflict resolution, relaxation training, role-playing, communication skills training, problem solving, assertiveness training, and perspective taking to adolescents.

First, we ask the people we are training to identify what they are looking for from the training. Do they want to develop a comprehensive program for use in the classroom? Are they looking for individual strategies to use with particularly problematic clients? Are they working in residential treatment or prison settings with violent adolescents? Are they hoping to find techniques to integrate into family counseling or perhaps to use with their own children? Do they work with community youth groups? It is important to identify the setting and the subjects you will be working with. All of the techniques can be adapted to any setting, but some lend themselves better to some situations than others.

Next, we share our own experiences with anger and anger management. We give many examples of the various settings in which we have worked with youth and how we have shared our own stories with these adolescents. We point out that modeling is an important part of training, especially with adolescents. Sharing one's own experiences builds credibility and also offers ideas for new coping strategies. It builds the repertoire of strategies teens can draw from. It also subtly acknowledges that feelings of anger are natural, normal responses. The feelings themselves are nothing to be ashamed of and can be channeled in constructive ways. Learning how to manage the feelings and deal with anger constructively is the purpose of the training. We then encourage our participants to construct their own stories of times they have been extremely angry and how they have managed to deal with it constructively. They tell these stories to each other and develop them for future reference in their own training work.

Next, we provide guidelines and strategies, providing as many examples as possible. We emphasize the importance of building rapport with the group, and also among the group. Activities like the "blind fall" and "group poetry" described previously can be integrated into this program. Telling stories about one's own experiences with anger as an adolescent is also useful for building rapport.

We talk about various "styles" of anger and show ways of helping students to identify their particular "style." We also provide ideas for working effectively with adolescents from educational psychology, including using novelty and surprise to engage attention and ways of demonstrating a nonthreatening sense of boundary combined with understanding and empathy. We share stories and poetry that can be especially useful, such as Richard LaGravenese's *Fisher King* and Carl Sandburg's *Wilderness*. We also integrate examples of music adolescents are familiar with that expresses anger and demonstrate art therapy techniques.

We discuss traditional behavioral strategies such as "time out" and reframe these as "acts of will." Willed introversion gives more of a sense of personal control than time-out, for example. Something as simple as the labeling can make a difference. We also demonstrate relaxation techniques and martial arts techniques that are useful and a variety of other techniques such as mirroring, matching, pacing, primal scream, and verbal aikido. Use of ritual is stressed. Journals, writing, and creative expression are emphasized. Simple means of biofeedback monitoring are taught. Physical activity and its role in releasing anger are discussed. Meditation, yoga, guided relaxation, and other techniques are shared.

We also discuss the role of values and spirituality in reactions to anger, and we demonstrate connections between depression, loss, fear, and angry reactions. We model systematic desensitization and role-play techniques. We look at ways of integrating critical thinking, problem solving, and brainstorming techniques. Developing hobbies that allow release and distance from anger, modifying the environment, social interactions, and the use of labeling and positive self-talk are examined.

We encourage anyone who works with adolescents to become familiar with anger management training techniques and to attend training sessions for teaching anger management techniques. As experiential techniques work best with adolescents, experiential training is also necessary. This summary, we hope, has piqued enough interest for the reader to become a trainer and join the "anger management corps." Lots of adolescents need assistance to develop these skills!

Although anger may frequently be demonstrated in the home, anger management is generally less explicitly relayed to adolescents by parents. Parenting, whether good or otherwise, is a critically important factor in the level of adolescent violence we see in modern times. No one, of course, sets out to be a bad parent, but this is one vital task that our society generally offers no training for. We train and license drivers, but not parents. We train and certify teachers, psychologists, and other professionals, but not parents. Integrating both anger management training and courses on parenting skills and child development into public education may be a useful strategy for reducing adolescent violence. In the next chapter, we examine the role of parents in depth.

CHAPTER 7

PROACTIVE PARENTING IN A CHANGING WORLD

Edith Grotberg, Augustus "Skip" Little, and Suzanne Little are acknowledged for their valuable contributions to this chapter.

Parents are, ideally, the strongest socializing factor in the lives of adolescents. For many reasons, though, this potential is often not realized. Peer culture supersedes parental influence for many adolescents. The majority of time is spent with peers rather than family. This chapter looks at resources to support parents of teens and strategies for making adolescents resilient against violence. The first contribution to this effort comes from Dr. Skip and Suzanne Little, whom you already "met" in previous chapters. They share the following valuable information:

As parents of six children, we realize the world our children live in is a distorted reflection of the world we were born into in the United States a generation ago. Gone are "Ozzie and Harriet" and "Leave It to Beaver" and the values they represented. We now have reality television and filters attempting to block inappropriate information from entering our homes through the Internet, which our children take as a challenge to dismantle. Today's children have watched as television delivered images into their homes of jets being flown into the World Trade Center towers and bodies of dead soldiers lying in faraway desert battlefields in which their siblings, cousins, and friends are fighting.

Those same televisions bring children images of distorted realities, with children placed in roles acting much older than their chronological ages. Even many "family networks" air commercials with seven- to nine-year-olds dressed and acting as we would expect to see twelve- to fifteen-year-olds. These inappropriate life images and violent activities that children see many minutes of their day are also enhanced by Internet sites, video games, computer Web sites, movies, rap music, and magazines.

Compounding the media barrage of inappropriate behavior and violence children view, they are also increasingly living in homes and communities froth with violence. All this contributes to the facts that:

- *Almost 16 million teens have witnessed some form of violent assault.*
- *About one in eight people murdered in the United States each year are younger than 18 years old.*
- *Research shows a link between violent television programs and aggressive behavior in teens who watch those programs.*
- *Most injuries and violent deaths occur between people who know each other.*
- *If there is violence in your family, it increases the risk of your teen becoming involved in future violence.*
- *A gun in the home is more likely to be used to kill a family member or friend than to kill an intruder.*

Many mothers and fathers pulled by the demands of modern living and the demands of adolescents often find themselves at the brink of their existence in dealing with their adolescent child. It is hoped that the information shared in this chapter will enable more parents to be proactive with their children in today's changing world.

Marshfield Clinic Psychiatrist Charles J. Van Der Heide, MD, of Palo Alto Medical Foundation, says that parents and other adults should watch for the following signs of potential violence in adolescents:

- *Intense anger/frequent loss of temper*
- *Extreme irritability*
- *Impulsiveness*
- *Easy frustration*
- *Cruelty to animals*
- *Aggressive behavior*
- *Fire setting*
- *Bullying*
- *Unusual defiance*

Factors that increase the risk include:

- *Past violent/aggressive behavior*
- *Access to guns*

- *Weapons at school*
- *Past suicide attempts*
- *Family history of violent behavior*
- *Unwillingness to accept responsibility for one's actions*
- *Recent shameful experience, disciplinary crisis, or humiliation*
- *A history of bullying/intimidating peers or younger children*

The Center of Education for Young Adults offers parents and others who work with adolescents 26 tips for proactively working with adolescents who exhibit any of these behaviors. Many seem simple, but are not occurring as they need to in the lives of these teens. Here is the suggested list of activities:

1. *Talk*

   Anything that can be done to increase communication with your children is time well spent. Talking will decrease the need for external rules and increase the interpersonal comfort level.

2. *"I" Messages*

   If you want to be less confrontational and make a point without threatening or offending when communicating with teens, try an "I" message. Example: "I feel angry when you borrow my shirt without asking. I need you to ask before you borrow things."

3. *Bad News-Good News*

   Share bad news right up front. That communicates honesty and a willingness to confront issues head on. End the conversation on a positive note.

4. *Put Good News in Writing*

   When there is good news to communicate, share it in writing. It makes the good news more formal and is something that can be posted as a visual reminder of accomplishment. Bad news should be communicated verbally and in a nonthreatening manner.

5. *Certificates and Ceremonies*

   Adolescents can really get down on themselves, so it is important to provide kids with visible, tangible symbols of accomplishment and success. Ceremonies can be as simple as a touch or a hand slap. Help teens to develop self-esteem for the right reasons.

6. *Be Positive*

   Look at the bright side whenever possible. There are many times when negative comments seem to dominate parents' communication with adolescents. It is important to remember that children at this age are full of energy, enthusiasm, and curiosity. They also tend to be quite sensitive to criticism or remarks that they interpret to be critical.

7. *Full Name, First Name, Nickname*

Adolescents appreciate subtle communication. That is why parents for many generations have communicated their feelings by using different names for different types of address. The use of the nickname is a signal that all is well, the full first name often signals a bit of concern, and the full name means there is trouble brewing. There are some cultural differences, of course, and the use of nicknames is more formalized in some cultural groups and countries than others. But developing a friendly "pet name" for your child and using it in private family communication may be a useful way of enhancing warmth between you.

8. *Display Good Work*

Adolescents may tell you they have outgrown this practice, that it is not cool to keep posting good work. However, they are usually very pleased with the honor.

9. *Humor*

Adolescents tell us that the single characteristic they admire most in teachers is a sense of humor. However, you do not have to be a great joke teller. Your intention and attitude will be as much appreciated as the quality of your humor. Remember that it is hard to be angry with someone who can laugh at himself or herself.

10. *Self-Esteem*

Help children develop a positive self-image. They need to feel good about themselves. This can be especially difficult for a young adolescent who is often experiencing a larger and more challenging school environment and a growing and more challenging body at about the same time. We need to help them to experience success and to avoid situations where failure is likely.

11. *Don't Use Indirect Communication or Sarcasm to Relay Important Information*

The majority of young adolescents operate at a concrete mental level. That means they tend to understand what is said at face value of the words used.

12. *Secret Signal*

Many young adolescents have reported the feeling of being "in a goldfish bowl." They feel that everyone is watching them. This leads to being self-conscious. A secret signal allows you to communicate with your children in groups at times when they may be embarrassed otherwise.

13. *Body Language*

Because young adolescents are experiencing rapid physical change, they tend to be very much aware of the body and of body language. Be aware of what your body is saying. Don't forget that your facial expression is an important part of body language, too.

14. *Problems*

   Children need to know that they are valued as people, as human beings. Their opinions, ideas, and problems are very important to them even though they may seem small to us. As parents, we need to be empathetic and not minimize or devalue the feelings and concerns our children share with us.

15. *Visibility*

   For many adolescents, if they can't see you, you're not available. Let them see you and know you are there. Visibility means you are there for them and you care about them.

16. *Support*

   Your support for the adolescents in your life is meaningful and important. Adolescents are seeking an identity of self and exploring new interests. Attend extracurricular activities; they may say that you don't have to come, but go anyway! They want you there and need your support.

17. *Don't Discipline in Anger*

   Don't become emotional or lose your temper. We are all more likely to do something that we will regret later if we act under the stress or influence of emotion.

18. *Consistency*

   Most adolescents are concrete thinkers and very often see their world in terms of right and wrong, black and white. Because they think that way, it is important that you approach them with consistency. Structure, dependability, and predictability at home are important for adolescents.

19. *Behavior Log*

   If you are frustrated with the behavior of an adolescent, you may want to keep a behavior log. If the child is in denial or really doesn't seem to understand what he or she has been doing, a written record is more difficult to deny than the spoken word. The behavior log helps to reveal the cumulative nature of the things we do.

20. *Don't Take It Personally*

   Adolescence is a time of physical growth and psychological weaning. This is a natural time to test limits, find out where the boundaries are, and to establish personal space. Don't be offended by this. Your children are not rejecting you; they are finding themselves.

21. *Don't Over-react*

   Some behaviors are exhibited for the purpose of attracting attention; others are tests used to determine how adults will react. Don't over-react! Many annoying behaviors will go away if they are ignored.

22. *Planned Surprises*

   Adolescents love surprises. A gift for no reason, a special meal, or an unplanned activity that is meaningful to them will mean a great deal. Surprises do not need to be frequent; they should be occasional, sincere expressions of love and concern.

23. *Contracts*

   Many adults have used contracts as a means of formalizing agreements or understandings. They should be simple and clearly understood by all involved. Expectations or behaviors must be specified in measurable terms. A time frame should be identified and the consequences should be straightforward. Remember that positive consequences are more effective than punishment.

24. *Labeling*

   When you are describing something you don't like that your adolescents do, such as the way they act, be careful not to label them with a name Describe what it is that they do that you do not like but don't use name calling or labels. Labels are likely to be hurtful rather than helpful. For example, calling your child a "slob" for not cleaning up is unwise. Instead, simply state that you feel it is important for the area to be tidy and organized and would appreciate assistance in keeping it so.

25. *Rehearse*

   This may sound silly, but you should rehearse conversations that you will have with your adolescents, especially if you foresee that they may be stressful or emotional. This can help improve communication skills.

26. *Modeling*

   Whether or not they appear to be watching, adolescents are aware of your every move, word, and comment. Work to model the same behaviors you expect of them.

   Using these strategies is likely to make parenting easier and more beneficial. Here are 12 more simple things parents can do to protect their children and keep them from becoming involved in violence as suggested by the National Youth Violence Prevention Resource Center, National Parent Teachers Association, U.S. Department of Justice, and U.S. Department of Education.

   1. *Give your children consistent love and attention.*

      Every child needs a strong, loving, relationship with a parent or other adult to feel safe and secure and to develop a sense of trust.

   2. *Communicate openly with your children, and encourage them to talk about all aspects of their lives: school, social activities, and their interests and concerns.*

Listen respectfully and solicit their opinions. Then, if a problem or crisis arises, they will be more likely to come to you.

3. *Start talking about ways to reduce or eliminate violence.*

   Communication is an essential component of child rearing and a constant challenge. Being available and being approachable are as important as having the answer to a question or providing the best guidance with a problem. Consistency, honesty, and understanding are critical to creating a climate conducive to sharing. Talking with your children shows you care about them and gives them an opportunity to share their concerns, interests, fears, and activities. It may also give you some ideas about aspects of their school and personal life that can be improved. Everyday conversations also create natural opportunities for you to teach your children social skills, anger management, problem-solving skills, and ways to avoid becoming a victim. Team up with other parents and get involved in your community; join your neighbors in activities to reduce violence. Talk to your teen about ways to solve arguments and fights without weapons or violence. Advise your teen to talk to you or a trusted adult to avoid potentially violent situations. If you suspect a problem with your teen, start talking about it.

4. *Set clear standards for your children's behavior, and be consistent about rules and discipline.*

   Involve your children in the setting of rules whenever possible, and discuss the reasons for rules with them. Make sure they understand what you expect and the consequences for disobedience, and then enforce rules consistently.

5. *Make sure your children are supervised.*

   Insist on knowing where your children are at all times and who their friends are. Try to get to know their friends' parents and your children's teachers. Encourage your children to participate in supervised after-school activities such as sports teams, tutoring programs, or organized recreation.

6. *Promote peaceful resolutions to conflict by being a good role model.*

   Deal with conflict at home calmly, considerately, and quickly. Manage your anger without violence. Talk with your children about handling disagreements, and help your children learn how to examine and find nonaggressive solutions to problems. Model prosocial behavior. One of the best ways to teach a child is by demonstration. Through their everyday actions, parents teach their children how to interact socially, handle competition and defeat, discuss differences, resolve conflicts, deal with frustration in solving problems, and cope with stress and anger. Children also learn from the other adults in their lives and may need help understanding different behavior responses to similar situations. Inevitable exposure of children to negative influences makes the parent's role as a model of prosocial behavior even more important.

   Help your teen deal with anger. Anger is a normal feeling. Anger does not have to be bad if it is expressed appropriately. Teach your teen that it is okay to be angry, but it's not okay to throw a punch. Parents and others who care for young people can help them learn to deal with emotions without using violence. Because violence results from conflicts between people, it can be prevented by learning nonviolent ways to control anger and solve problems. Teaching your teen, through words and actions, that violence is never an acceptable form of behavior is important.

- *People must control their anger before they can control a situation.*
- *Sometimes counseling is necessary to help teens deal with their anger appropriately.*

Be a role model by handling problems in nonviolent ways and seeking counseling yourself if necessary.

- *Don't hit your teen. Model nonphysical solutions to problem solving.*
- *Count to 10. Cool off. If you can't control your anger, tell your teen you need some time to get your thoughts and feelings under control.*
- *Problem solve with your teen. Think together about options and consequences for behaviors.*
- *Set limits, make sure your teen knows the rules and consequences, and follow through.*
- *Don't carry a gun. This sends a message to your teen that using guns solves problems.*

7. *Reduce the threat of gun-related violence to your teen.*

   Make certain that your teen does not have access to guns. If you own firearms, make sure that they are unloaded, locked up, and inaccessible to children. Other dangerous weapons should also be kept out of the reach of children. Talk to your children about the consequences of drug and weapon use, gang participation, and violence. If you have a gun, remove it from your home or store it unloaded and locked up. Lock and store bullets separately.

   - *Tell your teen to stay away from potentially dangerous situations and from guns in homes of friends or places where he or she may visit or play.*
   - *Keep in mind that teens don't always follow the rules. Also, teens are attracted to guns and see guns as symbols of power. Because you can't always count on teens to stay away from guns, you have to keep guns away from them.*

8. *Try to limit your children's exposure to violence in the media.*

   Limiting a child's exposure to crime and violence is a difficult but important task for every parent. Children are exposed to both real and simulated depictions of violence and other crime in many ways. They find it on television, in movies, in newspapers, on the radio, on the Internet, in plays, in neighborhoods, in homes, in schools, at athletic events, in video games, in music, and many other places. Some children do not fully understand or successfully cope with their exposure to crime and violence. Because of frequent and unrealistic media depictions, they may think that violent events are more common than they really are. They may not fully appreciate the true consequences of violent behaviors. As a result, children may pretend to be violent in their play with little harm, yet when they become frustrated or angry, these behaviors may take a more serious form in some children. Monitor the programs your children watch, the music they listen to, and the video games they play. Take time to watch television programs with your children and discuss any violence with them. Is the violence realistic? What would be the real-life consequences of such violence?

9. *Monitor the media.*

    - *Limit the amount of television your teen watches to one to two hours a day (including music videos and video games).*
    - *Do not allow your teen to watch violent movies or TV programs.*
    - *If something violent comes on the TV, talk about the program and how the situation could have been handled in a nonviolent way.*

10. *Try to limit your children's exposure to violence in the home or community.*

    Work toward making your home a safe, nonviolent place, and always discourage violent behavior or hostile, aggressive arguments between family members. If the people in your home physically or verbally hurt and abuse each other, get help from a psychologist or counselor in your community. If your children are exposed to violence in the street, at school, or at home, they may need help in dealing with these frightening experiences. A psychologist, a counselor at school, or a member of the clergy are among those who can help them cope with their feelings.

11. *Take the initiative to make your school and community safer.*

    Join up with other parents through school and neighborhood associations, religious organizations, civic groups, and youth activity groups. Talk together about your concerns about youth in the community, including issues related to alcohol, drugs, and violence, and share your common parenting concerns. Support the development and implementation of school and community plans to address the needs of youth. Get involved with school and community organizations and activities. Becoming active in a child's school and community life brings many benefits. It allows parents to see more of what their children see, providing parents with a deeper understanding of their child's needs. Situations arise that will provide opportunities for reinforcing what is taught in the home. The presence of parents can give some continuity in moving from one setting to another. Being involved also gives parents the opportunity to get to know teachers, childcare providers, and coaches, and to work with them to ensure that their child's needs are met when parents are not present.

    Here are a few examples of things parents can do to in the school and community to promote prosocial behavior and to make the most of learning opportunities:

    - *Make sure children attend class and complete assigned homework.*
    - *Get to know teachers and administrators.*

- *Actively continue a child's education in the summer.*
- *Encourage children to participate in extracurricular activities.*
- *Volunteer with the school or community programs the child attends.*
- *Know the school's discipline policy and discuss it.*
- *Attend parent-teacher conferences, school board meetings, and community meetings.*
- *Work with school staff when a child has been aggressive or victimized at school.*
- *Work with other parents and organizations to ensure that children are safe when going to and from school or community activities.*
- *Serve on a school safety committee or the Parent Teacher Association (PTA).*

Each community will have many more opportunities to get involved; finding them will be worth the effort.

12. *Participate in family management training or counseling opportunities.*

   Participating in formal training programs in family management is a good way to get extra help. Family counseling is an appropriate option for some, and others benefit from less structured assistance. Specific skills can be learned to reduce the stress and challenges of raising children, including problem solving, communication, coping with anger and stress, and conflict mediation. Training may be available through the school, faith communities, or in the broader community. Seeking help from friends or family members who are experienced parents is another way to better meet your child's needs.

13. *Be clear and consistent in disciplining your child.*

   When establishing rules for children, it is important for parents to think through their views on crime, violence, weapons, and appropriate self-defense, and be clear in communicating them to their children. Children also need to know parents support school discipline policies and any reasonable punishments that are administered by the school. Children need to understand the rationale for household, school, and other rules and behavioral expectations. If a child misbehaves, consequences are more effective if they are consistent and appropriate to the severity and frequency of the offense and administered with a gentle voice and with full explanation.

   Teaching self-discipline is more useful than punishment. Involving children in activities that teach constructive skills such as responsibility, appropriate play behavior, self-control, and goal setting is as important as sanctioning them for inappropriate behavior. Parents can devise rewards and incentives for desired behaviors to prevent future rule violations and to urge constructive behaviors.

We realize that, given the stress and pressure of modern life and the variety of communities in which we live, some of this advice may be difficult to implement. We certainly learned this in our own experience as parents of teens. One factor that makes parenting particularly challenging is the mobility of modern society and the need many families have to relocate—sometimes multiple times—for work-related reasons. This high mobility makes on-going, daily contact with extended family difficult, if not impossible.

Except in the case of highly dysfunctional extended family situations, this is unfortunate for teens, who benefit from a strong, loosely knit support system that allows them to interact with many family members of many ages. Grandparents, cousins, aunts, and uncles are a valuable pool of possible role models for teens. They can provide a different type of communication and support than parents, serve as "safe refuges" when needed, and otherwise assist teens with the difficult process of growing up. Parents also benefit from the "time off" that grandparents, aunts, and uncles can provide. The fact is, today in the United States, few families with teens live near the extended family. This has changed gradually over the last century, although from the fifteenth century on, many who settled in the New World of the Americas from Africa, Asia, and Europe began their family histories here, whether willingly or unwillingly, by cutting ties to extended family. Perhaps that is one reason that high mobility and distance from family has generally been acceptable to many Americans. High mobility, though, does have a price, especially to children and teens who are uprooted from the support of extended family.

Not only does the process of leaving a secure home and community mean that ties with family are lost, it also means that ties to friends, so important during adolescence, and to the security of daily routine, is also sacrificed. Leaving a community and relocating cause a type of grief that, in many teens, expresses itself (as grief often does for adults as well) as stress, anger, aggressiveness, depression, or self-destructive behavior. Poverty also results in frequent forced relocation or even homelessness, and "following the job" may of course be the most reasonable option. Even so, parents should be aware that the readjustment period for teens is likely to be rocky. This is a time when friendships with other uprooted teens who are also having adjustment problems can create a less than ideal peer group during a time when peer group interaction is very influential on adolescent behavior. Because parents may also be under increased stress during a relocation period, this is a time to take special care to enhance positive family dynamics. Establishing strong ties to the new community quickly is also important for all family members. The suburban "stranger next door" syndrome is part of the puzzling dynamics that explain tragic situations such as occurred at Columbine.

The role parents play in creating a healthy community and a safe, nonviolent future cannot be emphasized enough. Dr. Edith Grotberg writes the following in this regard:

Parents are the frontier of the next generation. They determine the future of the world. They are in a powerful position to reshape society. They have control of how their children are raised and no one can equal their power. They do things with and for their children from the day they are born and give them the support they need to develop their inner strengths and values. They help them to acquire interpersonal and problem-solving skills to deal with the challenges and adversities in their lives. In short, parents are the first promoters of resilience. They should be, at any rate.

A supportive relationship between parents and their youth is imperative if youth are to become resilient and have a much-needed sense of well-being. Parents play many major roles that provide the foundation for resilient youth. These include:

1. *Relationships and connectedness*

   When youth have a trusting and loving relationship with their parents, they tend to have good social skills, do well in school, and show lower rates of risk-taking behavior than their peers. It seems clear that having one resilience factor promoted permits other resilience factors to be promoted. Unfortunately, youth who have poor relationships with their parents are more likely to have problems, including problems with mental health.

2. *Modeling*

   Teens and youth still look to their parents as models of how to behave. What family members do, what they say, and how they prepare for and respond to adversities are models of behavior that influence the promotion of resilience in youth. The most powerful example of the impact of role modeling on children came from a study in Peru conducted by Giselle Silva (1999). Her study, using the resilience paradigm, I Have, I Am, I Can, examined the role of parents in helping their children and youth deal with effects of political violence and the role of resilience in that effort. She examined the reaction of parents to trauma and the impact of parents as role models on the resilience of their children and youth.

   Many parents became poor as they escaped the violence, moving from the countryside and the mountains to the city and lower lands. They were required to make a new life in the new setting and raise their children there. Two major reactions to trauma distinguished families who were modeling and promoting resilience in their children from those who were not.

Some of the families focused their attention on the trauma of the violence and the necessity of escaping to the new environment. The focus of these families was on the violent events the family had experienced. The orientation was toward the past. Close relationships in the family were negatively affected. Social relationships were affected by a lack of confidence. Feelings of fear and isolation predominated. There was no adaptation to the new setting. Fantasies focused on returning to the former home. Deep feelings of nostalgia were experienced, with a major focus on memories.

Most children and youth of these families did not become resilient, and, in fact, many developed severe social and psychological problems, adapting many of their parents' behaviors. In addition, the children and youth showed lack of confidence in others, changed their relationships with their parents in negative ways, experienced frequent feelings of sorrow over the losses from the violence, frequently engaged in games repeating the trauma, and had difficulty in communicating with others.

In contrast, other parents focused their attention on the new environment. They sought out opportunities in the new setting (jobs, education, friends). These parents refused to allow the trauma to affect family relationships, focused on the here and now and the future, and were receptive to new relationships with neighbors. They adapted and adjusted to the new setting, and although they remembered sad experiences of the past, they used them to encourage progress. These parents were role models of resilience for their children.

The children and youth of these families were optimistic about the future, made plans, attended school for the first time, learned Spanish for the first time, helped out in the family during vacations, and talked through their experiences of violence. They sometimes showed fear and uncertainty, but they could recover. They were resilient. Modeling is a powerful tool for developing resilience in the young.

3. *Awareness*

   Parents help their children and youth become resilient by knowing about their activities, who their friends are, where they are going, and setting limits on hours out of the home. Clearly, youth need to reexamine with their parents the rules, as youth will need to gradually take increasing responsibility for their behavior as they become older.

   Waiting until they leave home for college or a job is too late to learn all these responsibilities and expectations. The home is the place where certain behaviors are promoted and expected. And changes in how these are accomplished as children become teens and teens become young adults are necessary. However, the general expectations for adolescent behavior should be these:

   a. *A sense of responsibility*
   b. *Feeling empathy and caring for people*

    c. Expressing thoughts and feelings honestly
    d. Resolving conflicts with family member and friends
    e. Building friendships
    f. Sharing, taking turns
    g. Demonstrating interests and skills independent of school
    h. Having a sense of humor
    i. Feeling confident
    j. Being flexible
    k. Increasing autonomy and self-management
    l. Becoming socialized both in and outside the family

Parents who are supportive and caring while monitoring and enforcing family rules, tend to motivate their youth to be successful and provide a sense of well-being and self-esteem. Parents who are overly strict do not give their youth room for developing a sense of independence. These children tend to engage in more risk-taking behavior. By contrast, parents who are caring but also permissive tend to have youth who act impulsively and are likely to take risks. The literature on authoritative parenting, in contrast to authoritarian or permissive parenting, is a challenge for any parent to master, and well worth reading!

The role of parents in the promotion of resilience in youth takes on new significance, however, when the family faces a major adversity. Father is out of the country, engaged in war or peace keeping. Mother has just lost her job and there is a question about the ability to go to college. A brother has died and the family is having difficulty dealing with the grief. The youth was bullied by some of the kids in school. A parent, in spite of feelings of sadness, fear, and concern, must help the youth get through the current adversity, whatever it is. Here are some of the ways suggested by the American Psychological Association to deal with such situations:

    1. Talk with adolescents, asking them their opinions about what is happening. Also, ask for their advice on how the family can deal with the adversity. And offer advice when youth seems to be having difficulty deciding what to do. Let them feel part of the solution. Discuss, more than tell, what some of the things that might be done are, and the advantages and disadvantages of each.

    2. See your home as a place of safety from whatever outside adversities are occurring, whether it be a sniper threat, violence in the neighborhood, or a bully who is really frightening.

    3. If adolescents are watching or reading too much about bad things that happen, suggest they take a "news break." Continuous watching adds stress while providing nothing new. Further, you can use watching the news together as an opportunity to share thoughts and feelings with them, especially about how they are handling fears and stress in their lives.

4. *Reassure youth by your behavior and words that they will be OK, that the family is there to protect the members, and that everything possible will be done to make everyone feel safe.*

5. *Watch for signs of fear or anxiety that the youth may not be able to put into words. If they lose interest in school or in a team they belong to, if they get poorer grades, or if they seem depressed, something must be done. Outside help may be needed. Involve the youth in activities you are involved in, especially community work. Tutoring middle-school students, helping in a food kitchen, joining a hiking organization—things that provide a better perspective of their lives are valuable activities.*

6. *Be optimistic. Model optimism. If you portray that "We know things are going to be OK," this provides an atmosphere of confidence that influences behavior. When someone says, "We'll never get there without an accident," the atmosphere is one of fear and insecurity, and the driving often reflects that uncertainty. By contrast, when someone says, "We're going to make this, you'll see," the atmosphere changes. When people are more relaxed, things do go better.*

Families can make decisions together about how they will get through the adversities they are facing. They can reexamine what they are doing to see if changes need to be made as the adversity continues. They can learn from what they have been doing what is working and what needs to be changed.

Children and adolescents develop strategies for resilience based on what they experience with family members. Still, even when families do not transmit these skills, other community members can intervene and play important roles. In light of the recent findings about the role of the environment in counteracting the genes that appear to be markers of depression, the work of William Beardslee and others (Beardslee et al., 1997) is particularly poignant. His research on children of depressed parents found that these children faced four to six more times the risk of developing the illness than those from nondepressed families, and their risk increased over time. Now in its third decade, his program has focused on breaking this cycle by increasing the children's self-understanding, their awareness that something is wrong with their parent and that they are not to blame.

The project tested two strategies for impacting self-understanding: lectures and family counseling sessions. Both approaches communicated the same information, but the counseling was more intensive (six rather than three sessions) and also linked the information directly to the individual family's experience. It proved to be more effective. As family members began discussing what had previously been unmentionable—the parents' depression—communication about other subjects became easier. Communication, in turn, brought optimism about family relationships and the will to make small changes that impacted the lives of children and youth. Beardslee, the project's principal investigator, points out that those families sustaining the changes carried them into their daily lives. He called this "the emergence of the healer within." Beardslee is also an advocate of resilience; he recognizes that his work is, in fact, promoting resilience.

Other research in developmental psychology supports the importance that a mentor—a teacher or other community member—can have in building resilience. An extensive longitudinal study conducted more than 20 years ago in Hawaii showed that adolescents who came from highly dysfunctional, poverty-ridden homes and were able to cite at least one adult who they respected, to whom they felt close and could rely on for help, were much more likely to succeed. They were more likely to graduate from high school and less likely to develop mental illness or be arrested. Parents may be the most important cushion against adolescent violence, but when that cushion fails, other community members can also have a beneficial influence.

Before turning to the role of the community at large in promoting resilience, however, here is a list of valuable references and resources for parents who face family adversity compiled by Skip and Suzanne Little and based on their own experiences as teachers, psychologists, and parents:

> *Parenting Resources for the 21st Century*—Coordinating Council on Juvenile Justice and Delinquency Prevention
>
> This group links parents and other adults responsible for the care of a child with information on issues covering the full spectrum of parenting. It strives to help families meet the formidable challenges of raising a child today by addressing topics that include school violence, child development, home schooling, organized sports, child abuse, and the juvenile justice system.
>
> *Parents Matter: Helping Your Children Navigate Their Teen Years* (2000)—White House Council on Youth Violence.
>
> This guidebook provides parents with answers to typical "teen development" questions, including information on how to handle tough situations, such as bullying, substance use, school failure, depression, and anger and violence, and how to get help for your teen.
>
> *Raising Children to Resist Violence: What You Can Do* (1995)—American Psychological Association and the American Academy of Pediatrics.
>
> This public education brochure suggests ways that parents, family members, and others can help children learn to solve problems and to deal with emotions without using violence.

Here Is What We Can All Do for Our Children: A Guide for Parents—Children's Safety Network.

This brochure reviews steps that parents can take to ensure that their children stay violence-free. It includes tips for peaceful solutions to arguments.

Understanding Child Development as a Violence Prevention Tool (2001)—American Psychological Association

This brochure outlines important information about children's typical abilities and behaviors at various ages until age 8 years. By providing comprehensive information pertaining to child development, the brochure enables adults to modify their expectations and behaviors regarding young children.

What Makes Kids Care? Teaching Gentleness in a Violent World (1996)—American Psychological Association.

A three-page consumer-oriented fact sheet offers parents some techniques and suggestions for teaching their children to become gentler in their behavior despite their exposure to violence in their environment.

Make Time to Listen—Take Time to Talk (2000)—Center for Mental Health Services, Substance Abuse and Mental Health Services Administration

This brochure offers tips for parents and caregivers to communicate with children about drugs and violence.

These resources are available on-line and can be located by a simple title search in any common search engine. There are also a number of hotlines that can provide you with immediate crisis counseling, information, and referral services. Some of the key crisis hotlines in the United States are:

National Hopeline Network—This hotline offers crisis counseling, information, and referral services for those considering suicide and those who care about them.

1-800-SUICIDE (1-800-784-2433)

National Runaway Switchboard—The switchboard provides confidential information, referral, and counseling services to runaway and homeless youth, youth in crisis, and their families.

1-800-621-4000 (24 hours per day)

Girls and Boys Town National Hotline—This hotline offers help, hope, and healing to troubled teens and their families. Callers talk to highly trained professional counselors who listen and give "right now" answers.

1-800-448-3000

National Organization for Victim Assistance—This hotline offers crisis counseling and referral services to victims of crime and their families.

1-800-879-6682

National Domestic Violence Hotline—This hotline offers information and referral services, counseling, and assistance to victims of domestic violence (and dating violence), their children, other family members, and the public.

1-800-799-SAFE (1-800-799-7233)

To learn about other hotlines and referral sources, visit these Web sites:

List of Crisis Hotlines—National Clearinghouse on Families & Youth, Administration for Children and Families (ACF)

Lists contact information for a number of national crisis hotlines.

Resources and Referrals—National Clearinghouse on Alcohol and Drug Information, SAMHSA

This Web site links you to sources for more information and help on a variety of issues. It includes links to crisis lines and self-help organizations for people with alcohol and substance abuse problems, emotional problems, and for those who have been victims of abuse or crimes.

Center for Substance Abuse Treatment—Substance Abuse and Mental Health Services Administration

This Web site has a *Substance Abuse Treatment Facility Locator* that will help you to find the right drug abuse treatment program or alcohol abuse treatment program. This searchable directory of drug and alcohol treatment programs shows the location of more than 11,000 facilities around the country that treat alcoholism, alcohol abuse, and drug abuse problems. The Center for Substance Abuse Treatment also runs a 24-hour, 7-day-a-week National Helpline that offers free and confidential substance abuse and addiction-related information and treatment referrals.

1-800-662-HELP

Knowledge Education Network (KEN)—Center for Mental Health Services, SAMHSA

KEN staff are skilled at listening and responding to questions from the public and professionals. KEN staff members quickly direct callers to federal, state, and local organizations dedicated to treating and preventing mental and emotional problems.

1-800-789-2647 Spanish available (M–F 8:30–5:00 EST)

Perhaps changing technology, particularly the Internet, will offer some advantages for parents now and in the future. Information and assistance are more readily available. In addition, families who are separated because of moving long distances can more easily maintain contact. Children and adolescents can keep in touch with friends and family members more easily. Parenting remains a worthy challenge, though, and certainly is one of the most influential factors, for good or ill, on the amount and expression of adolescent aggression in society.

CHAPTER 8

Teens, Violence, and the "3 Rs": Resilience, Rehabilitation, and Recovery

Dr. Edith Grotberg made substantial contributions to this chapter.

The role of parents in preventing teen violence is certainly critical. We also know that, for a variety of reasons, parents are not always able to provide the type of environment and nurturing required for developing nonviolent, prosocial adolescents. Poor parenting, for whatever reasons, does not doom anyone to a life of violence or despair, however, any more than genetic markers might. Because of the dynamic interaction of biological, social, and personality factors under the umbrella of individual will, resilience, rehabilitation, and recovery are the "3 Rs" that can always be realized in adolescent development. Given the current level of adolescent aggression in society, it is certainly time for public education to begin to focus on these "3 Rs," at least as consistently as the more traditional academic variety. Research in all of these areas reveals many successful strategies.

Courtesy of Dr. Edith Grotberg, this chapter begins by offering more research and information about the first of these "3 Rs," resilience, as well as some useful strategies for promoting resilience in adolescents to reduce aggression.

The Role of Resilience

There is sufficient evidence that youth, as well as other age groups over the life span, benefit from the promotion of resilience. That is, those who have been given support, those who have developed inner strength, and those who have acquired interpersonal and problem-solving skill, are more able to deal with adversities successfully. They are resilient. What is resilience?

Resilience is the human capacity to face, overcome, be strengthened by, and even transformed by experiences of adversity. Some adversities are external, such as fires, earthquakes, floods, drought, bombing, war, and violence. Some are within the family, such as divorce, abuse, neglect, abandonment, or loss of a job, home, or a loved one. And some of them are within the individual, such as fear of rejection, loss of love, harm, failure, or illness.

Of course, there are differences in what is perceived as an adversity, particularly in personal experiences. One person may perceive divorce as an adversity, whereas another may see it as an opportunity to be free to pursue travel, more education, or a less stressful job. But when anyone has an experience that causes great stress, fear, or alienation, that person may well perceive the experience to be an adversity. Resilience provides the tools and the behaviors to deal with adversities

Resilience is not magic; it is not found only in certain people and it is not a gift from unknown sources. All humans have the capacity to become resilient. Obviously, there are many individual differences, depending on such things as age, stage of development, the number and frequency of adversities faced, and the resources available to deal with them. But the process of becoming resilient can begin at any age or stage of a person's life.

The resilience factors that can be promoted and used in dynamic interaction in dealing with an adversity consist of (1) external supports, labeled by the author as I Have; (2) inner strengths, labeled I Am, and (3) interpersonal and problem-solving skills, labeled I Can (Grotberg, 1995). Each factor can be promoted separately or in combination. These factors derive from the pioneering work of Norman Garmezy (1974) and Michael Rutter (1979).

Developing Resilience in Adolescents

In working with adolescents, it is often useful to examine these factors Dr. Grotberg refers to, then draw on and emphasize those that are already in place. Labeling the sources of support that are available, verbally acknowledging them, and being consistently reminded of them can help adolescents to trust their abilities more and to become more resilient.

I Have factors that promote resilience include:

1. One or more persons within my family I can trust and who love me without reservation

2. One or more persons outside my family I can trust without reservation
3. Limits to my behavior
4. People who encourage me to be independent
5. Good role models
6. Access to health, education, and the social and security services I need
7. A stable family and community

I Am factors that promote resilience include:

1. A person most people like
2. Generally calm and good-natured
3. An achiever who plans for the future
4. A person who respects myself and others
5. Empathic and caring of others
6. Responsible for my own behavior and accepting of the consequences
7. A confident, optimistic, hopeful person

I Can factors that promote resilience include:

1. Generate new ideas or new ways to do things
2. Stay with a task until it is finished
3. See the humor in life and use it to reduce tension
4. Express thoughts and feelings in communication with others
5. Solve problems in various settings: academic, job-related, personal, and social
6. Manage my behavior: feelings, impulses, acting-out
7. Reach out for help when I need it

Although the I Have factors are a worthwhile goal to work for as a society, it is certain that many adolescents are not provided with all, or even most, of them. Street kids, children raised in traumatic situations during war, and even those in economically stable locations not under attack but living in dysfunctional homes may not have many I Have factors available. But those factors that are in place can be emphasized, and rescue workers, teachers, friends, mental health providers, criminal justice agents, and social service professionals can seek to remedy those that are not in place. In the meantime, programs aimed at building I Am and I Can skills can be emphasized. Throughout the process, communication of strengths should continue. Dr. Grotberg continues:

Because language does not have the precision of mathematics in communicating ideas, some of the words used in identifying resilience factors do not cover all the words currently in usage—self-efficacy is one, faith is another, competence is another, and connections is yet another. However, the resilience factors identified serve to communicate what resilience is and form an acceptable base for the promotion and use of resilience (Grotberg, 2000).

These resilience factors are especially important for youth engaged in aggressive activities who clearly lack the resilience to deal with the adversities that tend to elicit a response of violence. So much of violence is tied to one emotion—anger—that a starting place for promoting resilience in youth is to address two factors of resilience: express my thoughts and feelings in constructive communication with others, and manage my impulsive behavior Both are acquired skills that can be taught. Youth who learn to share their thoughts and feelings are in a better position to resolve conflicts, to express caring, and to enrich relationships with others.

Many of the anger management strategies covered in Chapter 6 are useful for promoting resilience in this regard. The school-based programs to enhance critical thinking and emotional intelligence highlighted in future chapters are also aimed at promoting resilience by building I Can and I Am skills among adolescents. Emotions and emotional control are particularly relevant during adolescent development, as previously described. Physical and hormonal changes, cognitive development, and identity formation all enhance the emotions of adolescents, making them more intensely felt. Because of the constant daily emphasis on war, terror, and threat that modern adolescents are bombarded with, fear is another emotion that needs to be addressed. According to Dr. Grotberg:

Youth who can manage their behavior—feelings, impulses, acting out—are in charge of their lives and are more acceptable to others. To share thoughts and feelings, however, youth will have to recognize and label feelings not only in themselves, but also in others. This requires the building of a vocabulary of emotions, with examples of how the emotions are expressed.

A good starting place for developing an emotional vocabulary is the emotion of fear. Fear is a basic and important emotion to recognize and learn to manage. We all rely on feelings of fear to alert us when something is happening that is threatening our physical or emotional well-being. We rely on feelings of fear to give us the emergency energy to avoid hitting a string of cars stopped on a major highway because a duck and her ducklings are crossing the road. We rely on fear to give us the quick energy to run when someone is throwing stones at us. We rely on fear when we see a child at risk for being hit by a car.

The emotion of fear gives us extra energy in hormonal form—adrenaline—to move fast, and do things we normally could not do. We have probably all heard the story of the mother whose teenage son is trapped under a car that had rolled off a jack and pinned him down. There was no one around to help. She weighed 125 pounds. Her fear gave her that added energy so that she lifted up the front of the car to let him roll out. She has no idea how she did it. She feared loss of her son—that was all it took.

The same can be said for the role of fear in promoting violence. A great deal of violence is a reaction to fear: fear of harm, fear of being seen as weak, fear of future harm, fear of losing status with peers, fear of being vulnerable. Youth who learn to recognize their feelings of fear are in a good position to think about ways to deal with that fear without risking retaliation from the person or group causing the fear. Youth are primarily concerned about their sense of identity. They are asking questions such as:

> *Who am I?*
>
> *How do I stack up against other teens?*
>
> *What are my new relationships with my parents?*
>
> *What have I accomplished?*
>
> *Where do I go from here?*

In addition to these questions, youth are becoming sexually mature and are developing their higher mental capabilities of analysis and reflection. Adolescents can become resilient in ways that address their changing concerns and needs.

Here is a prototype of ways to help promote resilience in youth and to encourage them to promote their own resilience through practice: Begin by providing the adolescents you work with scripts that focus on developing resilience or, even better, guide them in writing their own. Have them read these together in psychodrama format, memorize them to deliver as a skit, and then continue to read and repeat them often. This can be done easily in a group or family counseling format and can also be integrated into language arts and theater classes. Psychodrama is an effective therapeutic tool when working with adolescents. Some suggested models for psychodrama scripts related to the various resilience factors appear next courtesy of Dr. Grotberg:

I Have

One or more persons I can trust and who love me without reservation

I know this is true because I receive unconditional love from my parents or from someone else. I can always count on them to be there for me. They often tell me how much they love me and how proud they are to have me as their teenager. I trust my parents to love me even when I do something wrong or when I am in a bad mood. They try to comfort me and help me feel better. We can talk about what may be bothering me, and they leave me alone when they know I am not ready to talk. I have trusting relationships with other people too, such as a teacher or other adult or a teen friend. I need these relationships to feel safe and secure.

Help youth to extend this script. You can implement it in written/read dialogue or role-play formats and use it individually or with groups, including the following elements:

There is someone in my family I know I can turn to and trust during an adversity, but I will not take that person for granted. I will also begin thinking about someone else in the family with whom I can build another trusting relationship, because the one I trust most now may be facing adversities of his or her own that prevents giving help to me. Who else can fill the bill? No one? OK, then, let me see who outside the family I can trust completely. Do they live close by? Are they available to talk to and share thoughts and feelings with? Can they give me the support I need in most situations or only some? Should I look for somebody else who can help me in different ways? I will look around at the people I know and decide who is most likely to give me such a connection.

I have to give trust to receive it. I'll take the risk and begin some casual conversations with the person I've selected and see how the person responds. If the response is friendly enough so that it seems safe to talk about something personal, I'll suggest doing something together. I'll try telling the person something more personal and ask that it not be repeated so I can see if my confidence is respected.

Exercises and activities like these are very helpful for youth who need to build resilience. If no one has ever modeled these skills, and they have not come from a family environment that provided them naturally, it is important that they receive instruction like that demonstrated here to learn how to function effectively. Understanding behavioral limits is another area that frequently needs to be addressed. Here is a scripted dialogue to develop that skill.

There are limits to my behavior that are negotiable. As I show I can respect these limits, I am ready for more freedom. I like to be with my friends and I want increasing freedom to go where I want with my friends. I know the rules (and the reasons for the rules), just as I know why we have rules for driving. My parents set limits on hours out and for friends that are acceptable versus not acceptable. If they do not, I should do so myself. There are consequences when I break the rules, but I am able to talk in an adult way about what I did and why.

This script can be extended to discussing potential consequences. These may range from illness resulting from lack of sleep and overexertion, failure to complete required school or work tasks adequately, legal problems caused by curfew violations, or to sanctions imposed by parents or other adults. A further activity can examine how to deal with consequences by developing support from others, including friends, family members, teachers, and others in the community. Here are practice questions for dialogue directed at this skill.

Do I know how far I can go in asking for or expecting support from someone? Do I know how far I can go in becoming dependent on someone else to deal with the experiences of adversity I have? I may need to practice thinking about and setting limits for my own behavior as I seek supports. To use rules effectively in experiences of adversity, I'll need to think about their value and their limits. Breaking rules can often lead to unwanted outcomes. I'll use my intelligence to decide what the rules are for and how I can use them—or at least respect them—as I express my freedom.

I still see my parents as models of how to behave in different situations, but I am more critical now and sometimes think they are not being fair. I can ask them why they did something and I can talk about it with them. I am becoming a more critical thinker and increasingly make decisions about just who my role models should or shouldn't be. I am shaping my own ideas about how to behave.

Are the role models I am using still the ones I want or need? Do they guide me as I become mature and have more experience? Have my interests and concerns in life changed sufficiently so that I need to find new role models? Where do I find new ones? In the news? In books? On screen? In history? Among my friends? Can a relative be a role model? Perhaps I should read about how someone else behaved in an adversity I once faced or am likely to face in the future. Also, what exactly are my role models modeling that I like? Is it the way they dress? The way they treat others? The way they solve problems? I will list my role models on a piece of paper and think about why I want to model myself after them. Do I draw on everything they do and are, or only some things? Am I a role model for others? Who are they and what do I do that makes them want to use me as a role model? Do I model behaviors that help in dealing with adversities?

There is a continuing conflict with how much I need to be dependent on my parents to make my decisions. My goal is to become independent and responsible, but to draw on the help of others when I need it. I do not know everything and I am not invincible, so I need to be dependent at times, but there are people around me who encourage me to try to solve problems as much as I am able to on my own, so that I can grow to be more independent.

Do the people I look to for support do things for me or do they encourage me to try to solve the adversity myself? I must not become overly dependent on others, so I need to practice thinking through how I can take care of things myself. Then, I can think about how much support I need. I must become conscious about my tendency to expect solutions from others. I know I don't like myself very much when I do that. Am I able to tell by people's reactions—body language, voice, and behavior—whether or not I am depending too much on them to solve problems? Do I feel comfortable asking them what I am doing that upsets them and asking for advice on how I can learn to deal with these problems on my own?

Dialogues like this will eventually become internalized and self-governing. Engaging adolescents in activities such as these develops resilience and coping skills. One of the best places to integrate them into is public schools through required group sessions for all students. They can also be integrated into language arts courses through structured journal writing assignments or discussion of literature—particularly the genre of young adult literature that deals specifically with day-to-day problems of youth in a realistic and current context.

Other places these activities can be integrated include church or community youth groups. Of course they are also readily integrated into group counseling sessions, which should be required for any adolescents who have come into contact with the police for potentially illegal activities and their families. At that level they become strategies for the second R, *rehabilitation*. It is best to build resilience first so that rehabilitation is unnecessary later.

We increasingly put more money into criminal justice agencies and prisons and less into public education. This approach works against the more efficient use of resources to accomplish the task of constructively channeling adolescent aggression before the chain of violence begins. No matter where in the chain of violence activities like these are introduced, however, they can help to break the chain. Here is another scripted activity suggested by Dr. Grotberg:

I have schools, health centers, police and fire stations, and many social services that I can use. I feel secure when I know I can draw on outside services. I use them and my family uses them when we need help.

Are the health services I need available? Do I need to find some additional ones? Is my favorite doctor moving or retiring? Do I feel as safe as I used to or do I need to find some greater security at my school or at my house? Do I know where to find the stores, libraries, employment centers, and other services I need? For, example, do I know how to find a job? Can I find a police officer? Do I know how to get emergency help when someone is having a heart attack? If I am injured or have burned myself, do I know who to describe my condition to and what help I think I need? Do I have a directory of services that I know how to use?

You can probably see, just by looking at these activities, how much the greater social environment—what psychologist Uri Bronfenbrenner (1994) refers to as the mesosystem and macrosystem—influences the development of resilience in adolescents. If medical services are available, police protection is a reality and not danger in and of itself, and social services are available, then a sense of resilience is more likely to ensue. The great variability from region to region and among various economic classes, especially in the United States, in how adolescents answer these questions goes a long way toward explaining the relationship between poverty and aggression—and by extension, the perceived but illusory connection between race and violence in the United States today.

Environment is unquestionably a critical factor in adolescent aggression, but it is not insurmountable in building resilience even among youth in very negative social circumstances. Psychodrama is a powerful therapeutic tool, especially with this age group, when it comes to addressing all of the "3 Rs." Because adolescents tend to feel like they are "on stage" anyway, it is a natural venue. Just be attuned to who among of the adolescents you work with are most comfortable as actors and who are most comfortable as audience, and do not force anyone into a role that he or she does not naturally seem comfortable with. Here are some more basic models for scripts related to building the other resiliency skills Dr. Grotberg highlights—I Am and I Can.

I Am

A person most people like

I am seen as pleasant and generally good natured. I make friends easily or I focus on a few friends who like me. I try to do nice things to help people who are having problems. I am sensitive to how people are feeling and try to show my concern without seeming patronizing. I understand that people are more willing to accept me and help me when they see me as lovable, but I don't want to take advantage of that.

Am I friendly enough? Do I make new friends easily? Do I show my acceptance of people I meet? Do I need to change any of the ways I communicate my friendships to others? To practice, I will smile at people I interact with, praise someone who aced a test, and bring some humor to the lunch table or to a meeting to help people feel relaxed. Nothing breaks tension like humor.

I Am

Empathic and caring of others

I am aware of how other people feel and can give words to what seem to be their feelings. I care about what has happened to them and want to help them. I show my caring by what I say and do, and I am able to feel some of the pain they are feelings when they are sad or troubled.

Do I show I empathize with a person's suffering or pain? Do I do nice things for people to show I care? Do I give them the help they need and express my concern? If I have trouble in these areas, I should practice by first finding empathic people in books or movies and think about the ways in which they show it. Then I can emulate them, in small ways at first, and gauge the response I receive.

I Am

A person who respects myself and others

I respect myself and expect others to respect me. I am proud of who I am and what I achieve, and I will not do things that make me ashamed of myself. If I do something wrong, I try to correct it so that I feel good about myself again. I know others respect me because they can see I care about them as well as myself.

Sometimes parents encourage aggressive and problematic behavior without realizing it and thereby undermine resilience skills. The following script base illustrates this in relation to the skills of respect and empathy/caring for adolescents.

A senior high school student was thoroughly enjoying confrontations with his English teacher. His mother was telling a friend about it and found it very funny. The friend, a smart woman, was alarmed. Here was the exchange.

Mother:	*It was so funny. Arthur told us last night that he tries to catch every mistake his English teacher makes just to show her she is not so smart. He does this in class and so other kids get a laugh.*
Friend:	*Let me get this straight. Arthur deliberately aggravates the teacher?*
Mother:	*Well, yes. Why do you ask?*
Friend:	*Doesn't Arthur want to go to college?*
Mother:	*Yes, of course. He is planning to go to the state college where they have a good engineering school.*

Friend:	He needs good grades, doesn't he?
Mother:	*(the smile is gone) Yes, of course.*
Friend:	*Well, who is being hurt here? The teacher knows the material; Arthur is learning. The teacher gives the grades; Arthur receives them. The teacher can lower his grade because of his behavior, and he takes the consequences. If Arthur were my son, I would tell him to grow up and get all he can from his teacher. Frankly, what Arthur is doing sounds kind of cruel. Maybe I shouldn't say that, but showing respect is very important. I doubt Arthur realizes how he comes across.*
Mother:	*I never thought of it that way. We'll have a good talk when he gets home. He really has his heart set on becoming an engineer. I hadn't seen the cruelty, the thoughtlessness in his behavior. This being a mother is a real trip!*

This can be followed by, or integrated with, a script based on the following questions:

Do I show enough respect for myself and for others? I can't be proud of myself if I don't respect myself because then I wouldn't care how I did things. I could fail and it wouldn't matter. But the feeling of joy at doing something well, helping someone in trouble, is so sweet that it is great to be proud of myself. Do I show enough respect for others? Am I proud of their achievements and of what they do to help others? What are some of the new ways I can show respect for others? I can make sure I give my full attention to someone who is speaking to me. I can make positive comments to someone I am talking to and soften the criticisms by such words as, "Have you thought of this approach to the problem?" I will watch that people don't put me down so that I am not respected and my pride in myself is threatened. I will set some limits on how people treat me.

I Am

Responsible for my own behavior and accept the consequences

My parents, teachers, and friends have helped me become more independent by letting me make my own decisions and learn from the consequences. I know that I can do more things on my own but that my responsibilities increase, too. What I do affects what others do and the outcome of events. I can't blame others when it is my fault that things went wrong. I am also learning how to separate what I did to affect outcomes and what others did. This helps me know where the responsibility lies. I try to correct what I did wrong or apologize.

Am I aware of what has happened and who is responsible in most situations? Do I find it hard to assume responsibility and easier to blame someone else? What have I done lately for which I was at fault but did not assume the responsibility? Do I need to reexamine my behavior more carefully so that I make more accurate assessments of responsibility? The first thing I have to do is recognize when an action I took was thoughtless, dangerous, cruel, unfair, or had an unwanted outcome. If I have trouble recognizing this, I'll need to ask people I trust for their assessment.

Responsibility is hard to accept because it suggests the person who did harm is a bad person, and a bad person should be punished. No one likes to be punished. Not only is there fear of harm, but there is fear that the person will be ostracized from society, will have trouble finding friends, and might as well be dead. The high rate of suicide among incarcerated youth attests to that fact. You can see by reading the papers or watching TV court how few people are willing to admit their mistakes and assume responsibility for their behavior. So many times, the person who has borrowed the money, destroyed property, or even let a dog dig out of the yard to bite a child denies any responsibility. "It was a gift, not a loan, and this is being done because I broke up with him." "They refused to come and get their property and so I threw it away"—even though the accused knew the person had to go out of town because of an ill mother. "They were nasty neighbors and are falsely accusing the dog"—even though their dog had dug under the fence a number of times before and was known to have bitten others.

Parents often see themselves as protectors of their children—as they are, of course—but carry it to denying their child threw the stones that broke the car windows. "My son does not do things like that," says the father, even though the judge interacts with the boy and the boy finally admits his acts. The boy admits he lied to his dad. Now, why would he lie to his dad?

Certainly he wants to be loved, wants to be seen as a lovable child. He needs that, but if he is willing to lie to preserve that, he must think it is only when he is good that he is loved. Have you ever heard a parent say, "Mommy won't love you if you break that glass," or "Daddy won't love you if you don't stop bugging me?" The message is clear. Be seen as a good person and you will be loved; be seen as doing bad things and you will not be loved. No wonder there is so much telling lies to parents and others. I know unconditional love is important, but sometimes parents do not.

Accepting responsibility is an important but difficult skill to address. Research on locus of control actually suggests that the ancient Greek

Golden Mean, moderation in all things, may be a good guideline. Research indicates that adolescents and adults who accept too much responsibility, or, in psychological terms, who have an internal locus of control for most situations, are more prone to depression. They are also more likely to be high achievers, though, at least in terms of academic success. Those who have a primarily external locus of control most of the time are more likely to get arrested, at least in the United States, although this is not the case in other countries, including Brazil. Regardless, accepting responsibility for everything may not necessarily be any more adaptive than accepting no responsibility. In this case the common 12-step program prayer probably applies:

> *God grant me the serenity to accept the things I cannot change, the ability to change the things that I can—and the wisdom to know the difference.*

Because there are so many shades of gray in knowing just what can and can't be changed in life and because adolescents are usually more literal, binary reasoners, this is a difficult skill to teach, especially because no one wants to accept responsibility for acts of violence. The task of the teacher, counselor, or parent involved in developing a sense of responsibility in youth is difficult. Be aware of these pitfalls. Too much responsibility may be as psychologically unhealthy as too little, and how much responsibility can legitimately be accepted varies greatly based on sociocultural and other environmental factors. Keeping this caution in mind, here is a script extension to address responsibility developed by Dr. Grotberg:

Others do not want to be responsible for the results of acts of violence. Two college students are playing with two others in a game that involves taking bets. They have been drinking while they play. They lose and both are very angry about that. One happens to bump into the other and a fight starts, becoming more violent by the minute. Finally, both are on the floor, badly bruised, and needing immediate medical attention. They are rushed to the hospital, sewn up, and returned home. One of the two takes the other to court to get money for the medical bills. He feels the other guy started it and therefore should pay his expenses. The fact that he willingly joined the fray was completely missed by him and he is sent home with the message: If you willingly engage in fighting, you take the responsibility and the consequences.

It's a good script for discussion, but complicated by the fact that the messages students get from the adversarial justice system currently in force in the United States doesn't always make such lessons clear. In reality, the person who has the means to employ the better attorney or has the better public connections is often not sanctioned for acts of violence, as the O.J. Simpson case may have been perceived to illustrate by some adolescents. At any rate, be prepared for discussion when you use this script and use good judgment in how it is best modified. Now, let's move on to Dr. Grotberg's script for the last of the I Am skills.

I Am

A confident, optimistic, and hopeful person

I have confidence that things will turn out all right and that my future looks good. I accept my responsibility in making my future good. Even when I make mistakes, I have faith that things can be corrected and will be all right. I know more about what is right and what is wrong because I can think more critically, but I am also aware that people do not always agree about what is right and what is wrong.

Do I feel that things will work out all right if I do my best to deal with them? Do I visualize positive outcomes? Even when situations are bleak, do I still have the faith that there will be a resolution I can live with? Do I have faith in others and join them in church services, spiritual retreats, or other ways of talking about hope for the future? Am I willing to take calculated risks because I have the confidence to benefit from them?

Allow the adolescents you work with to personalize and creatively develop the scripts based on the preceding models, while making sure that the appropriate questions are integrated and the focus remains on the skill. Here are scripts for the last of the three aspects of resiliency development, I Can.

I Can

Express thoughts and feelings in communication with others

I can talk with people about my growing independence, my future, what is expected of me, what my needs are, and what others want from me. I can discuss different points of view and negotiate solutions to problems in our relationships. I can communicate with my friends, as well as with my family, and share my thoughts and feelings.

Am I able to express my thoughts and feelings without too much embarrassment or hesitation? Do I need to enlarge my vocabulary for describing emotions? Can I pick up the emotional tone of someone I am listening to? Can I help the person clarify thoughts and feelings as the person talks with me? I will practice what I am going to say to someone who has upset me so that I am calm and have the right words. I can build a vocabulary of words that describe my feelings so that when I express them to someone, they really convey my feelings.

I Can

Solve problems in various settings

I am often able to see all sides of a problem and understand what it is about. This is true for problems that deal with my education, as well as interpersonal problems. I can take the time to test out solutions with thoughts and words before I act. I am a more critical person than before, which means I am able to assess what someone else has done from a larger moral perspective.

One challenging way to solve problems is by taking calculated risks. Do I take the time to see an adversity from all sides so that I have a clear picture of what is happening before I decide what to do and what risks to take? Do I understand the dangers and downside of any action I take? Can I play out in my mind different scenarios of what might happen if I do this or what might happen if I do that? Do I understand that I am risking not only my physical well-being, but also if I fail, making a fool of myself or harming someone? Do I need to slow down and spend more time thinking before taking the risk? Do I tend to keep so focused on the task I want to do that I fail to notice other risks around me? For example, if I take the risk of jumping into a pool that seems a little shallow by doing a surface dive, do I not notice the guy who is swimming across the pool? Do I see the field around the task?

As you can see from the content of this task, resilience skills are also connected with moral development and critical thinking skills. Developing critical thinking and moral reasoning skills in adolescents is a good inoculation against unnecessary acts of violence. These skills are explored further in later chapters. For now, here is a script for the next of the I Can skills. This skill, incidentally, is also addressed in great depth by the anger management training strategies described in the previous chapter.

I Can

Manage my feelings and behavior

I am able to recognize my feelings and name them. I can usually recognize and label the feelings of others, too. Then, I try to find out what has made me feel like this or made the other person feel the way he or she does, because this helps me when I want to express my thoughts and feelings. By listening to the other person's thoughts and feelings, I can show the person I care about his or her side of the conflict and we can begin to resolve it. I try to manage any tendency to react too soon or too strongly, and to calm myself down and think before acting our impulsively. This is particularly true when I date.

What techniques am I using to manage my feelings? Do I rely on control or even repression of my feelings? Am I able to manage my feelings without acting out? What helps me express my thoughts and feelings without doing something impulsive and dangerous? Do I slow down my reactions? Maybe I can practice counting to 10 or more before acting on a feeling, or taking deep belly-breaths, inhaling and exhaling slowly while pushing my stomach out and letting it come back in. Maybe I could practice writing down all my feelings before I confront somebody about something I'm angry about. Do I need to practice reading body language? Can I tell by facial expressions and other body movements what mood a person is in? Am I in the habit of using it as a gauge to know when to approach someone and when to leave them alone?

The script base for the next of the skills may actually be useful to develop in conjunction with the earlier script on responsibility. Those who demonstrate an extremely high locus of control are also less likely to be willing to depend on others. This skill is related to knowing when it is useful to do so and how to go about it. Developing a script involving both skills may be a way to address the "gray areas" adolescents are otherwise likely to miss. This may encourage youth to develop a locus of control that is more healthy—that is, in the average to above average range on the Rotter scales.

I Can

Reach out for help when I need it

I can find someone I trust to help me. I am learning to seek out those people when I am troubled, do not understand what is happening, or need to share my hopes and dreams. I can always go to my parents, but I also have others I can trust to help me.

I am facing the issue of whether I will go to college or take a year off and work. I do not know which to choose, as each has so many appeals. Who could help me with this? I am sure the counselor will suggest going to college. After all, all these teachers and staff have been to college so I'll probably get directed that way. Who do I know who chose to work for a year and then went to college? Oh, yeah, Jack did that. I'll talk to him and see what the down side is, as well as the up side. I can also talk to my parents because they will have to help me with finances if I go to college now. So, I'd better get going by calling Jack tonight and talking to my parents as soon as possible.

Psychodrama is a therapeutic technique that has been supported as effective in working with troubled adolescents in both in- and out-placement settings consistently over the last 50 years. It is also easily integrated into counseling sessions in school settings as a "preventive" measure and even in the classroom when content allows (language arts and literature courses often do). Community support groups and probation officers can also use psychodrama beneficially. You are encouraged to find training in this technique. It is generally readily available in continuing education courses at most major conferences and in private seminars.

A key to promoting resilience in adolescents is to find ways of routinely including training in skills that promote resilience into places where nearly all adolescents are likely to benefit. Public schools are the first venue for this. Psychodrama as described previously is a good starting point, especially if first implemented by competent school psychologists. These professionals can train teachers in how to use these techniques within their own classrooms and also deliver structured groups focused on resiliency-building strategies to *all* students in some type of *required* life skills course. This course may also focus, among other things, on parenting skills, career development, problem solving, and critical thinking.

There are currently several programs designed for integration into public skills to build resilience, although these are not implemented with any systematic regularity. As a parent, educator, or community member, lobbying to have some type of program that builds resilience implemented into the local school is a good starting point to contribute to reducing adolescent violence. Here are some other programs noted by Dr. Grotberg to promote resilience to consider.

Successful Programs for the Promotion of Resilience

Programs to promote resilience in youth and to prevent youth violence involve the home, school, and community. Here are a few examples from a major report on youth violence presented by the Surgeon General of the United States. The report includes the results of examining numerous programs developed to address the serious problem of adolescent violence in the United States. The criteria for selecting effective programs were rigid. Programs tested but found ineffective were identified as well. Here are a few of the best programs. Some involve parents, others involve the schools, and still others involve the entire community.

1. *PATHS* (Promoting Alternative THinking Strategies)

   The PATHS program consists of a curriculum taught to elementary school students beginning in U.S. grade 5 (about 10 or 11 years of age). Lessons targeting emotional competence (expression, understanding, and regulation), self-control, social competence, positive peer relations, and interpersonal problem-solving skills are delivered three times a week in 20- to 30-minute sessions. Evaluations show that this program has positive effects on several risk factors associated with violence, including aggressive behavior, anxiety and depression, conduct problems, and lack of self-control. The effectiveness of the program has been demonstrated for both regular education and special education students.

2. *I Can Problem Solve*

   I Can Problem Solve has been used effectively with students in preschool, elementary school, and middle school. The main goal of the program is to train children to use problem-solving skills to find solutions to interpersonal problems. In evaluations, the program has improved classroom behavior and children's problem solving measured up to four years after the intervention ended. This program is appropriate for all children, but it has been most effective with children living in poor, urban areas.

3. *The Seattle Development Project*

   The Seattle Social Development Project is an excellent example of a program that includes classroom behavior management among its core components. The goal of the program is to enhance elementary school students' bond with school and their families while decreasing a number of early risk factors for violence. The initiative includes both individual and environmental change approaches and multiple components known to improve the effectiveness of violence prevention efforts. In addition to classroom behavior management, the components include child skills training and parent training.

   The program reduces the initiation of alcohol, marijuana, and tobacco use by grade 6 and improves attachment and commitment to school. At age 18, youth who participated in the full five-year program have lower rates of violence, heavy drinking, and sexual activity. They also demonstrate better academic performance than controls. The program has been used effectively in both general populations of youth and high-risk children attending elementary and middle school.

4. *Big Brothers/Big Sisters and Other Mentoring Programs*

   Mentoring programs, such as Big Brothers/Big Sisters, have trusting relationships at their core. These programs are successful as long as mentors make long-term commitment to their role. Breaks in these relationships have negative results. Each time the trusting relationship is broken, repair is more difficult than the time before. Problems with attachment, already predominant among adolescents who benefit from such programs, are magnified.

5. *The Teen Outreach Program (TOP) and other Service Learning Programs*

   Programs that focus on strengthening the individual rather than changing one narrow behavior, such as drug use or promiscuity, not only build resilience but also reduce the problem behavior. TOP is a good example. There were two goals for the program: to prevent teenage pregnancy and to help young people succeed in school. Rather than provide sex education and academic tutoring, however, TOP engaged students in service learning. Service learning is a guided practice activity in which students volunteer services at an agency or center related to something they are studying, and then discuss their experiences and complete relevant assignments.

Students participated in volunteer programs supervised by trained staff and adult volunteers. They helped out in hospitals and nursing homes, tutored their peers, and raised money for worthy causes through a variety of organized events. In addition, they attended structured group sessions aimed at building the self-confidence, social skills, and self-discipline they need to succeed in their volunteer missions and helping them cope with the general challenges of life as an adolescent.

In an evaluation that compared TOP to a more traditional teen pregnancy prevention program, TOP participants had a 41 percent lower rate of teen pregnancy, a 39 percent lower rate of school failure, and a 42 percent lower rate of school suspension. The more time students spent in volunteering, the better the outcome. Further, the program appeared to be equally effective with children of different races, socioeconomic status, family composition, and grade levels. This program connects the youth with the community, enlarging the perspective of the youth.

6. *Bullying Prevention Program*

   The Bullying Prevention Program targets students in elementary, middle, and junior high school. It begins with an anonymous student questionnaire designed to assess bullying problems in individual schools. Using the information, parents and teachers implement school-, classroom-, and individual-level interventions designed to address the bullying problems identified in the questionnaire, including individual work with students who are identified as bullies or as victims. At the classroom level, teachers and students work together to establish and reinforce a set of rules about behavior and bullying, creating a positive, antibullying climate. In one use of the program, in elementary and junior high school, bullying problems were cut in half two years after the intervention. Antisocial behavior, including theft, vandalism, and truancy, also dropped during these years, and the social climate of the school improved. Replications of this program have been equally successful.

7. *Preventive Treatment Program*

   The Preventive Treatment Program is a two-year intervention aimed at preventing delinquency among 7- to 9-year-old boys from low-income families who have been identified as disruptive. The program has two major components: school-based social skills training and parent training. The parent-training sessions, provided every two weeks for the duration of the intervention, teach parents to read with their children, monitor and reinforce their children's behavior, use effective discipline, and manage family crises. A long-term follow-up study of boys enrolled in this program found positive effects on academic achievement and avoidance of gang involvement, drug and alcohol use, and delinquency up to age 15 years.

8. *Multisystemic Therapy (MST)*

The MST is an intensive family- and community-based treatment that addresses multiple determinants of antisocial behavior. This goal is accomplished within a network of systems that include one or more of the following contexts: individual, family, peer, school, or neighborhood.

The program targets families with adolescent children who have become involved with the juvenile justice system for violence, substance abuse, chronic offenses, or high risk of out-of-home placement for a variety of reasons. Family therapy, behavioral parent training, structural family therapy, and cognitive-behavioral therapy are all incorporated in treatment. Program outcomes included reductions in long-term rates of re-arrest, reductions in out-of-home placements, improvements in family functioning, and reductions in mental health problems among treated youth compared to controls.

All of these programs worked. A major problem with developing, testing, and finding successful programs to adopt is that they depend on what makes this process possible—money. Unfortunately, most programs end when the money dries up. They often originate based on grant money from federal entities, but are not sustained afterwards. There are short-term gains but no long-term sustenance of success. It seems that we need to consider a way to help youth become successful and happy by helping them learn to deal with the inevitable adversities they face and will continue to face in a way that is continually sustainable. And that way involves resilience training infused into public school curricula.

Ways to promote resilience can be incorporated into any training program that includes interaction with others. This is especially true for all service providers, and especially for teachers. Courses in human growth and development lend themselves easily to incorporating the promotion of resilience. Curricula for those in psychology, nursing, medicine, and police should incorporate the promotion of resilience among adolescents. The classroom, of course, is an ideal place to promote resilience, but if teachers do not know how to do this and increasingly avoid interactions with students, then the classroom is no longer a place where individuals are respected, or empathy and caring are manifest. These teachers then begin to contribute to the problem, not the solution, and that has certainly happened. However, other service providers are also a part of either the problem or the solution.

Every interaction with a client or a patient requires the demonstration of resilience behavior. In workshops for medical students, I found dramatic changes in behaviors when the students grasped the value of resilience and applied it to their interactions with patients and their families.

Each of these programs should be considered in finding ways to inoculate against increasing adolescent aggression through systematic training programs. It is important, of course, to tailor the programs to individual communities. Initial research is required to examine the specific needs of each school and to determine which combination of techniques will be most effective. This should be followed by continual data collection after implementation to assess outcomes and allow these programs to be modified as needed. Directing more public money to projects like this and less to enforcement and punishment in criminal justice would, in the long run, not only save money but enhance building a safer, saner future world. Other school-based programs to redirect adolescent aggression into constructive channels are examined in the next chapter.

CHAPTER 9

INTEGRATING PROGRAMS AND PRACTICES TO REDUCE AGGRESSION

We gratefully acknowledge the contributions of Dr. Edith Grotberg to this chapter.

The previous chapter summarized programs for use in public schools specifically aimed at increasing resilience. This chapter describes other strategies that can be integrated into schools and community services. The following strategies build coping skills and resilience, and redirect aggression into positive channels: (1) mentoring programs, (2) programs that enhance emotional and social intelligence, (3) life skills programs that reduce aggression and develop self-control, and (4) programs and activities that provide constructive outlets for pain and anger, thereby reducing inappropriate aggression. Suggestions for implementing these programs are included, as well. The fifth important strategy for reducing inappropriate acts of aggression is developing critical thinking skills and meta-cognitive awareness. This strategy is explained in depth in Chapter 11.

Mentoring Programs

Studies of resilience have consistently demonstrated that the best inoculation against tragic outcomes for at-risk youth is the presence of at least one caring adult mentor who takes an active interest. Whether the mentor is a family member, teacher, neighbor, coach, or other community member does not seem to matter. What does seem to matter is that adolescents need at least one adult with whom they feel comfortable talking honestly about life events and decisions. This person must be someone they respect and wish to emulate. Creating opportunities for youth and adults to interact in nonthreatening, equal-status ways helps encourage the development of such relationships.

Programs such as Big Brothers and Big Sisters are one way to develop these relationships, which are so important for socializing youth who otherwise lack appropriate role models. The caution here, though, is that volunteers must be committed to long-term interaction. Establishing trust and closeness with an adult mentor is often difficult for youth who already have attachment problems because of desertion of one or both parents or dysfunctional interaction with family members. Adolescents benefit from such programs, but it is risky, as well. Establishing a close relationship with another adult, only to be torn from that adult, too, because he or she no longer has time to volunteer or, more likely, moves to another area, can be emotionally traumatic. This can create more attachment difficulties for adolescents rather than helping. Perhaps a better means of developing mentoring-type relationships than programs such as Big Brothers is through engaging adolescents in short-term, task-focused activities at school that provide opportunities for interacting with adults. These adults can later serve as good role models and supportive friends in a way that will not be perceived as violating trust if the relationship is unable to continue because of circumstances.

One strategy for building such relationships is to give adolescents the task of writing the personality profile of a particular adult. Students may meet the adult as a guest speaker in class or at a community or church group. Alternatively, teachers may assign particular community members to students for interview assignments. These community members may have attended the same school as the student, may work in a field of interest to the student, or may be an older adult from a local geriatric center (Beyersdorfer & Schauer, 1992; Hamilton, 1990). Based on principles of identification, modeling, and transfer of knowledge, such methods may be fertile avenues for future exploration.

Job-shadowing through assignments related to career exploration is another option for developing mentoring relationships. The use of the Internet in instruction offers even more possibilities. Students may communicate with authors or public figures they admire, relatives who are a great distance away, sports and entertainment figures, and other adults. If integrated into instruction appropriately, this provides a great opportunity for developing mentoring relationships that help youth maintain a connection to society and an acceptance of diversity.

It is best to cast a wide net when it comes to providing mentoring opportunities to troubled adolescents. Criminal justice agencies assign probation or parole officers (POs) to troubled adolescents routinely. These POs are in a position to address this need, but to do so, the approach of the current system needs to be modified. A trusting, high rapport mentoring relationship should be encouraged to develop, rather than the authoritarian "good" jailer to "bad" jailee relationship that often characterizes the dynamics adolescents perceive between themselves and their POs at present. To facilitate this, criminal justice agencies need to address screening, hiring, and training processes. They must also change the agency perceptions and dynamics toward the youth they are responsible for. Taking a client out to lunch to discuss life issues on a regular basis would go much further than forcing a prisoner to wear a detention bracelet for constant monitoring. Environmental control may be useful for curbing inappropriate behaviors on a short-term basis, but it is not a tool that encourages internalization of appropriate values and self-control. Internalized values and self-control are what these adolescents truly need for rehabilitation.

Developing treatment models that offer integration with 12-step programs, counseling, and positive, structured peer activities, such as the drug court models described earlier, is a far more effective and, in the long term, less expensive strategy for dealing with violent adolescents than locking them up in jail when they are young. Early incarceration begins the socialization pattern that will cause them to return to detention facilities and be involved in criminal activities for the remainder of their lives.

It is disturbing that the current trend in much of the rest of the world is tending to gradually follow the American punishment/ incarceration model for adolescent offenders rather than maintaining a focus on rehabilitation. In truth, rehabilitation efforts are still far more focused and punishment is regarded as less of a solution in most countries, but it is important that this be maintained rather than undermined. Adolescents will not find effective, prosocial mentors in prisons, generally. Dynamics such as those evident in the Stanford prison studies and others spanning over a century (Zimbardo, 2002) make it clear this is nearly impossible to expect. Using POs as mentors, integrated into school and community programs that work with all adolescents rather than just those who have been convicted, would be a more effective means of redirecting inappropriate adolescent aggression.

Public high schools are natural venues in which to connect youth to potential mentors. The following case study, developed in a large public high school in a gang-ridden, poverty-stricken area in the United States, illustrates how this process might occur. The process is divided into steps to make it easier to follow. We encourage you to become actively involved in developing such programs. They go a long way toward preventing adolescent aggression and strengthening the community.

1. Approach teachers, parents, and community members. Share background on the importance of mentoring adolescents that is provided in this book. School board meetings, parent-teacher association meetings, faculty meetings, church groups, community centers, and neighborhood watch/safety council meetings are all appropriate places to begin this process. In this particular case study, all were involved.

2. In cooperation with teachers, school psychologists, counselors, and administrators, examine the current required curriculum at the public high school and find creative ways to tie the mentoring program to the curriculum. In this particular case, courses in two subjects—a career exploration unit, tied to a required social studies class, and writing skills instruction, tied to a required English composition class—were used as the beginning points for the program.

3. Involve teachers in creative planning of the program. A one-month intensive summer curriculum workshop was used in this case to prepare the curriculum. The curriculum began like this: English and social studies teachers of students in grade 10 (age approximately 16 years) began the program. In social studies, students studied the various careers and agencies required for a community to function. The counselors then visited students in their classes. Each student then completed appropriate vocational aptitude and assessment tests.

The English composition instructors, in the meantime, used daily journal writing that involved both structured and free response for composition practice. Structured questions used for this assignment during the career study included self-reflective questions that led the adolescents to consider their own possible career choices, and to identify the career paths of adult family members and friends with whom they were familiar. This technique served two purposes. First, because adolescence is a time of identity formation, as previously mentioned, youth are more motivated by and engaged in activities that center on "who I am." Reflecting on possibilities, choices, and career assessment information made available to them were high-interest activities that were psychologically important. Second, by writing about the various career paths of family members and friends in the community, students provided teachers a "pool" of adults to use as resources later in the unit.

4. Composition teachers then began a unit on questioning and interviewing skills. The assignment for this unit was to find an adult in the community who was working in one of the career fields students had identified as interesting. During this time, all of the agencies and community groups referred to previously were contacted for volunteers who were willing to be interviewed. Community and family members identified in the earlier journal writing assignments were also contacted, as were the friends and associates of teachers and school personnel. Teachers and counselors assisted students in finding an appropriate person to interview. Once students were matched with a person to interview, the assignment began. Students were required to meet with the people being interviewed at least once per week for one month. Then, the interviews were written, shared with the class in an editing group process derived from the National Writing Project, and published in a booklet that was printed and distributed by the school to students and community members. One copy was made for each of the students and one copy for each of the mentors. The journalism, graphic arts, and yearbook classes were involved in producing the booklet. Support to cover costs was solicited from local businesses that were also able to place advertisements in the booklet. Because many of the people interviewed owned or worked in local businesses, contributions, though small, were readily offered and the cost was covered.

5. Once the booklet was ready for distribution, all interviewees were invited to attend a special dinner and awards ceremony with students. Each participant and each interviewee were recognized publicly for the successful collaboration and given a booklet at the dinner. During the dinner, teachers and school administrators also talked to the community participants and asked for their continuing commitment to the program. They gathered contact information and signatures of commitment from each and explained that they would be contacted by the student they had assisted periodically through the remainder of the school year for additional assignments and again the next year for additional assistance.

6. Social studies and English teachers cooperated through the remainder of the year in planning to ensure that at least one assignment per month required brief contact with the adult who had been interviewed.

7. The next school year, the program continued with the following addition: At the beginning of the unit, interviewees and the student who had interviewed them participated in "career seminars" for the new sophomore class. Students who had completed the unit the previous year and their cooperating community members attended sessions where they talked about various careers. Attrition, students moving, and new students beginning were problematic, but the school was able to cope with this. The previous volunteers generally remained with the students from the previous year, and new mentors were found for the younger group. Some community volunteers, however, worked with new students as they continued with their previous students. The continuing students (now juniors, age 17 years) were eventually assigned to a sophomore student interested in the same career path. Thus, the sophomores had a peer mentor, as well as two potential adult mentors as the program continued. Social studies and English teachers working with juniors planned lessons together to ensure at least one assignment per month required contact with the adults.

8. During the final year of high school, seniors (age 18 years) were required to complete a service learning activity with the adults they had now been in contact with for the previous two years. This assignment required them to volunteer an average of at least five hours per month throughout the school year, volunteering their time to work with the "mentor," either in the workplace or local volunteer agencies. Assignments related to this were integrated into a required social studies class (government and free enterprise). The cycle then began again, with the mentors who were still willing to remain involved (most were!) being assigned to new students at the sophomore level.

This program was a powerful tool for community cohesiveness and renovation. It increased cooperation among schools, families, and businesses; made education for students more relevant; and encouraged the development of long-term mentoring relationships for youth in a troubled area. Interesting side effects were a reduced high school drop-out rate, more students continuing to college after graduation, and higher employment rates among those who remained in the community after completing high school.

This is an example of one way such a program can be structured. As previously noted, each school and each community have particular needs, strengths, and weaknesses. It is important to develop such efforts collaboratively and independently in each unique school environment. Developing such programs and sustaining them are ultimately worthwhile efforts in refocusing adolescent aggression.

Emotional and Social Intelligence

Mentoring and positive contact with appropriate role models are essential for socializing youth into healthy roles. Another area that needs additional attention in schools is the development of social and emotional intelligence. Increasingly, the trend has been to focus on basic academic education and cognitive skills in public education, especially at the secondary or high school level. This is a mistake from a psychological perspective. Many adolescents do not have the support they need at home and in the community to develop social skills and manage their emotions. Even when they do, programs that allow them to explore these areas in a more independent way, away from family, are beneficial. Adolescents need more emotional and social support at school than younger children, not less. From this standpoint, the current system does exactly the opposite of what is required. Students become more anonymous and adrift in competitive classes with no single teacher to rely on. High school teachers are required to teach so many students (150 or more per semester on average in the United States) that developing the types of personal relationships so important for adolescents becomes impossible. Still, the teachers become scapegoats for the problems. The system itself needs to be reexamined and restructured, as many experts in education have been asserting for decades. For now, though, even without restructuring, mentoring programs like the one described here are helpful. Another helpful strategy is providing students with the training and resources necessary to develop social skills and emotional intelligence. Regarding this, Dr. Grotberg writes:

Most of the institutions that are involved with youth are not very concerned about social-emotional intelligence. This is particularly true of the schools that are more focused on the cognitive and academic parts of youth. The schools want mastery of reading and math, and later, more specific academic subjects. States and the federal government are in accord with this focus. Further, states are required to test students to decide if they are ready to graduate, having met certain standards, especially in the designated areas. And the federal government makes decisions about funding states to help in the educational endeavor. Teachers, who are trained in particular subjects for middle and senior high schools, have little time or interest in the social-emotional intelligence of students. This situation is understandable but does not help teachers who have students who cannot pay attention, who cause problems, and who drop out of school.

There is a real problem and the solution is still obscure, but do teacher-training programs need to include learning how to promote resilience (which is true for all service providers in Argentina) in children, as well as in teachers? It's an idea worth exploring. The schools are not only academic institutions; they are also social institutions. Most teens become socialized with peers at the school, and to prevent "The Lord of the Flies" solution to social problems, the schools must reexamine their role in socialization.

It may be helpful to start with a definition of social-emotional intelligence, which is so important for youth. D. Goleman (1995), a pioneer in this area, defined such intelligence as being able to motivate oneself and persist in the face of frustrations; to control impulses and delay gratification; and to keep distress from swamping the ability to think, empathize, and hope. Such intelligence is manifested by people who know and manage their own feelings well, who read and deal effectively with other people's feelings, and who are altruistic and willing to help others. Dr. Goleman provided a test for the general reader to determine social-emotional intelligence. The items are consistent with resilience:

> *I am aware of what I am feeling (Inner Strength—I Am)*
>
> *I know my strengths and weaknesses (Inner Strength—I Am)*
>
> *I deal calmly with stress (Skills—I Can)*
>
> *I believe the future will be better than the past (Inner Strength—I Am)*
>
> *I deal with changes easily (Skills—I Can)*
>
> *I set measurable goals when I have a project (Skills—I Can)*
>
> *Others say I understand and am sensitive to them (Skills—I Can)*
>
> *Others say I resolve conflicts (Skills—I Can)*
>
> *Others say I build and maintain relationship (Skills—I Can)*
>
> *Others say I inspire them (Skills—I Can)*
>
> *Others say I am a team player (Skills—I Can)*
>
> *Others say I helped to develop their abilities (Skills—I Can)*

Those with social-emotional intelligence have promoted or were helped to promote many of the resilience factors, regardless of external supports—I Have. We do not know who helped them develop this social-emotional intelligence. The resilience literature, by contrast, is concerned about the role of outside help in promoting social-emotional intelligence. Role models, learning limits of behavior, being encouraged to be independent, providing services—all the resilience factors of I Have contribute to developing social-emotional intelligence. Parents may play the major role in the social-emotional development of their children and youth. Surely, teachers need to play a role as well.

The increase in the incidence of encouraging students who are not academically successful to go for a graduate equivalency diploma (GED) instead of graduating, or waiting for them to become dropouts ignores the reality of the consequences of such actions. Another group of youth is bypassed in favor of those who demonstrate specific knowledge and skills. Obviously, there are no easy responses to this continued focus on the cognitive, academic development of youth and ignoring their social-emotional development. But, it behooves society to rethink its tendency to compartmentalize the development of youth and to see youth as social-emotional people, as well as cognitive people. It must be said, however, that even our researchers have trouble giving up such compartmentalization.

If we wish to stop the growing tide of adolescent aggression, we need to incorporate systematic training to prevent it. Allowing youth to grow up in a violent society with many media images and events that encourage and condone violence and trigger emotions such as fear that make violent aggression more likely to occur, and then offering no information about how to understand and control emotions but instead focusing just on "basic skills," is not a solution. Literacy suffers as a result; it is not enhanced. Adolescents who are focused on primitive survival needs in an emotional and physiological sense are not tuned in to academics. At present, there is no guarantee that many adolescents will ever have the opportunity to acquire the skills that lead to emotional and social intelligence. In many cases, family, church, and community groups may, indeed, provide these. In other cases, especially with street kids and adolescents from dysfunctional and isolated family units, they do not. It is up to the schools to step in. An interesting historical observation is that the former Soviet Union faced similar problems nearly a century ago, and the schools did step in successfully as socializing agents for the large numbers of abandoned children and street kids there. This, of course, has now changed somewhat because of economic realities and policy changes, and Russia again shares this problem with the rest of the world.

To address this problem, it is necessary to begin viewing our public schools not just as institutions that teach academic subjects but also as institutions that teach life skills. Programs to develop emotional and social intelligence, tolerance education, arts and humanities education to provide constructive emotional outlets, and anger management training should all be included in the definition of life skills if we wish to curb youth violence.

Life Skills Programs

Life skills programs have been successfully integrated into special education programs in the United States for the last several decades. These programs often include not just the more traditional life skills associated with special education among young, developmentally challenged children, such as tying shoes, basic hygiene, and, later cooking, shopping, and balancing a checkbook, but also often include social components focused on appropriate conduct, conversation skills, and developing friendships. It is no secret that more and more children in the United States have been identified as in need of special education over the last few decades for a variety of reasons. Learning disabilities, emotional disorders, and attention deficit/hyperactivity disorders top the list, and the diagnosis is often accompanied by prescriptions for medication. The now psychotropically-subdued children and adolescents then receive training in social skills and the "normal" classroom is returned to "normal." If the trend continues, it will soon be more "normal" to be medicated and in a special education classroom than in a regular classroom. There is a trend among psychologists and educators in other countries to slowly imitate this trend, but we suggest it would be far more effective to examine the social causes. We also suggest it would be wise to include a variety of social skills, emotion-management, and tolerance education programs in the general education programs of all public schools. One illustration for this need comes from the research on *bullying* in public schools. Dr. Grotberg describes this below:

Bullying is a good example of a common occurrence in the schools that rouses fear. There are few schools where students don't experience or witness acts of bullying. It is so prevalent as a form of violence and aggression that studies are being conducted to determine the experiences students have and the problems they encounter dealing with bullying. Some critical information was gathered from focus groups with junior high students who reported on experiences with bullying. The focus groups were representative of all the major ethnic groups in the United States. Here are the results of the sessions. These statements were all generated by the adolescents and agreed on. This is what they concluded, in their own words, about the problem of bullying in American junior highs (grades 7 through 9; student ages 12 to 15).

a. Bullying happens all the time

b. Bullying happens to everyone: Even the popular ones get bullied.

c. Kids who are different are most frequently victims: Usually it's stuff that you can't control, maybe you are smarter than they are, or there is this girl who has no hair, or this kid has a birthmark under his eye, or the kid who is seen as gay. These are the people who get picked on most. And usually no one stops it.

Why doesn't anyone intervene?
No one intervenes because of:

1. *Fear: If you say something, then they will beat you up, too.*
2. *They don't want to be involved; besides, it won't make a difference and you might be the next victim.*
3. *It's fun and entertaining to watch bullying.*
4. *We don't know how to deal with bullying—when to tell or whom to tell.*

What would it take for you to intervene?

1. *Confidence: I would have to know it is the right thing to do.*
2. *Courage: I would have to be willing to do something that might get me beat up or in trouble.*
3. *Close relationship: If it is a friend or family member or a good acquaintance, then I would be more likely to help.*
4. *A crowd that agreed with me: You can't do it alone; you need a group and tell the bully, "NO! Stop it!"*

These comments are enlightening. Many adolescents are fearful of attending public schools for reasons like these. Truancy is often related to a phobia of school. In fact, many adolescent psychologists in the United States deal with this problem now. Combined with public tragedies such as school shootings that cause both parents and adolescents to be fearful of attending school, the reality of bullying increases the fear. In schools with large gang populations, the fear is escalated, for nonmembers are likely to be at high risk. Given this environment, the increasing trends toward home schooling and charter or private school attendance in the United States are not surprising. Neither are increasing high school drop-out rates in some areas and the trend for many students to receive GEDs and continue at community colleges rather than completing high school. To make public schools safe again, we need to incorporate programs that reduce bullying. Bringing in armed police—perceived by adolescents often as just another type of bully—is not the way to proceed. Integrating social

skills training and tolerance education throughout the curriculum
would be far more effective. Dr. Grotberg continues:

*Youth benefit from gaining an understanding of bullies. Bullies generally
have low self-esteem; they lack self-confidence; they seek power and control.
Youth can also benefit from recognizing the consequences of bullying: Bullies,
as well as those who are frequent victims, tend to become sexually promiscuous, to more frequently commit suicide, to be depressed, to have poor grades,
and to be unmotivated and engage in violence to others. Bullying and acts
of violence have a basic characteristic in common: They are cruel. Not all
bullying is physical. Much is verbal or behavioral. Girls are more likely to
say nasty things about another girl, spread rumors, or ridicule some behavior another girl engages in. Girls may ignore another girl, make a point of
turning away or walking away, keep another girl out of the clique, or refuse
to sit by someone they do not like. As with physical bullying, verbal and
behavioral bullying is also cruel.*

*A 14-year-old girl from the bullying study says: "Some of us frequently
backstabbed other girls. We named one girl 'The Tooth' because she really
annoyed us. We talked about 'our toothache' and 'getting it pulled,' telling
her she had to get out of here. I realize now that this was stupid and cruel,
real middle-school stuff. When we're in high school, my friends and I will
have a great time without backstabbing."*

*Youth who engage in cruel behavior may not be aware of their cruelty, and
to label them as cruel individuals is very damaging to their own identity.
What they need to understand is that they have engaged in a cruel act, not
that they are cruel people. Personal labeling shatters the self-confidence and
rouses the defenses of the labeled one. It is more important to separate the
behavior from the character of the person. When dealing with adolescents
who are bullying others, focus on the act, not the individual. For example,
say: "What you did when you pushed Bob down the stairs was a cruel act,
Joe, and I know you are not a cruel person. Let's see what we can do to help
you find ways to talk about what's going on that bothers you and what you
can do so your behavior doesn't come out looking cruel." Labeling a person
implies that the label describes who that person is, and reactions usually consist of denial or resentment or, worse, acceptance of the label, none of which
is desired.*

*It is more important to focus on behavior and help youth find ways to
change their responses to events than to make them feel vulnerable. They are
having enough trouble answering the question: Who am I? It is useful for
youth to think about what they are feeling and to name the emotions: I feel
sad, concerned, angry, frightened, belittled, ignored, controlled, encouraged,
criticized, protected, manipulated, rejected, approved, accepted, loved, good,*

bad, optimistic, self-confident, safe, caring, responsible, insecure, etc. When youth know their emotions, have words for them, and recognize when the emotions are felt, then they can talk about them or just think about them and learn how to manage them. One sure-fire way to manage them is to stop and think before acting.

In other words, incorporating courses into public schools focused on management of emotions and appropriate behaviors is warranted. This should not be in a punishment mode, or "after-the-fact" fashion, as so frequently is now the case, but in a systematic way to reach all students before such problems arise. Training teachers to incorporate these ideas into their academic courses—even requiring that they do so—could be beneficial. Dr. Grotberg illustrates an example here of how such a lesson might be structured. It could be used as a psycho-drama script, in journal writing, as part of a literature assignment related to character analysis in a particular novel, as part of a small-group counseling session, or in other ways. Here is the script:

Good questions to ask before acting are these:

Q: What am I feeling?

A: I'm feeling angry and humiliated.

Q: What about the event makes me have these feelings?

A: George seems to have deliberately ignored me when I tried to ask him a question about a class assignment. He actually said, "I don't have time for you."

Q: What can I do so that the feelings will not make me do something I will regret?

A: I can calm down so that my feelings don't take over, and think about what I can do so that these feelings are no longer necessary.

Q: How can I approach the person who has roused these feeling? Do I need to share my reaction to what the person did?

A: I should express my feeling, but I can keep it light and say: Hey, that remark has me spinning. It would be cool if you could tell me when you have time to answer my question.

Using activities like this helps to provide skills that may not develop naturally in adolescents. It is a mistake to assume that proso-cial, acceptable behavior is a natural trait; that anyone who does not have it is flawed and should be punished; and that schools, parents, and society need assume no responsibility. This attitude is ridiculous from the standpoint of adolescent psychology and the information we have about societal influences on socialization; yet it is an argument that often seems accepted by the public and touted by politicians. The

answer is prayer, say some. The answer is stricter laws, zero tolerance, and tough love, say others. The answer is prison cry still more.
No! The answer is a cohesive community that embraces, models, and
teaches nonviolent, prosocial behavior. Understanding the connections between the various "systems" within society, as Bronfenbrenner
(1994) explains, is critical. Otherwise, what results is a game of laying
blame. "The parents are to blame," say schools and other social forces.
The parents are devastated, suffer esteem problems themselves, and
turn against their own children to save their own esteem and social
status. They give power to schools, police agencies, or psychiatric
hospitals. "The schools are to blame," say others. Lawsuits ensue and
school personnel become even less likely to intervene in ways that
may help the situation. "The media is to blame." "The church is to
blame." "The politicians are to blame." There is never a shortage of
ideas on who or what to blame, it seems, but there does seem to be
a shortage of constructive ideas for solutions that are implemented.
Integrating life skills and social skills into schools is one such idea.
Dr. Grotberg continues:

*Recognizing feelings is an important part of social interaction. No one
wants to be isolated from others unless there is a critical reason. Most youth
want to interact with others, especially other youth, and many are not aware
of the skills necessary to succeed. Here is what it takes for an adolescent to be
seen as appropriately socialized in our present society:*

1. *Make friends easily. Youth who are friendly are not afraid of people. They do
   not fear rejection but assume acceptance, and greet others with a "Hello."*

2. *Feel empathy for those having special problems. Those who are empathetic
   offer some words of comfort or understanding, providing help if it is
   desired.*

3. *Give honest reactions. Youth talk to others who upset them, but do not hold
   a grudge or wait to get even. They can tell others what is bothering them
   about their behavior, with the goal of bringing about some changes in the
   relationship so that they can go on being friends.*

4. *Manage negative emotions. Appropriately socialized youth know that others are distressed by anger, fear, and desire for revenge; but they try to use
   discussion, negotiation, and resolution for problems causing strong, negative
   emotions.*

5. *Expect fairness. Youth assume fairness in relationships and are quite willing
   to address any seeming violation of fairness.*

6. *Demonstrate affection. Youth, primarily boys, are often reluctant to demonstrate affection, except to hit or hug a team player who has just made a basket*

important to winning the game. Football also shows players demonstrating affection after they have won a game or one member has been particularly clever in a play. But in the classroom or on campus this behavior is unacceptable. So, smiles and greetings best express affection at school.

7. *Listen. Youth give full attention to someone who is talking. They respond, asking questions to clarify what was said or asking a new question to add to their knowledge.*

8. *Start conversations. Youth are willing to start a conversation with someone else or in a group. This shows a friendly recognition of another person and affirms the other as an individual human being.*

9. *Ask for help. Youth trust others enough to feel free to ask for help. They usually have a network of supports to help when those inevitable adversities show up.*

As noted previously, these are skills and behaviors that are developed in interaction with all of the socializing agents in the greater cultural milieu—family, schools, peers, parents, media, church, and more. Even when these skills are not appropriately developed through natural interactions, they can be learned. These skills are not inborn traits that either are or are not present in each person. Programs to develop these skills and behaviors are, arguably, far more important in school than programs to teach phonics, reading, and basic mathematics. Emotional literacy is a functional skill that many of our youth lack for a variety of reasons. This lack needs to be addressed and remedied.

Integrating Art, Music, Dance, and Sports to Reduce Aggression

Lewis (1981) noted that Plato and, later, Aristotle, both emphasized the value of education to socialize youth for productive and happy lives. Both stressed the importance of "molding children through stories, music and gymnastics." Plato thought the study of mathematics was particularly important during adolescence to prepare the mind for abstract reasoning. Aristotle placed slightly less value on the study of mathematics during adolescence and more value on reading, writing, and drawing as tools to facilitate clear thinking. All are important.

Logic and mathematics both play important roles in developing formal operational reasoning, in a Piagetian sense. This type of reasoning is necessary for critical thinking and decision making. But teaching logic, mathematics, decoding, and other basic curriculum alone is not enough to prepare adolescents to handle their emotions and constructively channel aggression. Sports and physical activities, too, are necessary. It is probably not accidental that research in the United States indicates that adolescents who are active in athletics during high school are also less likely to be arrested. Reading physical cues appropriately and developing useful and socially acceptable outlets for aggressive energy are important skills. Sports activity also has inherent risks, of course. When competition and winning are stressed at all costs, including use of steroids and unfair play, they serve to exacerbate aggression. In general, however, participation in team and individual sports both serve as effective ways to constructively channel frustration, anger, and aggression. Coaches naturally assume the role of mentor, so important to adolescents as previously discussed. The rest of the team serves as a natural, supportive peer group. The physical training teaches control and body awareness, useful in anger management. If used appropriately, sports are an important part of adolescent education. The classical emphasis on "gymnastics," referred to by both Plato and Aristotle, should be maintained.

In U.S. high schools at present, athletics in the school are supported and well funded, but they are presented as extracurricular activities, highly competitive, and available only to a small percentage of students. Many who could benefit are shut off from this potentially beneficial part of education. The current Russian educational system, despite limited resources, seems to do a better job of integrating physical training throughout the curriculum and including all students in a mode that is more cooperative than competitive. The rest of the world could perhaps learn from this model.

Another important aspect of education is humanities, what the classical philosophers referred to as the importance of "stories and music in molding youth," and what Aristotle also expanded to include drawing and creative writing. Humanities education includes literature, music, creative writing, drawing, and other forms of art production. These areas not only offer an important perspective on the higher, aesthetic values inherent in humanity but also are a natural way to train for the appropriate outlet of aggressive energy. Powerful emotions can be released through painting, poetry, and music. Providing adolescents with the skills to use the arts as an outlet for what may otherwise become potentially destructive emotional energy is important. Encouraging them to make use of these outlets—in private, certainly, even if not in public—is essential.

Although at one time, humanities education in U.S. schools was integrated and these skills were provided, that practice has changed over the last couple of decades. Most schools still offer some type of art or music education, but it is not available to all students and is increasingly being eliminated altogether. Rather than courses in the elementary schools that teach students how to draw, paint, and play musical instruments, it is more common to see music available only as an extracurricular activity, generally funded at least partially by parents who must buy instruments and provide lessons. General art and music teachers at this level may see students for less than 40 minutes per week. They are able to do little more than teach a few melodies for singing, offer basic "art appreciation" information, or perhaps work with classroom teachers to produce a school play once each year, which is often operated more in a competitive rather than a cooperative mode from the students' perspective. Such instruction offers additional stress rather than a strategy for stress release. In addition, most art and music teachers at this level work in more than one school and with more than 500 students at a time, making it impossible to develop close relationships with students.

When students move on to junior high and high school, these courses are offered only as electives and selected by relatively few students. Thus, they have not been provided with the necessary skills or experiences to use art and music as a means to rechannel aggressive energy unless it has been through private lessons offered by parents. Depending on how these experiences were offered, they may have been perceived as stressful rather than helpful. Problems of overscheduling children and pressuring them to achieve have been discussed elsewhere. Some elementary teachers do integrate art, music, and drama into their lessons naturally and effectively, but changing policies toward "standards" and "exit tests" makes it increasingly difficult to do so.

Many adolescents crave the outlets that can be offered through visual arts, music, and writing, but they are offered no opportunity to develop the skills necessary for these outlets. These adolescents may end up in prison or perhaps in adolescent treatment facilities for substance abusers before they acquire any opportunity for using these outlets, perhaps through music or art therapy or through rehabilitation programs. How much more efficient and humane it would be to emphasize them in the schools and give them at least equal status with the "basics!"

Again, the current educational system in Russia offers some good practices in art, music, and drama throughout the elementary and secondary curriculum. Several magnet schools within the United States still offer superb training in the humanities. Many private and public schools probably still do, as well. But the trend, especially in high poverty areas where these programs would be most beneficial, is to cut these programs and focus on other areas. This is a dangerous trend. As noted in the chapter on anger management training, finding appropriate outlets for emotions through art, music, and physical activities is instrumental in reducing violence and inappropriate expressions of aggression. Not only are humanities programs effective for providing constructive channels for aggression, they are also tools in moral development and values education, as illustrated in the next chapter. It is imperative that such programs remain integral parts of public education.

CHAPTER 10

CULTURAL ASPECTS OF MORAL DEVELOPMENT AND IMPULSE CONTROL

Parts of this chapter were presented at psychological conferences, including the International Council of Psychologists 2003 Convention in Toronto, the International Union of Psychological Sciences 2004 Meeting in Beijing, China, and the International Association of Cross-Cultural Psychology Convention in India in 2002. Dr. Jas Jafar, Dr. Carlo Prandini, Dr. Natalia Parnyuk, Frank Hollingsworth, Dr. Valerie Sitnikov, Dr. Veronika Artemeyeva, Dr. William Kolodinsky, and Dr. Vincent Schroeder all assisted with the research recounted here.

Moral Development

Morals and values are the inner mechanisms that govern external behavior. From that standpoint, moral development and values education are important aspects to consider when it comes to rechanneling adolescent aggression. Most developmental psychologists believe that moral and cognitive development are correlated. General reasoning skills and moral reasoning skills both develop gradually, in stages, based on a combination of environmental experiences and cues combined with biological brain development. Piaget (1932) postulated that children's development of moral judgment follows the same basic pattern as that of cognitive development. The development of moral reasoning depends on such cognitive skills as the perception of reality, the organization and evaluation of experiences, perspective-taking ability, and abstract reasoning. Piaget noted that a remarkable change in the quality of moral reasoning generally occurs at the time of puberty (Muss, 1996).

Lawrence Kohlberg was a psychologist who made important contributions to the theory of moral development, and his work still underpins much of the research in this area. Piaget and Kohlberg were primarily interested in moral judgment, which refers to the intellectual ability to evaluate the correctness of a course of action. Kohlberg (Kohlberg & Eifenbein, 1981) defined moral judgment in terms of Kant's categorical imperative: *Act only according to that maxim by which you can at the same time will that it should become a universal law and treat each person as an end, not a means.* In other words, people should act only in ways that would be acceptable to them if the actions could be held up as universally required for all and were not ever intended to harm or manipulate another human being.

Building on this Kantian foundation, Kohlberg incorporated aspects of Plato and Dewey to find guiding principles governing moral judgment. From Plato, he adopted the notion of justice as the ultimate goal of morality. From Dewey, he adopted the concept that education contributes to moral development. Although he asserted that development was not tied to cultural aspects, later research indicates that it is (Hallpike, 2004).

Kohlberg describes the development of moral judgment as a process in which people pass through three levels and six qualitatively different stages in a universal and invariant sequence (Kohlberg, 1969). Level of moral reasoning is assessed by analyzing responses to a series of moral dilemmas, and determining which of the stages of moral reasoning described by Kohlberg best characterizes the responses. These levels and stages include:

1. Level 1: Preconventional or Premoral Reasoning

    This stage is most prevalent during childhood and is concerned only with external, concrete consequences of acts.

    Stage 1: Heteronomous Morality

    At the first stage of level one, rules are obeyed to avoid punishment and obtain gratification. Kohlberg referred to this stage as "obedience and punishment orientation."

    Stage 2: Individualistic, Instrumental Morality

    At the second stage of level one, children begin to distinguish between physical damage and psychosocial intent of actions. This is still a hedonistic orientation, in which morally right behavior is determined by what satisfies individual desires. People who reason at this stage are not able to objectively consider the perspectives and objectives of others.

2. Level 2: Conventional or Moral Reasoning

At this level, concern becomes focused on meeting social expectations. In this sense, it is still an external orientation. It is based on acceptance of the existing social order. Conformity to social standards determines behavior. There is a strong desire to maintain, support, and justify the existing social order. According to Kohlberg, most adolescents and adults function at this level, at Stage 3 or 4, in terms of their moral reasoning.

Stage 3: Interpersonally Normative Morality

At this stage, an egocentric orientation is replaced by a socio-centric orientation. Kohlberg referred to this as the "good boy-good girl" approval-seeking orientation, governed by adherence to the golden rule of "Do unto others as you would have them do unto you." Personal needs can be distinguished from morality at this stage, but social approval becomes the mark of morality. Living up to the expectations of others becomes the most important criterion, and good behavior is seen as that which pleases or helps others. Winning the approval of others becomes of paramount importance. The need to win the approval of the immediate social group and to live up to perceived expectations becomes the yardstick for moral decision making. People at this level conform to what they believe to be the opinions of those they identify with. As you can see, adolescents at this stage (which is the stage where most adolescents are in terms of development, even though they may later pass beyond this stage) make their decisions based on approval of peers and role models. They imitate the actions with those in whom they are in contact and judge their behavior according to others. Peer-culture and role-models/mentors are both important determinants of adolescents' moral reasoning and behavior.

Stage 4: Social Systems Morality

This stage is characterized by a strong belief in law, order, duty, and legitimate authority. Maintaining the existing social order is viewed as the primary value. The focus is on duty rather than on approval. However, the rules one follows are still perceived as concrete rather than abstract. Breaking laws produces guilt and shame. This moral orientation includes unquestioning belief in existing authority, obeying the law, doing one's duty, showing respect for authority, and maintaining the social order. It is worth noting that military training often serves as a type of "moral education" that brings adolescents and adults to this stage of moral reasoning.

3. Level 3: Postconventional or Autonomous Level

A person reasoning at this level identifies the primary value to be adherence to carefully considered and self-selected moral principles. Moral reasoning is not based on selfish needs, fear, reward, need for approval, or need for conformity. It is not based on authority or adherence to social structures and demonstrates more internal congruence than reasoning and behavior at the earlier levels.

Stage 5: Human Rights and Social Welfare Morality

Individual rights, human dignity, mutual obligations, and contractual agreements are important considerations at this stage. Moral behavior reflects a concern for the welfare of the larger community and a desire to further community respect. Because individual fairness and dignity are paramount, a desire to change unfair laws and social conditions that violate these principles replaces a blind adherence to authority. Laws are viewed as contracts that can and should be renegotiated when necessary, not as concrete rules that justify themselves. A person at this stage will work to change laws that seem unfair or unjust as long as the changes reflect consensus, follow rational deliberation, and consider social utility and justice.

Stage 6: Morality of Universalizable, Reversible, and Prescriptive General Ethical Principles

At Kohlberg's highest stage of moral reasoning, conscience and reasoning are based on carefully considered and self-chosen ethical principles that place the highest values on humanity, life, fairness, and dignity. Rules are binding only to the extent that they agree with these ethical principles. Rules that violate these principles must be broken, and any penalty that ensues will be accepted. *The concept of justice at this stage extends beyond any existing social order.* Consistency, logical comprehensiveness, and universal applicability characterize Stage 6 reasoning. According to Kohlberg, no one can operate at this stage without having first operated at the social contractual level of his or her society and without having clearly understood the basic contractual nature of the existing social order. A person at this stage may practice civil disobedience, not out of disrespect for the law, but out of respect for higher moral principles.

This orientation is beautifully expressed in the following excerpt from Martin Luther King's "Letter from Birmingham Jail." He wrote in 1964:

> I do not advocate evading or defying the law, as would a rabid segregationist. That would lead to anarchy. One who breaks an unjust law must do so openly, lovingly and with willingness to accept the penalty. An individual who breaks a law that conscience tells him is unjust and who willingly accepts the penalty of imprisonment in order to arouse the conscience of the community over its injustice is in reality expressing the highest possible respect for the law.

Historical figures such as Ghandi, Hans and Sophie Scholl, and Nelsen Mandela have also exemplified this orientation. So have many religious figures and saints from many denominations over the ages, and even more controversial recent figures such as Timothy Leary and Dr. Kavorkian who took moral stands against laws they viewed as opposed to human rights and dignity. Kohlberg estimated that less than 20 percent of the adult population would ever attain this stage of moral reasoning. It is based on consistent use of the following: (1) choice, (2) hierarchy, (3) intrinsic value, (4) prescriptivity, (5) universality, (6) freedom, (7) reversibility, (8) mutual respect, and (9) constructivism.

Kohlberg hypothesized that each individual moves sequentially through these six stages, although for the majority of individuals, development is arrested at Stage 3 or Stage 4. Individuals move through the stages at different rates, but the movement is invariant and sequential. This invariant sequence is hierarchical in nature and each higher stage incorporates and adds to the elements of the next lower stage. These stages were originally measured through verbal responses to moral dilemmas presented to less than 300 male college students, as part of Kohlberg's doctoral dissertation. Since then, his findings have been replicated many times all over the world.

Behavior is related to this cognitive verbal structure of moral reasoning, but not identical to it. Just because a person can identify morally sound behavior, it does not mean the person will always act in accordance. However, studies indicate there is a positive relationship between the level of moral reasoning and moral behavior (Rubin & Schneider, 1973) and that juvenile delinquents score lower on cognitive moral reasoning tasks than their peers (Hains & Miller, 1980; Kohlberg, 1969).

Kohlberg also asserted that moral judgment is not significantly determined by sociocultural context. He felt his stages were universal, and unaffected by cultural, religious, or social contexts (Kohlberg, 1981). This notion has been criticized by many, most notably Gilligan (1977). In support of his claim of universality of stages, research conducted in places as far afield as the United Kingdom, Honduras, India, Israel, Kenya, Mexico, Nigeria, Taiwan, Turkey, New Zealand, and other countries seemed to support the sequence. There is no doubt, however, that cultural factors influence how rapidly individuals move through the stages he postulates, and at what stage the majority of individuals in any given culture stop their developmental trajectory (Hallpike, 2004). For example, Lei and Cheng (1987) found that some Chinese cultural values such as the maintenance of harmony, obedience, and filial piety do affect Chinese adolescents' moral judgments. Snarey (1985) found that communal equity and collective happiness are important in Israel while compassion and detachment are predominant in the moral judgments of Tibetan monks (Gielen & Kelly, 1983; Heubner & Garrod, 1993). In addition, Maqsud (1977) found that culture and religious values have effects on moral judgment. Other cultural factors that play a role in affecting moral judgment are language, cultural context, rules, and expectations (Rogoff, 1990; Tappan & Packer, 1991).

Researchers in the new emerging discipline of cross-cultural psychology have started to look carefully not only at the moral stages, but also at the kinds of reasoning that individuals from different cultures bring to moral discourse. From the perspective of cross-cultural psychology, social and cultural context is the key factor affecting moral development of individuals. Individual moral development refers to how one develops skill in understanding, managing, and adhering to the moral expectations of one's culture (Shweder, 1990; Stigler, Shweder, & Herdt, 1990). Shweder (1990) and Shweder, Mahapatra, and Miller (1987) argued that a highly principled member of a Brahman community in India reasons differently, using different justifications from Americans to explain moral judgments. The researchers concluded that in an Indian society, moral events cannot be easily distinguished from social conventions. Thus, some moral principles that are shared across cultures do not characteristically lead to similar judgments about right or wrong. Other cross-cultural studies also indicate the strong impact of culture on moral reasoning. Some researchers find the existence of cultural variability in justice morality (Keller, Edelstein, Fang, & Fang,1998; Edwards, 1994; Harkness, Edwards, & Super,

1981; Hutz, Conti, & Vargas, 1994; Miller & Bersoff, 1992; Snarey, 1985) while other studies identify types of postconventional outlooks that emphasize moralities of community (Dien, 1982; Gorsuch & Barnes, 1973; Heubner & Garrod, 1993; Ma, 1989; Okonkwo, 1997; Tietjen & Walker, 1985; Vasudev, 1994). Other studies also increasingly highlight the importance of religious and spiritual orientations on morality (Bouhmama, 1984; Colby & Damon, 1992; Shweder & Much, 1987).

Similarly, Iwasa (1992), Miller (2001), and Mizuno (1999) also agree on the importance of culture in determining moral reasoning. Gender is also noted as a determinant of moral reasoning (see Gilligan, 1977, 1979, 1982), although it is unclear whether gender operates differently as a mediating variable according to cultural context. McCarthy, Jafar, and Artemeyeva (2004) found that among Russian adolescents, no significant differences in level of moral reasoning was apparent between males and females, whereas among Malay adolescents females generally demonstrated a higher level of moral reasoning. This finding contrasted to U.S. adolescents, where males demonstrated significantly higher levels, consistent with Kohlberg's initial work, which was also completed with North Americans. It is also worth mentioning that of the three cultural groups studied, there were significant differences in overall stage of moral reasoning apparent among adolescents. Russian adolescents demonstrated the highest levels, generally at Kohlberg's Stage 4 and above. Malay youth scored, on average, below Russian youth but above U.S. adolescents at Stage 3. Adolescents from the United States were more likely to be at Stage 2 (McCarthy et al., 2004; Jafar, McCarthy, Kolodinsky, & Schroeder, 2003).

In sum, researchers who have been focusing their work on the impact of cultural factors acknowledge that greater attention and weight should be paid to understanding the impact of culture on moral development. Given the importance that role models and peers may play in adolescents' moral development, it is not surprising that moral reasoning reflects cultural values. In the studies mentioned previously, religious teachings were more frequently cited by Malay adolescents, and Americans adolescents were more concerned with personal consequences of actions, equitable exchange, and self-interest. Adherence to traditional social norms in Malay culture is characterized by following religious principles; in American society, traditional values to which adolescents are socialized include exchange theory, economic self-interest, freedom, autonomy, and fear of punishment. Russian youth emphasized personal relationships, personal and family honor, philosophical and moral principles, and social responsibility.

All three groups mentioned religion, but they were mentioned in different ways. Russian youth seldom cited religion, and only when referring to ethics and principles; Malay youth cited religion in reference to laws and social norms; U.S. youth generally cited religion in reference to fear of punishment from God. In other words, the Malay adolescents' referral to religious principles has to be understood in terms of deeply held and socially grounded principles. To maintain harmony in all aspects of life, a Malay has to behave in a certain appropriate way. Demonstrating some traditional behavior like *balas budi* and following a religious code, *adat*, coexists with the religion, Islam. As in the studies by Maqsud (1977), Simmons and Simmons (1994) on Nigerian and Saudi Arabian Muslims, and Bouhmama (1984) on Algerian Muslims, results of this study suggest that the respondents' moral judgments are largely determined by the commandments in the Holy Quran. Therefore, there are strong grounds to believe that religious principles determine the moral judgments of the Malays who, by their adherence to principles of religious duty, reflect the characteristics of Stage 3 moral reasoning.

Although American adolescents also frequently demonstrate reasoning based on social contract, their more frequent use of Stage 2 reasoning can also be explained within the context of the society in which they live. American society is concerned with individual rights and responsibilities and with self-interest, economic and otherwise. Adherence to authority based on a reward/punishment orientation is also stressed in American society. Extrinsic rewards are valued and are viewed as directly correlated to individual effort. The goodness or badness of a particular course of action is determined pragmatically by the physical consequences or outcome of that action. According to Kohlberg's theoretical model, an individual who demonstrates Stage 2 moral reasoning is basically concerned with the individual self and protecting one's own interest. American society also reflects this concern.

Although references to religious or moral principles were not entirely absent among Russian adolescents, they occurred with far less frequency than among the Malay and American adolescents. Russian youth frequently mentioned the importance of working hard, of doing the best thing for society, and of maintaining respectful, honorable, interpersonal relationships. There seemed to be an emphasis on the practical; there was only one direct reference to

God or religion, although indirect references to principles rooted in Christianity were more common. It is important to note, however, that lack of reference to God in answers does not imply a lack of religious influence in Russia. On the contrary, it can be argued that a strong religious tradition has been maintained through the family for the last century in Russia. A strong Soviet educational system actually maintained these underlying values rooted in religion through the emphasis of Russian literature written before Soviet times, all of which contained an underlying moral structure that reflects a value system based in Orthodox Christianity. As religion was banned and not discussed publicly under Stalin's regime, however, it is not surprising that adolescents still do not mention it.

Principles cited by Russian youth generally came from the Christian faith. For example, "Honor thy father and mother" was referred to several times, as was the importance of forgiveness, charity, and social equality. More general religious references such as sin, moral standards, and good character were also mentioned, as were principles such as the Hippocratic oath and the law of karma and reciprocity.

These studies showed that the Malay cultural and religious norms, values, and expectations influenced by the Muslim religion affected moral judgment among Malaysian adolescents. In contrast, U.S. responses did not reflect these concepts and principles in their reasoning but rather reflected values characteristic of the American sociocultural milieu. These values included individual freedom and responsibility, self-interest, self-protection, crime and punishment mentality, and reasoning governed by economic fairness. Correspondingly, principles, codes, and ethics, including those related to justifications for communism and social equity combined with a strong sense of family loyalty, characterized the Russian responses.

Others who have conducted studies on moral reasoning in non-Western cultures have noted similar, culturally specific influences on stages of reasoning (Gielen & Kelly, 1983; Heubner & Garrod, 1993; Shweder, 1990; Snarey, 1985; Miller, 2001). These studies lend credence to the growing number of studies that highlight the importance of culture and socialization in human development and moral reasoning.

Culturally mediated gender differences warrant additional discussion. It is clear that gender, in and of itself, is not, as has been previously asserted, an influence on reasoning level as assessed by Kohlbergian dilemmas. Russian adolescents demonstrated the highest levels of moral reasoning overall, and there were no differences between males and females. Perhaps this reflects the relatively long-standing economic and social equity of men and women in Russian society, or perhaps it reflects other underlying cultural values transmitted through school and family to both sexes equally. Malay females demonstrated the next highest level of reasoning. They seemed the most able to use clear Stage 3 reasoning. Perhaps the females in this culture are even more concerned with maintaining traditional religious and cultural values than the males, who did not seem to reason much differently than their American counterparts. The American females, in contrast, exhibited the lowest level of reasoning, scoring below their male counterparts as well as below both genders in the Malaysian sample. They demonstrated clear Stage 2 reasoning within their responses.

Perhaps this suggests that females are more likely to reflect societal values in their reasoning than males are, in line with Gilligan's theory that females are more concerned with social orientation and social aspects—perhaps even a societal orientation concerned with maintaining social norms. Or perhaps there are other explanations, such as a heightened competitiveness among American females resulting from perceptions of gender inequity in the job market and elsewhere. This could also account for more concern with fairness and self-protectiveness. A third possibility is that females are more likely than males to react to fear by demonstrating submission and conformity, and this reaction slows moral development. The emphasis on fear in U.S. society, where messages like "If you break the law you will go to jail and terrible things will happen," "The streets are not safe," or "We are constantly under attack by terrorists," are common. It may impact the moral development of females more than of males for biochemical reasons related to testosterone and adrenaline levels. Regardless, gender does not appear to make up a separate culture in and of itself, as Gilligan has suggested, although it does appear to differentially reflect culture. Additional studies, with larger samples and in other countries, are necessary to provide more insight. Overall, though, socialization within particular cultures does influence the development of moral reasoning.

Cultural context is an important consideration when assessing adolescents' level of moral reasoning. These findings point to the importance of culture in determining all aspects of life, including moral judgments. This, in turn, highlights the importance of the macrosystem (Bronfenbrenner, 1994) and the greater social milieu in either exacerbating or escalating adolescent acts of aggression.

A form of moral, values education occurs within each society regardless of whether it is formally acknowledged and planned, delivered through schools, religious or military training, or serendipitously. To prevent escalating youth violence, it is logical to make the moral aspects of education systematic, acknowledged, planned, and delivered through the socializing agent most likely to be encountered—in this case, public schools.

Values Education

Using public schools as socializing agents to promote moral development is controversial, at least in the United States, where so many religions, beliefs, and attitudes coexist. Still, what appears to have happened, at least in terms of adolescent aggression in this country, is that many children have "fallen through the cracks." Because public schools and state agencies are so careful *not* to impose any values education, and because many youth do not receive such education through other means such as family or church, a violent peer culture results. Russia, too, as a result of the changes that country has undergone over the last two decades, is also beginning to see such problems. Two well-known Russian psychologists, Dr. Valerie Sitnikov and Dr. Natalia Parnyuk, write this about the current socialization of Russian adolescents:

Social cataclysms of Russian society, the destruction of an established system of values within society, and rapid changes in personal and social relations have resulted in problems in individuals' socialization. A gross break of the system of ruling government accompanied by deformation of social priorities, ideals, and stereotypes bring tension, aggression, self-distrust, and distrust toward others into the foreground. These changes have had a deep influence, especially on adolescent behavior.

During the 1990s, there were global social upheavals in post-Soviet territory. These upheavals nearly ruined the system of socializing a developing child, which had been in place for many years. The main influences on adolescents' socialization were state systems such as schools and the system of mass communication. Public organizations, neighborhood environment, and the immediate family—in other words, macro, meso, and micro systems—all exerted an influence, as well. During Soviet times, public organizations were practically the continuation of a government system, as was the Service of Mass Communications (SMC). These formed the macro environment within which a person was socialized. These organizations tried determinedly and not entirely fruitlessly to be the main institutions of influence on the rising generations. In many cases meso environment took second place in socialization. Adults—teachers, trainers, acquaintances and other older people—composed a small part of it. The leading position was often given to points of view of people of the same age: classmates, neighbors, and people with the same interests such as sports, music, art, and other hobbies. A family microenvironment played only the third role for most Soviet adolescents.

Note that, based on what has already been discussed about identity formation during adolescence, the natural distancing from family members that occurs as a result and the tendency to rely on the peer group, this system actually is quite compatible as a means of enhancing development and providing values education. It has since changed, however. Dr. Sitnikov and Dr. Parnyuk continue:

The meaning and role of these factors (macro, meso, and micro environment) changed diametrically after the disintegration of the Soviet Union. There was a destruction of the established government systems, including public organizations for children and youth. A major decrease of school funding and funding for daycare and social programs resulted in the rapid growth of street crime. Intrusive propaganda of private enterprise and individualism depreciated the value of intellectual labor and education.

During the 1990s in Russia, there was a negative change of the structure of macro environment and its influence on adolescents. A governmental-official system of ruling was penetrated by corruption and became indifferent to the fortunes of people. An abundance of dwarf political parties did not express the people's wishes and interests. A lack of actual youth organizations, on the one hand, and full ideologization of former values, empty inner development, lack of spirituality and a venal SMC, on the other hand, have derogated the influence of the macro environment.

During the last 10 years, the department of practical psychology (head, Professor Sitnikov) and the laboratory of problems of a person's socialization (head, Professor Rean) have been conducting research on these changes in socialization among youth. The findings reveal that modern Russian adolescents value good friends, work, and family. The same findings were revealed in research conducted at other Russian universities. The study, however, also uncovered several findings contradictory to previous research, showing that success and money are now highly valued by adolescents.

With regard to the obtained findings, we established that the leading factor of socialization for most adolescents has become family, regardless of whether or not a family is happy. Thus, the results of socialization have become more unpredictable. It has become more typical for adolescents to emancipate themselves earlier, leaving the family. Many express a desire for self-assertion and independence. Also, for the last 15 years there has been a harsh decrease in the quality of life and living conditions in many Russian families. This has contributed to increased family conflicts, leading to divorces and to adolescents leaving their families.

Research at the Russian State Pedagogical University, under the leadership of Regush, shows that the most serious life problem of modern Russian adolescents is their relations with parents. Regardless of interfamily conflicts and leaving the family, the seriousness is not decreased but even raised. The most sincere and gentle words about their parents can be heard from children whose parents have been deprived of their rights because of abuse. The most cordial and full-of-hope words we've heard were in a colony for female delinquents. Among the 600 girls there, only 3 were from so-called "wealthy" families.

In regard to this and other contradictions between reality and its reflection in the consciousness of adolescents, there seems to be a problem of social-perceptive reflection of adolescents and, in peculiar, the problem of specifics of reflection by them of their friends and enemies. Of special note in this regard are specifics of social-perceptive apperception of friends and enemies by adolescents who have been treated cruelly and raped. It is precisely because of this problem in perception that these adolescents later experience great difficulties in forming their own families. Such experiences may not even need to be directly experienced to have such an influence, however. Psychiatrist Chime F. Shatan has shown that, among people who have experienced catastrophes such as wars, violence, and destruction, these traumas have been communicated to children even though parents haven't intentionally done so.

Unfortunately, since the 1990s, family violence, including violence toward children and women, has become a major problem in Russia. Research shows that now Russian children are one of the most unprotected categories of people of the world. Precisely because of this, they have often become victims of abuse, contempt, and exploitation.

Children's exploitation in prostitution and pornography is a global industry being contributed to by poverty, cupidity, and a demand for cheap sex. Such sex provides great profits, second only to drugs and arms. As a consequence, the lives of millions of boys and girls, in both rich and poor countries, are ruined. In the 1970s, prostitution was common in Southeast Asian countries, but it has been rapidly spreading to countries of Eastern Europe and the former Soviet Union since the early 1990s. Customers of

Russian prostitutes and sex-industry consumers are primarily residents of more developed countries of the world. It appears, also, that family violence and abuse to women and children are more problematic in these countries, although it is rising in Russia, as well.

According to data from an independent charitable organization "Sisters" (a crisis center for women being violated), a rape is committed every six minutes in the United States. Every seven seconds there is violence in a family. About 1 million sex crimes are committed toward children annually. Victims of the pornography industry are often children between 7 and 12 years old. Data from American criminologists inform us that Americans between 12 and 19 years old become victims of nearly 2 million rapes, robberies, and assaults yearly. By the way, violence is not only an American problem. Roduen and Abarbanela in their book, As It Happens, provide data on violence in other Western developed countries. In Canada and Great Britain, it is estimated that one of every six women is a victim of rape. In Holland and Norway, nearly one-third of women experienced sexual acts or violence during childhood or adolescence.

In 1996, the entire world was shocked by these figures published at the First International Congress in Stockholm, which was devoted to protecting children from the pornography industry and prostitution. Children are widely used in pornographic films, which is also a form of sexual violence. It was noted that 1 million children yearly were involved in prostitution. In Finland and Sweden, there is a special service with information on St. Petersburg. It explains where and at what price a boy or a girl from 8 to 12 for a male and female can be found. Because of the vigorous growth of information technologies, the child pornography found on the Internet intensifies the situation.

In former countries of the Soviet Union, the problem of sexual violence has been ignored for a long time. Only recently has research devoted to psychological aspects of sexual violence been conducted. According to data from the information center of the Ministry of Internal Affairs (MIA), nearly 2,000 children are exposed to sexual violence yearly in Russia. But specialists of MIA admit that these figures don't reflect the real situation, because registration of the violence takes place only in such cases of violence when criminals have been arrested and punished. In an analytical report "Social Orphanhood in Modern Russia," Rean noted that an analysis of statistics of MIA of Russia showed a significant decrease in such kinds of crimes against minors since 1998; however, this had been achieved by passing an act decreasing the age of a minor from 16 to 14 years. The act in its core has "legalized" child prostitution and contributed to its spread. The range of this phenomenon is such that it has not only shocked society, but it has become accepted by those government establishments and public institutions that are to protect and guide childhood, upbringing, and education of children.

The problems of Russian adolescents that have escalated so rapidly over the last 20 years closely mirror those of their U.S. counterparts. In both countries, a central socializing agent is now lacking. Violence begets violence. Troubled families beget troubled adolescents. Socioeconomic difficulties are correlated to troubled families, as are a lack of commonly accepted communal values. Given the diversity of values common in most cultures, is there a solution?

The values education movement in the United States, though gaining momentum in many places, is still viewed by some as inappropriate, as part of a right-wing Christian agenda. In some cases, it may be. Separation of church and state has made agreeing on any standard values curriculum a difficult task. Still, to curb adolescent aggression, some mechanism needs to be developed to ensure that prosocial skills are transmitted. An interesting model to consider may be the one in place in Malaysian public schools. Malaysia is also a diverse society, where Muslim, Chinese, Christian, and Jewish belief systems coexist. To solve the controversy over values education—not to mention differing calendars of religious holidays—the solution has been to create separate public schools that adhere to each of the four major religious groups in terms of calendars and values education, and then include a diversity education curriculum in each to provide information about and contact with the other religious groups. Though not a perfect solution, this may certainly be preferable to a secular model where no values education occurs. In the United States and other countries, such a system exists informally with religious and private schools. The problem, however, is that often the students who need such education most do not get it, as their families either cannot afford to send them to private institutions or are too dysfunctional to care about the socialization of their children. Agreeing on some type of appropriate values curriculum acceptable to each community school is important. Working with the public school in your area to adopt some type of values education curriculum could be time well spent in curbing the rise of adolescent violence.

Impulse Control

Another area that requires attention is working to develop impulse control. Several studies in developmental psychology suggest that length of attention and ability to delay gratification, even when measured in infants and toddlers, are good predictors of later success or failure in school and of delinquency. These studies should not be interpreted, as they are by some, to mean that a life path, be it toward genius or jail, is determined at birth. Instead, they should be used to point out the importance of early screening and diagnosis for those who naturally cannot delay gratification and have low impulse control so that special attention to developing these abilities can be provided early. Parenting styles and strategies from the time of birth are important influences on whether or not these abilities develop. So are the ways in which rules and requirements are explained and justified in public school.

Working to establish intrinsic rather than extrinsic rewards for behavior and academic success is important in helping children learn to structure their own behaviors and responses and control their impulses. Although this is changing, the current normal strategies taught in teacher education systems are based in behaviorism and emphasize the importance of extrinsic rewards such as grades, stickers, special privileges, approval, and so forth, rather than intrinsic values. In fact, this system tends to undermine both intrinsic motivation and impulse control. When children are raised in situations where their behavior is always controlled for them, through punishment and rewards—and this applies to authoritarian parenting styles, the current criminal justice system, and behavior control strategies used in many schools—they are less likely to control their own impulses and behaviors when in situations where this structure is not in place. In short, part of the problem with adolescent aggression may be rooted in a system that focuses on extrinsic control and undermines the ability to control one's own impulses. Because of the external control that is relied on at home and in schools, when adolescents find themselves in situations with peers where the authoritarian controlling agents are absent, they act in extreme ways, unable to control their impulses. The moral reasoning, identity formation, and self-control needed to establish intrinsic motivation for prosocial behavior have never been allowed to develop.

Summarizing the work in this area and recommending how to change the socializing agents responsible would require another book. For now, though, the important point to remember is that an over-reliance on outside authority, punishment, and external behavioral control strategies with children and adolescents undermines intrinsic motivation and self-generated impulse control. Controls need to be internalized, not extrinsically given. Internal states such as shame, pride, sympathy, empathy, joy in acts of altruism, and desire to help others need to govern adolescent decisions and behaviors—not fear of punishment or desire for extrinsic rewards.

Shame and Pride among Adolescents

One of the tasks of social development for adolescents is identity development (Erickson, 1968). Self-other differentiation and self-awareness and perspective-taking ability all develop gradually as identity is achieved. Self-awareness plays an important role in social life, specifically in social relationships that also have their own developmental sequence of ordered levels. The highest levels of social relationships can be attained only when self-awareness is well established for all parties involved in social interaction. Self-awareness is usually defined as the ability to recognize one's own actions, purposes, states, and skills and to assess their impact on others.

For each level of development, there are correspondent emotions. The correspondent emotions for self-awareness are shame and pride. These are called self-conscious or self-evaluative emotions (Lewis, 1990; Lewis et al., 1989). From a developmental perspective, shame and pride appear only when self-awareness is established. These emotions require several cognitive skills, including the capacity to learn about the social world, internalize rules of conduct, and evaluate personal behavior according to these rules. Self-evaluative emotions are characterized by self-referential behavior. These emotions first occur when children become capable of evaluating their own actions against a standard. These emotional states have an important influence on children's social lives. Although social behavior is possible without self-evaluative emotions, such emotions are basic to establish mature, higher level human relationships (Lewis, 1990; Lewis, Sullivan, Stanger, & Weiss, 1989).

Investigating the development of self-evaluative emotions among adolescents growing up under harsh, stressful conditions can contribute to increased understanding of factors that increase resiliency and further social and emotional development. The knowledge derived from such studies can help develop more effective prevention and intervention programs designed to reduce violence and vulnerability and to increase protective factors that foster resilience. One study that examined this phenomenon interviewed 214 male adolescents from high-poverty households in southern Brazil. Adolescents were divided into two groups. The first group (n = 110) was composed of criminal offenders convicted of armed robbery, murder, rape, and other felonies. The second group (n = 104) was composed of students from the same neighborhoods, family backgrounds and economic circumstances who had never been involved in criminal activity. All participants lived in severely economically disadvantaged neighborhoods. Age range for both groups was 13 to 18 years. Mean age for both groups was 16 years.

Before being arrested, 98 (92%) of the adolescents in the delinquent group lived with family members, 8 (6%) lived alone, and 2 (2%) lived with friends. Before being arrested, 63 (61%) were unemployed. Forty adolescents in this group (38%) were first-time offenders. Eighty (77%) had been at an institution for more than 7 months, 19 (18%) between 7 and 12 months, 3 (3%) between 13 and 18 months, and 2 (2%) between 19 and 24 months. None of the adolescents in this group had been incarcerated for longer than 2 years. Adolescents in this group had attended school for an average of 4 years before conviction. Convictions were for violent crimes such as assault, armed robbery, and rape.

For the nondelinquent group of adolescents in this study matched according to living conditions and neighborhoods, 102 (98%) lived with their families. Fewer were employed than in the delinquent group; 85 (77%) were not working at the time of the study. Adolescents in this group had attended school for an average of six years, two years more than adolescents in the delinquent group. None of these adolescents had ever been convicted of a crime. Otherwise, in terms of neighborhood, family structure, and economic status, they were similar to the members of the other group studied.

Adolescents were interviewed individually either in institutions for juvenile offenders or in public schools. The interviews were taped and transcribed to allow for content analysis of the material. During the interviews, participants provided personal data, life history, and criminal history. An effort was made to ascertain that the adolescents interviewed in the public schools had not been involved in crimes. Adolescents in both groups were asked to describe one situation or event that had happened to them that made them feel ashamed, and one event that made them feel proud. After interviews were conducted, transcripts were reviewed. Through content analysis, several categories for sources of shame experienced by delinquent and nondelinquent adolescents were identified.

The main sources of shame for delinquent adolescents were the crimes they had committed. Other sources of shame were the experience of being arrested or of being considered as a criminal by relatives or friends Since the nondelinquent group had not experienced these events, it is impossible to compare these dimensions, unless lack of social skills or transgression of social rules are considered to be similar experiences, differing in degree. Other sources of shame reported by both groups were similar and included sexual inexperience and inappropriate behavior (mostly fights with family members) and having a low-status job. About 20 percent of the delinquent group stated that they were not ashamed of anything compared with 35 percent of the nondelinquent group. Although this may suggest that some of the adolescents in this group are incapable of shame, as the comparison group reports no shame at an even higher rate, this is likely a developmental phenomenon present in all adolescents rather than an indication of borderline or sociopath tendencies in the delinquents

This study described events or situations that are perceived as sources of pride and shame to delinquents and nondelinquents living in adverse circumstances based on interview data. Pride and shame are called self-evaluative emotions, because they require the capacity to evaluate one's own behavior according social rules. The capacity for feeling ashamed or proud suggests a high level of social and emotional development. Both groups presented these self-conscious emotions.

In fact, adolescents in both groups reported many of the same sources of pride and shame. Both groups took pride in work, study, and helping others. These situations can be considered appropriate sources of pride according to social and cultural standards about what is acceptable behavior for an adolescent. The sources of shame mentioned for the two groups included behavior considered inadequate according to social rules including crimes, fights, and problems with relatives and drug use. These are also appropriate sources of shame according to social and cultural standards. Sexual inexperience and troubles with opposite sex were also mentioned as sources of shame in both groups. Research establishing issues of special concern to adolescence (Durkin, 1995; Feiring, 1996) suggests that these responses are typical of adolescents, tied to changes associated with puberty and sexual maturation, as well as to cultural expectations. In fact, sexual experience and competence are viewed as an important "rite of passage" into adulthood for many adolescents (McCarthy, Prandini, & Hollingsworth, 2001).

The absence of reporting a source of pride (18.3% of the delinquent group and 10% of the nondelinquent group) may suggest either a false modesty or low self-esteem in this population. According to Atwater (1988) low self-esteem is a common characteristic of many at-risk and delinquent adolescents. Delinquent adolescents were more likely to indicate that they felt no sense of pride. Social and emotional development of all adolescents investigated was similar. Thus, a model that labels delinquent youth as qualitatively different because of sociopathology or other psychiatric labels is totally inappropriate and counterproductive. Delinquent youth differ only in terms of experiences and are certainly capable of being rehabilitated by appropriate interventions.

Perhaps delinquent adolescents differed from their nondelinquent peers only in their prominent use of aggression and violence as problem-solving strategies. As both groups came from similar environments, competition for resources and frustration levels should be relatively equal among members of both groups unless mediating variables are present to account for the difference. Because the nondelinquent group had stayed in school longer and reported more achievements, it is possible that education is a mediating variable. Time of arrest for the delinquent group, however, may have been responsible for the more limited educational experiences and achievements, so this cannot necessarily be assumed to be the case. A more likely explanation is social modeling (Bandura, 1971) related to parenting styles or other role models.

In fact, this was supported by a later study that examined parenting styles used in the homes of delinquent and nondelinquent adolescents (Pacheco, 2004). This again highlights the role of the environment in enhancing impulse control. Authoritarian systems diminish personal control, while authoritative systems that focus on explanation, understanding, empathy, and developing perspective taking abilities, enhance responsibility for personal control. Positive attention and modeling develop impulse control and enable adolescents to better internalize the emotions and states that allow them to appropriately control their behavior.

Ideas to Encourage Moral Development and Reduce Violence

Many of the ideas already summarized in previous chapters are means of building moral development and reducing violence. Anger management strategies, art and music therapy, education, psychodrama, mentoring programs, and appropriate parenting all help to accomplish this, either directly or indirectly. Activities in school specifically tied to developmental issues adolescents face are also important. One example of such an activity, developed by two high school psychology instructors, Frank Hollingsworth and Carlo Prandini, is described next as an example. At the time this activity was developed, Hollingsworth taught psychology at a public high school in Pennsylvania and Prandini taught at a secondary school in Bologna, Italy. Both were working with students approximately 16 years old. The purposes of the activity included teaching content from their curriculum—in this case, research methods and aspects of developmental psychology—as well as encouraging cross-cultural dialogue and understanding, and developing self-reflection to encourage identity formation. This model can be used to help teachers develop similar types of activities in other content areas, as well as psychology that encourages prosocial development and cultural understanding. The lesson, developed by Prandini and Hollingsworth, is described next:

"I'm Not Old Enough To Love You" is the title of a famous Italian song of Gigliola Cinquetti. She was only 16 when she won the most popular festival in Italy (1964). This song is used to introduce the unit. Students in both countries listened to it, discussed what may have motivated her to write it, and reflect on whether or not they agree with the lyrics. These reflections are elicited via small group discussion followed by class discussion, and then a brief written essay. Next, students are presented with information about the concept of "rites of passage" from developmental psychology through the following questions and information. They are also simultaneously assigned readings in their textbook that correspond to this concept.

What comprises the boundary line between adolescence and adulthood?

According to an ingeniuous idea, this border is real and corresponds to the completion of psychological, social, and biological development. Nevertheless nowadays there's no general agreement on the role of social factors in the definition of life phases. As a class, we must try to understand:

- *Which features should a person present to be considered as an adult?*
- *Will these features be considered the same in all cultures and societies, or are they specific to a particular country or region?*
- *If we ask people (both adolescents and adults) what these features are, will they agree?*
- *Will there be differences in the answers depending on the age of the respondents?*
- *Do American and Italian high school students think the same on this theme?*

After reading, discussion, and library research on these questions, the activity proceeded according to these steps:

Activity Steps

1. *Theoretical work about the main approaches to psychological development and class discussion, as described previously, introduced the activity. Also, readings and discussion of qualitative and quantitative data collection and analysis in psychology were studied, focusing on the uses of interview and survey data. It is important to note that the steps described here were being completed simultaneously by the students in Pennsylvania and Italy, and the two instructors were in daily Internet contact to jointly discuss and plan the lessons.*

2. *Interviews on the essential features of adulthood with parents, peers, and community members were conducted. Each student was assigned to conduct a brief interview with a friend, an adult family member, and another adult community member to ask what it meant to that particular individual to consider someone an adult.*

3. *Based on the readings and the interview data, each class developed an interview. The American and Italian students then compared and collaboratively refined the interviews they had developed via electronic discussion. The result was an 18-item questionnaire designed by the students to collect data about various ideas of what it means to "come of age"—to go through the rites of passage that transform one from an adolescent to an adult.*

4. *Each class then collected data. Students in both the United States and Italy distributed the survey to five different age groups of 30 people each in their respective communities. These groups included preadolescents, high school students, college students, adults between 25 and 60 years old, and adults over 60 years old.*

5. *Classes shared their data, analyzed and interpreted the results, and discussed how their research compared to the other information they had read.*

6. *Students worked in small groups to write research reports summarizing the study.*

The objectives for the lesson were:

1. *To deal with issues related to students' experience*

2. *To offer discussion based on concrete experiences and data that were important to developing values and moral judgments*

3. *To compare different psychological approaches in the study of concrete problems*

4. *To teach students how to do research and to obtain new data*

5. *To deal with issues related to students' experience*

All of these objectives were met in this activity. The resulting data are of interest. Different age groups showed differences in the evaluation of some items, but, in general, the hierarchy was nearly the same. No significant differences were found between responses of American and Italian high school students, except for the greater importance attributed by the Italian group to *have had love affairs* and by the Americans to *driving a car.*

These data did not necessarily contradict the hypothesis of a strong cultural influence in the definition of the features of adulthood that students had read of in their texts and library research. Similarities found among different age groups and between American and Italian subjects were explained as an expression of the growing and pervading cultural homogenization we observe in Western societies, another concept students studied. On the other hand, there was also evidence of the survival of niche–cultural traits, as, for example, different sexual attitudes and different economic values.

The activity showed that both cultures shared similar views about rites of passage. Italians saw a first love affair as a rite of passage, and Americans saw a driver's license as a rite of passage. Otherwise, there were only slight differences. Having a child of one's own was seen to signal entry into adulthood more than any of the other events by both groups.

After completing the lesson, students evaluated the effects of the activity through a questionnaire. They believed this assignment increased their competence in planning and carrying out empirical research. Other marked positive judgments referred to the acquisition of statistical knowledge, to the increase of theoretical knowledge, and to the possibility to be engaged in an intellectual challenge. Most important, all noted that the activity improved their critical thinking skills. Critical thinking skills are discussed in the next chapter.

This activity is an example of the types of lessons that can be developed to help students examine their own lives and can also lead to discussions of values, so important in moral development. Not only should lessons teach academic content, they should also be relevant to daily life and decision making faced by adolescents. They should facilitate discussions and focus on moral judgment and life-planning skills. Creating lessons that serve these purposes is a worthy challenge for all teachers of adolescents.

CHAPTER 11

REDUCING ADOLESCENT AGGRESSION BY DEVELOPING CRITICAL THINKING SKILLS

Some of the information in this chapter originally appeared in articles by Sherri McCarthy in the Korean Journal of Thinking and Problem Solving *and in her doctoral dissertation, completed at Arizona State University in 1995 with Dr. Robert E. Grinder as chairperson.*

Critical Thinking Skills and Meta-cognitive Awareness

To the Greeks, critical thinking encompassed the combined abilities of logical reasoning and creative thought that allowed citizens to successfully execute self-governance. Engaging in Socratic dialogue was a means used to refine critical thinking (Robinson, 1921). Critical reasoning has been defined in many ways since ancient times, but the majority of philosophers who have studied the human mind believed that reasoning takes place according to laws governing logic. Such is the tradition that runs unbroken from Aristotle to Piaget (Hunt, 1982).

Piaget hypothesized a stage by stage progression of a child's ability to organize perceptions and adapt to the world. The developing brain interacts with the environment to build cognitive structures such as number, causality, and constancy. At each stage, the child reconstructs modes of thinking, remaking simple structures into more complex ones. The summit of this development is what Piaget called "formal operations." Formal operational thought is characterized by mature, systematic, and logical thinking. Much evidence suggests, however, that all individuals by no means attain formal operations. Evidence also suggests that, even when attained, it is not used equally well in all situations and that it develops quite differently cross culturally (Scribner, 1977). It appears that years of formal education are the greatest predictor of formal operational reasoning (Cole, 1979; Cole & Scribner, 1977; Cole, Sharp, & Lave, 1976), but one need only look at the daily newspaper to ascertain that even well-educated citizens do not consistently apply critical thought processes to social issues, laws, religion, and other areas. It may be that critical thinking is a skill acquired only in correspondence to the amount of practice with logic available in the environment. Like language, the capacity for critical thinking is acquired through a dynamic interaction between organism and environment. In other words, the human brain may be "prewired" to acquire critical thinking skills during adolescence just as it is "prewired" to acquire language during infancy and early childhood, but appropriate exposure to and practice with logic must occur for this acquisition to take place. If it does not, then critical thinking skills are unlikely to be evident during adulthood. The environment must supply necessary practice for critical thinking to develop just as, in a Piagetian sense, the environment must provide stimuli on which the organism acts to build mental structures or, in a Chomskian sense, the infant must hear spoken language to intuit the rules of grammar.

Our current society fails to provide adolescents with opportunities to observe, learn, or practice logic in any systematic way. Neither schools nor parents are likely to teach these skills to adolescents. This lack is certainly related to the irrational acts of violence we see committed on a daily basis. Formally teaching logic and critical thinking skills, and engaging adolescents in activities that build meta-cognitive awareness—the ability to analyze one's thoughts, emotions, and impulses before acting—are important strategies for redirecting adolescent aggression into constructive channels.

Brief History of Teaching Critical Thinking

Teaching logic and critical thinking to adolescents, either explicitly or implicitly, has actually been a common practice for the last several centuries, which only seems to have disappeared recently. The ancient Greeks maintained that the means to explore the nature of reality was through rigorous deductive thought. Mathematics, to the Greeks, was considered the purest form of reason. Plato believed an understanding of mathematics was prerequisite to the study of philosophy, and Aristotle termed mathematics divine because it dealt with timeless and perfect realities. Even when the experimental approach began to yield returns through the work of Sir Francis Bacon and others like him, many philosophers remained intent on deciphering the world through deductive reasoning. Spinoza, in the seventeenth century, developed his work through Euclidian proofs. Leibnez believed that logic could best answer both metaphysical and moral questions and hoped to develop a new form of mathematical logic to replace ordinary thinking so that, when disagreements occurred in daily life, disputants could sit down together with pen in hand and say "Let us calculate...."

In ancient Greece, an ideal education was based on apprenticeship to a recognized teacher-philosopher—Plato or Socrates, for example. Students were engaged in dialogues during which they were expected to apply information they had mastered to solve moral dilemmas and provide solutions for current problems. This process seemed to offer both instruction and practice of critical thinking.

Lewis (1981) noted that Plato and, later, Aristotle both emphasized the value of education. Both stressed the importance of "molding children through stories, music and gymnastics." Plato thought the study of mathematics was particularly important during adolescence to prepare the mind for abstract reasoning. Aristotle placed slightly less value on the study of mathematics during adolescence and more value on reading, writing, and drawing as tools to facilitate clear thinking. Because Roman education was based on the Greek model (Gibbon, 1960), similar practices were followed for educating Roman patricians.

From the fall of the Roman Empire until the Renaissance, Western educational practices were tied primarily to the Roman Catholic Church, and the majority of the populace was neither educated nor literate. In the late fifteenth century, clerics and government officials who had visited Italy and witnessed the intellectual movement flourishing there transported the influence of the Renaissance to England. This influence was responsible for the English humanists' view of education. It became the mission of prominent humanists such as Colet, Elyot, and Ascham to persuade the English gentry that their sons and daughters should study Latin and read the works of Terrence, Virgil, Horace, and Cicero. Studying the moral, philosophical, and political content provided therein was considered necessary to refine critical thinking skills (Abrams et al., 1974).

During the sixteenth century, education consisted of studying these classics and the Bible in a manner considered liberal yet practical. The curriculum was designed primarily to prepare elite citizens for duties in government and was presented by tutors who worked with small groups or with a single student at a time. Queen Elizabeth I, with her command of languages and her sense of diplomacy, is an example of the results of the educational system used for royalty in England during this time (Abrams et al., 1974).

Elizabethan education was based on the *quadrivium* (arithmetic, geometry, astronomy, and music) and the *trivium* (grammar, logic, and rhetoric). This seven-part curriculum survived as a model for the education of the upper classes in England and, later, in the United States for nearly four centuries. John Stuart Mill (1862), considered one of the most intelligent individuals in recent history, reported receiving an education based on the trivium and quadrivium during the nineteenth century. The curriculum was subsequently rearranged into "Arts & Letters" and "Mathematics & Sciences." It appears that what we now term "critical thinking skills" were incorporated primarily in the trivium, when the early form of the classical curriculum was used, and later divided between "Letters" and "Sciences," a division that, assuming critical thinking skills are taught at all in modern public schools, still exists today.

Early in this century, Alfred North Whitehead, Bertrand Russell, Rudolph Carnap, and other logical positivists took the view that laws of logic deal with relationships among statements; they are extremely valuable ways of handling information, but do not produce new knowledge or guarantee infallibility. Their work was based, in part, on Kant's view that pure reason can lead to contradictory conclusions.

Problems with the validity of deduction noted by these more recent philosophers, however, do not make it any less valuable a tool to human beings. As Lipmann pointed out earlier in this century, blind faith in irrational beliefs is not a better alternative. Processes of induction and deduction, which result in hypothetical-deductive reasoning, appear to be at the heart of critical thinking. If experience with these processes does not occur, it is unlikely that the capacity for critical thought will be acquired, either.

Our current society does not seem to offer many examples of hypothetical-deductive thought. Correspondingly, lack of critical thinking skills in American high school and college students is viewed as a problem by educators, businesses, and society at large (Arons, 1985; Barnes, 1992; Burns, 1983; Hartley, 1990). This suggests that experience with some of the fundamental processes requisite for critical thought are not being transmitted through education or socialization at present. The next section examines the role of American schools in teaching critical thinking during the last century.

Teaching Thinking Skills in Twentieth-Century U.S. Public Schools

During the twentieth century, the United States took on the complex task of attempting to educate *all* citizens born on her soil, along with numerous resident aliens and naturalized immigrants, in a public education system designed to allow everyone to acquire the skills needed to function in a republic. Whether this intent was ever purely in place is debatable. George Bernard Shaw's observation on English schools, as cited in Robinson (1921), may also be used to characterize the American system over the last century and even to the present day:

> We must teach citizenship and political science at school. But must we? There is no must about it, the hard fact being that we must NOT teach political science or citizenship at school. The schoolmaster who attempted it would soon find himself penniless in the streets without pupils, if not in the dock pleading to a pompously worded indictment for sedition against the exploiters. Our schools teach the morality of feudalism corrupted by commercialism and hold up the military conqueror, the robber baron and the profiteer as models of the illustrious and the successful. (p. 23)

As public education became accessible to more and more of the citizenry, however, the pupil population became increasingly heterogeneous. As the century progressed and the public school system grew to unwieldy proportions, teachers could no longer expect their students to arrive with common skills—or even with a common language. As American society became urbanized, more students were required to be in school and to stay in school longer. The overburdened educational system responded by "cutting corners." If industrialized American society required a high school diploma to access its port of entry, went the common scholastic reasoning, then it must be possible for every student to attain one; however, in some cases, that meant teaching less to more. The same logic was used in other countries with controversial results. In Brazil, for example, the number of years in school was reduced from 12 to 11. When changes like that are made, logic and rhetoric are generally among the first content areas to fall from standard high school curricula.

Other sociopolitical forces were also at work shaping the twentieth century curriculum—specifically, economic forces. An industrialized, compartmentalized, assembly line driven society (DeBerry, 1991, 1993) required citizens capable of following orders and completing rote tasks. Many public schools in the twentieth century began producing just such citizens. Whether through lobbying forces, funding, and the textbook industry, or incidentally, as a function of what G. Stanley Hall (1921) referred to as the "message of the zeitgeist," curricula became segmented and compartmentalized. Students memorized "facts" in English, which had little to do with "facts" memorized in science, which had little to do with "facts" memorized in social studies. A diploma ensured that these compartmentalized facts had been, at least temporarily, encoded in memory and, more important, implied that the unwritten curriculum—one of being to school on time, following directions and not questioning authority—had been mastered. Although a few schools, mostly private, still followed a classical curriculum for educating the children of the elite who would run the factories and the nation, public schools were, for the most part, engaged in the enterprise of producing workers, with no emphasis on critical thinking skills. Robinson (1921) noted this trend with concern, predicting that critical thinking would soon be abolished in public education:

> Businessmen, whether conspicuous in manufacture, trade or finance, are the leading figures of our age. They exercise a dominant influence in domestic and foreign policy, subsidize our education and exert unmistakable control over it. In other ages, a military or a religious caste enjoyed a similar pre-eminence.... In any case, economic issues are the chief and bitterest of our time. It is in connection with them that critical, free thinking is most difficult and apt to be misunderstood, for they easily become confused with the traditional reverences and sanctities of political fidelity, patriotism, morality and religion.... Once I feared that, given our current educational system, men might think too much. Now, I only dread lest they will think too little and far too timidly, for I now see that real thinking is difficult and that it needs every incentive in the face of discouragement and impediments.... Every youngster in school might be given some notion that neither private property nor capital is the real issue, but rather the new problem of supplying other than the traditional motives for industrial enterprise—namely, the slave-like docility and hard compulsion of the great masses of workers on the one

hand and speculative profits on the other which now dominate in our present business system. This existing organization is not only becoming more and more patently wasteful, heartless and unjust, but is beginning, for various reasons, to break down. (pp. 161–211)

Robinson's observations on both the assembly-line mentality of schools and the eventual breakdown of the industrial system from early in the century foreshadowed not only the changes in our public education system as the century progressed but also McCarthyism, the cold war, and the current global economy, which is resulting in massive restructuring for many multimillion-dollar corporations. As Robinson predicted, the former organization of these corporations has now "broken down due to waste" (Boroughs, 1990; Marshall, Yorks, & Pitera, 1993). The long suppression and recent reemergence of teaching critical thinking skills in public schools are, ironically, intricately interwoven with these economically driven, sociopolitical forces.

The era of McCarthyism—during the early 1950s—at the height of our society's rejection of all systems except capitalism probably also represented the height of suppression of critical thinking in public school curricula. Other than in hodge-podge fashion through isolated bits of instruction in science or literature, students were not encouraged to think. They were instead trained to internalize the values of current society and prepared to assume their roles in the post–World War II workforce. Then came Sputnik. Perhaps traceable to modifications in the Russian educational system made by Peter the Great which maintained vestiges of classical education including logic and rhetoric in the U.S.S.R. (Troyat, 1987), Russia's aerospace technology surpassed that of other nations. Neither business nor government interests in the United States were pleased. The nation needed to prepare to meet the future, and one means of preparation was by educating able students to, once more, become thinkers and inventors rather than assembly-line automatons. Thus began an increased focus on gifted education which serendipitously returned instruction in logic and critical thinking in various forms to the curriculum.

The "gifted education" movement, conceived in this country when Leta Hollingworth (Silverman, 1989) argued for special programs for bright students and born when Lewis Terman received a generous grant from the Commonwealth Fund of New York for the purpose of finding 1,000 subjects with IQs above 140, had been cyclic, sparing, and sporadic before the launch of the Russian satellite. The oldest continuing gifted education program in the United States originated in Cleveland in 1921, where pupils with high test scores devoted part of their school day to special curricula and methods that encouraged critical thinking. New York, the state that funded Terman's first grant, also has offered a variety of separate classes and schools for exceptionally bright children since the 1920s, most notably the experimental programs at Public School 500, where Leta Hollingworth developed the curricula. Selective magnet high schools for students with artistic or scientific talent have also existed in New York City since the 1920s, but such programs were rare in the rest of the United States for the first half of the twentieth century.

After Sputnik, however, support for gifted and talented (GT) education peaked. Legislatures and local school boards in the late 1950s moved hastily to improve education, especially for prospective scientists and engineers. Supporting federal legislation carried the title: "National Defense Education Act" (Laycock, 1979). Educational changes were encouraged and grants were provided for that purpose. Magnet schools for students deemed capable of exceptional achievements flourished. Science was emphasized in curriculums across the country. Special programs aimed at educating "rocket scientists of the future" were instituted. Critical thinking again had a place in our public schools—but only in GT programs.

Gifted education has been available in most public school districts since the 1960s. The Office of the Gifted and Talented, responsible for authorizing expenditures for model school programs, teacher training, research, and dissemination of information regarding the gifted was established by U.S. Commissioner of Education Sidney Marland in 1972. Federal expenditures on gifted education programs rose from about $300,000 that year to $2.6 million in 1977 (Laycock, 1979), and that level has since been maintained proportionally, adjusted by cost of living. Lobbying and legislation have resulted in continued support for gifted education programs for the last several decades.

Until the recent movement to teach critical thinking explicitly, spurred by economic concerns (Paul, 1992), GT programs were the only area of public school curriculum where a semblance of critical thinking skills were consistently taught. Much of this occurred almost serendipitously, as GT instructors were increasingly discouraged from covering information taught in "regular" subjects and sought materials with content that was not covered by other instructors. The "regular" public school curricula was segmented, departmentalized, watered down, and, as the report "A Nation At Risk" pointed out in the early 1980s, largely ineffectual and incapable of competing with the educational systems of other industrialized nations. Critical thinking instruction was seldom included anywhere, as evidenced by the fact that GT teachers could include the topic in some form without any other content area teachers becoming "territorial" over that particular domain of knowledge. It is possible that even the sporadic inclusion of logic and activities that focused on hypothetical deductive reasoning served to support and enhance the thinking skills of students in these programs, maintaining or enhancing their high scores on ability tests. This suggests that instruction in logical reasoning may result in increased performance on ability tests. Logic is certainly a key element of critical thinking, but it is not all of it.

Defining Critical Thinking

Critical thinking is a complex task, and so it seems to require a fairly complex definition. Critical thinking is composed of six abilities, attitudes, and affects. These are knowledge transfer, logical analysis, orientation, persistence, open-mindedness, and objectivity. Knowledge transfer is the ability to relate new information to what is already known. Analysis is the ability to make use of logic to compare, contrast, inspect, or establish propositions, which then promote speculation about probable relationships and new possibilities. Orientation is basically minimizing cognitive effort by distinguishing between trivial and critical data. Persistence is a willingness to maintain effort over time in searching for solutions. It requires self-regulation and the ability to delay gratification. Open-mindedness is being able to tolerate ambiguity and consider unconventional possibilities. In this sense, it also has a dimension of willingness to take risks. Objectivity is defined, in a long-range context, as the ability to decide dispassionately and deliberately which alternatives are most likely to effect a desirable cultural change over time.

If one conceives of critical thinking as a social activity, which our definition implies that it is, this suggests that a social-cognitive model is required to show how thinking skills develop. Many social-cognitive theorists lean toward a view in which cognition expressed in social forms is internalized as individual thought. Others favor a more Piagetian view of parallel but coordinated development on physical, individual, and social planes (Piaget, 1950). Environmental, social, and educational influences interact in complex ways with developmental change, so the study of this process is difficult. Researchers in human development are increasingly coming to agree that it requires methodology that allows the process of change to be observed over time.

Whether thinking skills can be taught explicitly or must be constructed implicitly by learners themselves through their own activities is unresolved (Damon, 1990), but it appears that, in a successful learning context, knowledge about what the learners themselves contribute to the process must be attended to. Cognitive developmental level must be considered, as must the broader social milieu in which the learners exist (Freire & Macedo, 1987; Okagaki & Sternberg, 1990).

An action oriented, social-relational approach to teaching critical thinking, which accounts for both cognitive developmental level and familial-cultural background, is thus suggested as most effective by theory and research in developmental psychology (Damon, 1990). This message may be thoroughly embedded in old pedagogical theories, as well as in several more current approaches to teaching critical thinking, but it is not a message that appears, as of yet, to have had much influence on traditional schooling.

The core assumption of a developmental social-relational approach is that children and adolescents bring away from their social interactions a number of "cognitive structures" acquired through observation, modeling, physical interaction with the environment, and discourse with others. While communicating with others, children learn necessary skills for survival, as well as values and basic mental processes. These basic mental processes range from acquisition of language to processes such as justification, questioning, invention, and logic itself.

This "world knowledge" acquired through social relations and observations builds the structures to which later acquired, "formal knowledge" connects. References to these processes have been explicated in Vygotskian theory (Wertsch, 1987). They have appeared in the writings of developmentalists for generations (Werner & Kaplan, 1963; Piaget, 1950).

Corollary to this social-relational assumption, but rarely explored, is the notion that social interactions are linked to the nature of the cognitive products arising from those interactions. In other words, not only do social relations create the context for cognitive growth, but they also determine the nature of the cognitive growth that ensues. For example, developmental studies with young children have shown that not much learning occurs unless the mother not only shares task responsibility with the child but also guides the child to some type of cognitive understanding and generalization beyond the actual task that mother and child are working on (Gauvin & Rogaff, 1989; Gauvin,

1989). This suggests that similar practices in our schools would most likely result in enhanced learning and critical thinking and may also encourage transfer of thinking skills across domains.

Just as young children acquire the language, or languages, to which they are exposed early in life, they may acquire the types of thinking to which they are exposed during childhood and adolescence. These would include skills in planning, verification, justification, explanation, evaluation, criticism, and formal logic. These skills then become essential components of critical thinking. It could be argued that, as logic and critical thinking have exited from the curriculum, children and adolescents are no longer exposed to these skills. Their parents and teachers have not been instructed in these skills during their own education and, hence, are unable to model them. Heroes and heroines in young adult literature do not model critical thinking skills (Harrison, 1984; DeHart & Bleaker, 1988). Models of critical thought are not to be found on television or in the media at large. Thus, unless students are fortunate enough to be placed in a GT program where instruction in critical thinking and formal logic remained, no social-cognitive basis for attaining these skills is available.

Just as one would not expect a child who grows up in an environment without language to learn to speak, it is unreasonable to expect a child who grows up in an environment bereft of logic and lacking examples of critical thinking to be able to reason well. The mind may be "wired" to learn to reason, just as it is "wired" to acquire language. There may, in fact, even be a "critical window" when this acquisition of reasoning skill most easily occurs. We may have two types of "LADs"—a language acquisition device from birth to middle childhood and a logic acquisition device from middle childhood through adolescence. If no exposure to logic occurs during this time, mastery of critical reasoning may not be acquired.

It appears that theory and research in developmental psychology offer a wealth of information to apply to teaching critical thinking, concerning both when and how such instruction is likely to be most effective. Elementary teachers should model behaviors for their students that include planning, categorizing, verifying, and evaluating. They should not, however, expect students to be able to immediately put such skills into practice, any more than a parent would expect an infant to engage in an extended conversation after listening to adults speaking to each other. The modeling is necessary but is part of a process that is not likely to be visible in products for a few years. In the case of language, extended conversations are not likely to occur until later in childhood. In the case of critical thinking skills, products are not likely to be visible until later in adolescence.

High school teachers should extend the base of information acquired from social interactions during elementary school by providing instruction in formal logic and rhetoric just as early childhood educators improve conversation skills through practice with language and vocabulary. By adolescence, students who have observed reasoning skills for several years through social interactions and observations should be capable of applying these skills to problem solving. Do these recommendations from developmental psychology appear to be followed in the present curriculum? A review of programs currently used to teach critical thinking suggests this is not the case.

"Direct attempts in our schools to produce a more intelligently critical and open-minded generation are likely to be far less feasible than indirect ones," Robinson (1921) wrote. This seems to have proved true. A thorough search of programs used in American public schools to enhance critical thinking has shown these programs to be indirect, at best. According to the curriculum director for a large southwestern high school district (Hathurn, 1993) and substantiated by the author's experiences teaching public school in two states, they are diffused with no particular order, rhyme, or reason throughout various content areas.

As noted earlier, when the trivium and quadrivium were split into "Arts & Letters" and "Mathematics & Sciences," critical thinking instruction seemed to be split, as well. More than 100 different programs for teaching critical thinking, other than those aimed specifically at gifted and talented groups, are currently published. Roughly half of these programs are divided between language arts and social studies, with slightly more in language arts. The remainder, with a few exceptions, is divided between mathematics and natural science. Programs from each of these areas, selected on the basis of extensiveness of use and research available on effectiveness, are described next to provide a sense of what is currently used to teach critical thinking in our schools and to offer ideas for use in local schools and programs.

Critical Thinking Programs in Language Arts and Social Studies

Aristotle stressed the importance of reading and writing to develop critical thinking skills. Later, Thorndike (1917) stressed the link between reading and reasoning. Thus, including thinking skills instruction in language arts classes does have some historical precedence. More recently, Brown and Campione (1990) cited reading to be the domain in which thinking skills figure most prominently.

Many English teachers seek to follow the suggestions of Aristotle by teaching logic, reasoning, and critical thinking through essay assignments and classroom discussions of literature. The insistent cry from those in higher education that students are coming to college less able to write and think critically than ever before (Arons, 1985; Hirshberg, 1992; Heyman & Daly, 1992; Paul, 1992) suggests that something is missing in this approach. Despite this, many of the better-known programs to teach critical thinking skills are designed for use in the content areas of language arts and English.

Lipman, Sharp, and Oscanyan (1980), of the Institute for the Advancement of Philosophy, developed a program called "Philosophy for Children." Plato and Aristotle might consider introducing this subject to elementary school age children developmentally inappropriate. Both believed the study of philosophy to be pointless before the age of 50 years, when adequate knowledge structures had presumably been developed to deal with issues wrestled with by the discipline. Lipman's program, however, does involve one of the key instructional methods used by both Plato and Aristotle—the Socratic dialogue. The program is based on what Lipman calls "social inquiry" (Lipman & Sharp, 1980) and consists of assigning a story to be read by students in which the major character must make a critical choice, then discussing ways in which the character reached a decision. Although marketed as an original approach based in the discipline of philosophy, similar practices are used by teachers from early elementary school through college to enhance reading comprehension and thinking skills. Such strategies are taught to preservice teachers in English, reading, and language arts methods courses.

Many junior high and high school English instructors engage in the practice of discussing the motivations for decisions made by fictional characters through the genre of "young adult (YA) literature," which includes stories such as "The Outsiders." This strategy engages students in dialogue about social issues. Harrison (1984) and DeHart and Bleaker (1988), however, found that this practice often may fail to enhance students' thinking, because YA literature offers few, if any, characters who truly model critical thought processes and logical reasoning skills. Lipman's program addresses this lack by providing stories specifically written to include protagonists who *do* think critically. No systematic studies of the program have documented its success at developing critical thinking skills, however.

Okagaki and Sternberg (1993) illustrates major problems with "Philosophy for Children," and with the general approach used by many language arts teachers who use literary discussion to encourage critical thinking, as well. First, although modeling and identification are psychological principles on which the technique is based, a limited number of students will actually be able to identify with the characters in any particular story assigned for a variety of reasons, including background experiences, gender, socioeconomic status, and ethnicity. Second, the technique is not developmentally sound for use with preadolescents.

Lipman's program is designed for use in middle schools, although research suggests that few students in grades five through eight are capable of formal operations in a Piagetian sense. Some teachers may not even be capable of such thought processes (Jones & Norman, 1989). Yet, the skills Lipman's program is built on nearly all require formal operational logic. Here is a partial listing of the 30 skills he suggests that the program is designed to establish: (1) generalizing, (2) formulating cause-effect relationships, (3) drawing syllogistic inferences, (4) understanding consistency versus contradiction, (5) identifying underlying assumptions, (6) grasping part-whole connections, (7) working with analogies, (8) formulating problems, (9) comprehending nonreversibility of "All" statements, and (10) comprehending reversibility of "No" statements.

It is not reasonable to expect children operating at a concrete level of thought to master these skills (Otto, 1986). Thus, although the strategy of using literature to teach critical thinking offers the advantage of modeling social interactions that can build the foundations for critical thought processes, Lipman's program does not seem compatible with what we know of learning from a developmental perspective. Similar, commonly used methods in high school language arts may be more appropriate from a developmental perspective but fail to offer critically reasoning models with which students can identify. Thus, Lipman's program and the general approach of teaching critical thinking skills through literature are both problematic from a psychological perspective.

Another attempt to teach critical thinking through language arts is Chicago Mastery Learning (Jones, 1982). The Chicago Mastery Learning program is designed for use in grades five through eight. It is divided into four levels that contain units on sentence context, mood in reading and writing, organizing complex information, comparisons, character analysis, separating fact from opinion, and study skills. The program is based on the belief that almost all students can learn what only the best students currently learn, provided sufficient time and a variety of instructional tools are provided. This program has been shown to improve student skills in reading comprehension (Fenson & Fenson, 1992), although the extent to which improved reading comprehension generalizes to critical thinking skills has not been established.

Peer tutoring, grouping, formative and evaluative testing, reteaching, and enrichment are all components built into Chicago Mastery Learning. The peer-tutoring and cooperative learning components of the program may enhance critical thinking. Many current researchers in the area of critical thinking support these methods as effective means to build thinking skills (Brown & Campione, 1990; Damon, 1990; Paul, 1992). Beyond this, however, the Chicago program seems to train students in a very limited domain—that is, reading comprehension, and verbal skills. Unless research establishes, as Aristotle seemed to believe, that these skills generalize to critical thinking in other areas, the program may be viewed as effective in language arts, but questionable for establishing thinking skills in a broader sense.

Another thinking skills program that has received attention in both practice and research is Feuerstein's (1980) Instrumental Enrichment. Several levels of the program are available for students of varying abilities, from late elementary through early high school. This program, generally used in language arts, social studies, or special education classes, emphasizes what is referred to as meta-componential and performance-componential functioning. Instrumental Enrichment is designed to address and correct deficits that impair critical thinking through a series of units and tests that include orientation to dots and figures, categorization, temporal relations, numerical progressions, stencil designs, comparison of pictures, and following directions. Feuerstein's list of thinking deficits, which these activities supposedly correct, includes (1) unplanned, impulsive, and unsystematic exploratory behavior; (2) lack of, or impaired, capacity for considering two sources of information at once, reflected in dealing with data in a piecemeal fashion rather than as a unit of organized facts; (3) inadequacy in experiencing the existence of an actual problem and subsequently defining it; (4) lack of spontaneous comparative behavior or limitation of its appearance to a restricted field of need; (5) lack of, or impaired, strategies for hypothesis testing; (6) lack of orientation toward the need for logical evidence; (7) lack of, or impaired, planning behavior; and (8) an episodic grasp of reality. Feuerstein (1980) seeks to correct these deficits through his activities and tests, while at the same time increasing each student's intrinsic motivation and feeling of self-worth. His is one of the most widely studied programs, and there is evidence that its use tends to significantly raise student scores on measures of ability. This is most likely because most of the training exercises contain items similar or identical to those found on intelligence and aptitude tests. Thus, it is not surprising that intensive practice on such items should raise test scores.

The isolation of Feuerstein's problems from any working knowledge base or academic discipline raises questions concerning the transferability of skills to academic and real-world intellectual tasks. Transfer of knowledge is an important psychological consideration that must be addressed in instruction. Instrumental Enrichment seems to train primarily those abilities tapped by IQ tests rather than a broader spectrum of abilities and adaptabilities that go beyond what tests measure as intelligence.

Writing assignments, discussions, and debates focused on current events are viewed as important means of enhancing critical thinking skills in language arts and social studies classes (Bender & Leone, 1988; Fleming, 1982; Karolides, 1987; O'Banion, 1989; Oliver, 1985; Parker, 1989; Rosenbaum-Cale, 1992; Spicer, 1991; Stahl, 1988). If logical reasoning and critical thinking skills are not established before engaging in these activities, however, students are unlikely to succeed at these assignments. Further, no clear evidence exists to establish that such assignments enhance thinking skills. It may be more appropriate to instruct students in the components of logic and critical thinking before assigning tasks such as these, rather than making assignments that are impossible to complete accurately considering the lack of a critical knowledge base in most students and then bewailing the lack of reasoning skill students display (O'Banion, 1989; Oliver, 1985). To refer to the earlier metaphor of language acquisition, one would not expect a child who had grown up in an environment without any exposure to spoken language to adequately complete a vocabulary assignment on the first attempt.

Another strategy that has been used gives adolescents the task of writing a personality profile of a particular adult whom the students have interviewed or heard speak. This adult may be a community member who attended the same school as the student, a person currently working in a field of interest to the student, or an older adult from a local geriatric center (Beyersdorfer & Schauer, 1992;

Hamilton, 1990; Tjas, Nelsen, & Taylor, 1993). Although systematic research to determine whether such assignments enhance critical thinking has not yet been conducted, based on principles of identification, modeling, and transfer of knowledge, such methods may be fertile avenues for future exploration.

Although the preceding review is by no means an exhaustive summary of all critical thinking programs available for use in language arts and social studies, these programs are representative of the approaches currently used to enhance student thinking skills. One element from the classic trivium that seems to be missing in all of these programs (except, perhaps, Lipman's, where it is inappropriately introduced to children who are not developmentally ready to grasp it) is instruction in formal logic. Rhetoric has survived in the form of the discussion, reading, and writing assignments summarized previously, but without the foundation of logic on which it was traditionally based. Without this base, it may be of little value for enhancing critical thinking. One may discuss feelings and opinions exhaustively, but, without logic as a basis for such discussions, no reasonable means of evaluation exists. Mass opinion and consensus are likely to replace more solid foundations for decision making. Morris (1984) came to this conclusion when reviewing social studies and economics texts in Great Britain. He suggested that inclusion of logical reasoning instruction in the classroom would improve student performance.

Critical Thinking in Natural Sciences and Mathematics

Plato's strategy for developing abstract reasoning skills in adolescents involved instruction in mathematics. This philosophy may still be the underlying premise on which high school algebra requirements in our public schools are based. A number of programs to improve critical thinking skills in adolescents have been directed toward science and mathematics curricula.

A substantial body of research (Bitner, 1989, 1990; Blosser & Helgeson, 1984; Galotti & Komatsu, 1989) has established that skills in spatial reasoning ability, problem-solving skills, proportional reasoning, and probabilistic reasoning are highly correlated to student achievement in science and mathematics. Underlying these abilities is the Piagetian concept of formal operational reasoning, typically not available to students until at least adolescence and sometimes not available in all content areas, dependent on student knowledge structures, even then (Arons, 1984; Bitner, 1989, 1990; Blosser & Helgeson, 1984; Keating, 1988).

Programs aimed at enhancing thinking skills in science and mathematics are typically more compatible with developmental and other psychological theories than those designed for use in language arts and social studies. Science and mathematics programs are also more frequently studied systematically to assess results. Perhaps this is because educators in these areas are more familiar with the scientific method and more likely to read and apply research to curriculum development than educators in other content areas.

Methods courses in math and science also frequently include units on logical reasoning (Jones & Norman, 1989; Piburn & Baker, 1988). Regardless of causes, a survey of programs designed to teach critical thinking skills in science and math revealed that most do account for student developmental level. Most also tend to focus on enhancing specific requisite skills to scientific, visual-spatial, or mathematical reasoning. One example is Peterson's (1986) model to teach proportional reasoning to adolescents, which addresses both definitional and developmental concerns, and then proposes a hierarchy of several skills and mental processes required for proportional reasoning before presenting a series of science activities designed to teach and reinforce each of these skills.

Narode, Heiman, Lochhead, and Slomianko (1992) suggested several strategies for use in science and mathematics classes to enhance visual-spatial reasoning, including concept mapping and Venn diagrams. Arons (1982) successfully used these strategies to enhance visual-spatial reasoning in an introductory physics course. Linn (1989) found that combining content area instruction in human biology with instruction in logical reasoning, including syllogistic reasoning and Venn diagrams had a positive effect on student mastery of concepts. Crow and Haws (1985) had similar results in a geology course. Instruction in logic combined with content-area instruction enhanced student achievement in both critical thinking and mastery of geology. These studies provide support for the need to include instruction in formal logic in coursework for adolescents and young adults to refine thought processes and facilitate mastery of concepts and information.

In mathematics, units to improve visual-spatial reasoning are common, as are approaches to develop problem-solving skills based on solving mathematics word problems. Instruction in formal logic is also sometimes used (Miller, 1986; Heiman, Narode, Slomianko, & Lochhead, 1992). Logical reasoning ability has been found to have a high correlation with achievement in statistics (Harvey, 1985), matrix algebra and graphing, computer programming (Foreman, 1988), and geometry (Massachusetts, State Department of Education, 1987).

Others have carefully documented and researched a series of underlying logical reasoning hierarchies required in mathematics and established that mastery of these logical skills seems to be developmentally tied, in a Piagetian sense. Thus, most current elementary mathematics programs, such as "Math Their Way" and other hands-on math approaches, are based on developmental theory. Many secondary programs seek to incorporate instruction in logical reasoning to some extent (Baxandall, 1978; Michigan State Board of Education, 1988; Cook, 1989). Plato's assertion that adolescence is the appropriate time to focus on more abstract forms of mathematics and logic seems to be supported by this body of research.

Strategies used to teach logic in math and science include, but are not limited to, use of Euhler and Venn diagrams, practice with verbal and visual analogies, diagrammatic representation of information presented in word problems, and practice with the scientific method. Such activities can be found in most secondary math and science texts. They are typically included during preservice teacher instruction in math and science methods classes and are apparent in numerous supplementary materials published for math and science instruction (Seymour, 1992). A good source of examples of activities similar to those commonly used can be found in Baron and Sternberg (1990) and Sternberg (1985).

Two common problems in logic instruction in the areas of math and science are that (1) teachers focus on relating the skills presented only to their own subjects, thus limiting transfer of knowledge to other areas by students who do not make such connections independently; and (2) instruction in logic is inconsistently used from teacher to teacher, school to school, and district to district. Although logic is commonly included to some degree in district math and science curriculums, it is not consistently presented and few means are available to systematically introduce, teach, and practice logical reasoning skills from year to year (Miller, 1993). Consequently, because the instruction is content-tied and sporadic, students may have difficulty transferring it to daily life. It may be viewed as an isolated "fact" of science or mathematics rather than a strategy useful in daily life.

Teaching logical reasoning skills in conjunction with course content seems to be the preferred method and is supported by the research noted previously (Leary, 1993). Availability of materials to teach logic at the high school level is limited. Most effective units studied have been developed by teachers for use specifically in their own classrooms. Teachers, even those who are trained to do so, may not have sufficient time to develop units in logic to accompany their teaching, so finding a means to include logic in the curriculum is a current concern for public school curriculum developers and teacher trainers (Hathurn, 1993; Leyba, 1993; Spratlen-Mitchell, 1993).

Also, because of the "watering down of the curriculum" described earlier, instruction in logic is often seen as a "frill" for which there is no time while instructors are forced to encourage students to memorize "facts and formulas" for assorted district, state, and national assessments in their content areas. Thus, although the programs that do exist to teach critical thinking in science and mathematics tend to be consistent with psychological principles, such programs are unlikely to transfer to critical thinking skills in other areas.

Many university courses and curricula involve practice with critical thinking skills. Perhaps this partially explains why research indicates that increasing years of formal education is the best predictor of formal operational thought; however, not everyone goes to college, or even finishes high school. It is too late to start the task of developing critical thinking skills at the university level. Critical thinking skills have to be developed from early childhood and the schools should play a major role in this development. Schools should try to establish a contextualized logic curriculum, aimed at adolescents who would profit very much from such an experience. We do not mean to imply that there is an age after which you cannot learn to reason critically. In fact, we all learn and develop critical thinking skills throughout life, but many of the skills, abilities, and affects we have discussed here need to first be developed throughout childhood and adolescence. Logic seems to be especially appropriate to teach during adolescence, from a developmental perspective.

Instruction in Logic and Critical Thinking

Logic instruction is not absent in the high school curricula of most countries. In mathematics, classes on language, etymology, speaking skills, grammar, literature, science, and philosophy, elements of logic are inherent. Two common problems with current logic instruction, however, are that (1) teachers focus on relating the skills presented only to their own subjects, thus limiting transfer of knowledge to other areas by students who do not make such connections independently; and (2) instruction in logic is inconsistently used from teacher to teacher, school to school, and district to district. Although logic is commonly included to some degree in district curriculums, it is not consistently presented and few means are available to systematically introduce, teach, and practice logical reasoning skills from year to year. Consequently, because instruction is content-tied and sporadic, students may have difficulty transferring it to daily life. It may be viewed as an isolated "fact" rather than a strategy useful in daily life. Thus, finding a means to include logic in the curriculum is a current concern for public school curriculum developers and teacher trainers (Hathurn, 1993). Although many high schools offer instruction in meta-cognition and logic in some form such as elective courses in psychology, philosophy, semantics, and formal logic, these courses are typically only available to high-achieving students (McCarthy, 1999). Logic is no longer included in the standard high school curriculum in any systematic way for other students, so those most likely to need instruction are least likely to receive it. If practice with logic during early adolescence improves thinking skills, this lack of instruction in logic may, at least in part, be responsible for the current lack of critical thinking skills in society, which, in turn, is related to a lack of impulse control and aggressive acts. Formal operational thought may be possible in one domain but not another, as a result of the types of experiences, modeling, and activities to which students have been introduced. With proper direction and instruction, nearly all students are capable of appropriately transferring information from one area to another. Physical, social, and cognitive development seems to be sufficiently canalized by the environment for us to assume that we can effectively teach thinking skills. Intelligence, as suggested by Sternberg (1985), may indeed be far more malleable than psychology has traditionally assumed. It may be tied to thinking skills that are teachable and refinable throughout the life span. Developmental theory and research suggest, however, that certain periods of the life span may be more appropriate than others for teaching these skills and that certain approaches may be more beneficial than others. Adolescence certainly seems to be the critical period for teaching logic and critical thinking. Failure to do so has many consequences—one of which, in the current social milieu, is irrational acts of aggression.

Practice with logic needs to occur during adolescence, in a way that is compatible with the manner in which the brain processes information, for critical thinking skills to develop. Connecting logical reasoning to daily decision making is possible only when the fundamental bases of logical reasoning are first understood. Skill in logical analyses can best be established by providing systematic practice comparing, contrasting, and inspecting information to establish concepts, propositions, and syllogisms. This, in turn, promotes speculation about probable relationships and identification of new possibilities, which leads to critical thinking. If this is the case, including instruction in logic during the educational process should increase the probability that formal operational thought will be attained and critical thinking skills will be used.

In a study conducted with high school students in an inner city, high-risk neighborhood, this approach was demonstrated to be effective (McCarthy, 1995). Students who were instructed for one semester using a curriculum that included logic and reasoning skills not only performed better on standardized tests but also reported more confidence in graduating from high school and attending college.

Reintroducing logic into the curriculum during the first two years of high school may improve thinking skills. Improved thinking skills should lead to a greater likelihood of acquiring formal operational thought and also generalize to improved performance on standardized ability tests. This enhanced competence should, in turn, lead to increased self-perceptions concerning cognitive and academic achievement. Increased perceptions of ability may improve motivation, make students less likely to drop out of high school, and increase the likelihood that they will reach long- and short-term career goals and become valuable, contributing members of society.

Some researchers (Martin, 1983a, 1983b) suggest that the best way to improve critical thinking skills among students is to train teachers in formal logic and thinking skills so that they are able to impart these skills to students in whatever area they teach. This seems compatible with the suggestion that students be exposed to logical reasoning throughout their schooling, in all subject areas, so that they are able to internalize the thinking strategies involved.

Modeling is a powerful tool for teaching. Just as infants must hear language used constantly before they begin to speak, children may need to watch logical reasoning skills being applied continuously before they are able to think critically. Ensuring that all teachers understand, apply, and consistently model logical reasoning skills in their classes may be an appropriate means of assisting students to learn critical thinking skills. Another option is to establish a national requirement for a course that includes formal logic in public high schools. Although most high schools currently have an overload of required and recommended courses, the following comment from a freshman completing a unit on logic and cognition as part of a pilot study conducted at an inner city school offers a suggestion. After a discussion of knowledge structures, intensional and extensional features, and the hierarchical nature of information stored in memory, the student commented: "Is that true? Do people really think like that? Wow, I know I do—and since I know that, I think better than most of my friends 'cuz I can check to make sure things in my head are in the right place. That's psychology, man!"

Perhaps the most efficient place to include formal logic in the high school curriculum would be in a required psychology course at the freshman level that covered meta-cognition, life skills, career exploration, parenting skills, and human development, as well as units on the various components of formal logic as part of a "thinking skills" unit. Lessons on categorization; hierarchical organization; intensional and extensional meanings; propositional logic; Venn diagramming; hypothesis testing; and inductive, deductive, and analogical reasoning could be presented in the context of how the human brain organizes information. Transferring this knowledge to other classes and activities would thus be encouraged; logic would be viewed as a thinking skill we use consistently in all areas of our lives, rather than in just math or science. Such a reintroduction of logic into the high school curriculum would be efficient not only from the standpoint of knowledge transfer, as noted previously, but in other ways, as well. The required psychology class could meet one of the social studies requirements most high schools have. Psychology instructors, provided they are certified in the discipline and have had sufficient training, will already be familiar with formal reasoning and the scientific method, so required in-servicing would be minimal. Many of the current materials aimed at teaching critical thinking in logic courses were written by psychologists, so psychology instructors will be familiar with the perspectives presented and the terminology used.

Experience with some of the fundamental processes requisite for critical thought are not being transmitted through education or socialization at present. Reintroducing logic, one of the requisite skills for critical thought, into the curriculum during the first two years of high school when students are developmentally tuned to efficiently process the information may improve thinking skills (McCarthy, 1998). Improved thinking skills should, in turn, lead to a greater likelihood of acquiring formal operational thought and also generalize to an awareness of the probable consequences of one's actions—an important part of the meta-cognitive awareness that helps to develop impulse control and curb aggressive behavior.

CHAPTER 12

STREET KIDS, ANTISOCIAL BEHAVIOR, AND ADOLESCENT AGGRESSION

Some of the material in this chapter originally appeared in the Journal of Offender Rehabilitation *in an article by Sherri McCarthy and Tom Waters. Other information was presented at the International Congress of Psychology in Beijing in 2004, and at the International Council of Psychologists Convention in Toronto in 2003. Dr. Natalia Parnyuk, Dr. Valerie Sitnikov, and Dr. Tom Waters are acknowledged for their contributions.*

There are no reliable estimates of the number of street children in developing countries, especially in Brazil. The United Nations Infancy Fund estimated the number of street children in developing countries at around 30 million (UNICEF, 1991, 1993). There are reports, however, that in Latin America alone there may be up to 40 million street children (Aptekar, 1988a; Cosgrove, 1990). Some researchers state that there are between 7 and 10 million street children in Brazil (Barker & Knaul, 1991; Maciel, Schmidt, Santoro, Azevedo, & Guerra, 1991), but these numbers are probably very inflated (Forster, Barros, Tannhauser, & Tannhauser, 1992) and do not represent the real situation (Hutz & Koller, 1999). A few years ago a headcount in São Paulo, the largest Brazilian city with a population of more than 12 million, reported 4,520 street children (Rosemberg, 1994). Although numbers in the United States are lower, they are increasing.

The definition of who is a street child is a source of confusion that may account for some of the discrepancies regarding the estimates of their numbers (Hutz, Koller, Ruschel, & Forster, 1995). In most large cities in developing countries, there are many children and adolescents on the streets who look like drifters who ran away from home or who were abandoned by their families. Usually they wear shabby, dirty clothing and they seem to spend most of their time begging, performing menial chores, or just wandering, apparently without a purpose. Although these children look similar to each other, they belong to different groups; they have different characteristics, life histories, and prognoses (Hutz & Koller, 1999; Koller & Hutz, 2001).

Attempts to classify street children raise important methodological and epistemological problems and often are not very useful. Nevertheless, we have found some significant differences between two specific groups of street children that researchers in the field usually call *children of the streets* and *children in the streets.* Although this classification is problematic because children often move from one group to the other, and the within-group variability is very large, some differences between these groups seem to be stable (Hutz & Koller, 1999; Koller & Hutz, 2001).

Children of the streets do not have stable family links. They seldom see their parents and usually they do not go to school. They are children or adolescents who ran away or who were abandoned by their families and confined to the streets (Forster et al., 1992; Rosemberg, 1990). *Children in the streets,* despite the appearance of neglect and abandonment, live with their families, who may also be homeless. They spend most of the day on the streets, begging or working, trying to make some money for themselves and to help their families. These children go back home almost every evening. Occasionally they sleep on the streets, especially if they did not make enough money to bring back home. Some of them go to school, but many, usually coerced by the mother, have dropped out of school to have more time to work or to beg on the streets (Forster et al., 1992; Rosemberg, 1990; Koller & Hutz, 2001).

In a study 97 *children of the streets* (67 boys and 30 girls), between 9 and 17 years old (M = 12.3) in southern Brazil were interviewed. Family conflict was reported as the major reason to leave home. More than half the children said that they were in the streets because of constant fights at home, which frequently involved physical or sexual abuse by a parent or stepparent. Some left home because they could not stand the misery and the lack of food at home. About a fourth of the subjects said that they left home because life in the streets was much better than life at home.

Most subjects did some chores to earn money. Many of them sold fruits or flowers, polished shoes, cleaned, or "took care" of parked cars. Adolescents interviewed also said that sometimes they just wandered or played in the streets. More than a fourth of the subjects said that occasionally they would steal. The use of drugs (mostly inhalants) and prostitution were reported by several children. It is important to note that 11 percent of the children reported the use of drugs as an activity. In fact, almost all of them sniffed a mixture of ether, alcohol, and perfume.

How do these street children survive? Many often go to city, state, or religious institutions where they can have a meal, take a shower, sleep, or participate in recreational activities or in job skills training workshops. This emphasizes the need to maintain and develop social services for this group. Most of them actually do not sleep on the streets. About 50 percent of them said that they usually sleep in shelters, and 30 percent reported that occasionally they go to shelters. When they do not go to shelters, they sleep on the streets, and, sometimes, they may even go home to sleep. Only 20 percent of the children said that they always sleep on the streets. Some of these children are not accepted in the shelters anymore because of past aggressive behavior or drug use. A few children said they liked the streets better than the shelters.

Nearly 65 percent of the group reported occasional contact with the family. Of those, 44 percent said they had visited with a family member in the last week. Most of these children (75%) went to school for at least a short period and then dropped out, reflecting the difficulty of attending school when basic needs, such as food and shelter, are not met. These children are under pressure to go out to the streets and make as much money as possible. The parents, especially the mother, are often illiterate or, at best, have attended school for only one or two years. They do not perceive the school as important, and they do not think that their children can benefit from going. The children themselves do not see a link between going to school and having a better life in the future.

These findings about school attendance are similar to those of Forster et al. (1992). These researchers found that 10 percent of their subjects never went to school and that, among those who did attend, attendance was very brief. Only 2 percent reached the fifth or sixth grade. Most subjects (68%) went to school for about two years and dropped out without learning to read and write.

A large number of street children spend part of the day in institutions. Most of them go there for the food, but many end up participating voluntarily in workshops or in recreational activities. Those institutions could have an important role in sending street children back to school and in providing training for job skills that would allow them to enter the job market. We agree with Maciel et al. (1991) who stress the importance of developing specific projects to provide schooling for street children. Schools have an important role in the prevention of drug abuse and delinquent behavior, and can be helpful in providing a sense of stability that has been lost by this population.

It is unfortunate, however, that our public school curricula are so divorced from the reality faced by street children. The schools also demand behavior, language, respect for authority, and neatness, which are very discrepant from their experiences. Although the best solution to keep children off the streets and in the schools is to create jobs for the parents and to eradicate the abject misery in which millions of families live, much can be done to ameliorate the fate of the children. Community programs to reduce family violence, physical and sexual abuse, alcoholism, and drug use would be an effective means to stop the migration of children to the streets. We also need a new educational model to develop literacy and work skills, compatible with the expectations and limitations of this population.

Family violence and extreme poverty appear to be the main reasons for children to leave home and migrate to the streets. Once on the streets, they have limited options to survive. Many try to earn some money doing chores. There are not, however, many work opportunities for street children. Begging, stealing, and prostitution are often the only possibilities available.

Nearly a century ago, Russia faced similar problems with street children. Though these problems were nearly eliminated through social institutions and schooling in that country for part of the last century, they have now emerged as a problem once again. Social cataclysms of Russian society, the destruction of an established system of values within society, and rapid changes in personal and social relations have resulted in problems in adolescent socialization yet again. Dr. Valerie Sitnikov and Dr. Natalia Parnyuk describe the current situation like this:

A gross break of the system of ruling government accompanied by deformation of social priorities, ideals, and stereotypes brought tension, aggression, self-distrust, and distrust of others into the foreground. These changes have had a deep influence, especially on adolescents' behavior. Before the early 1990s, the main influences on adolescents' socialization in Russia were state systems through which a person was socialized. These organizations tried determinedly and not entirely fruitlessly to be the main influences on adolescents

This changed dramatically after the disintegration of the Soviet Union, after which there was destruction of the established government systems, including public organizations for children and youth. A major decrease of school funding and funding for daycare and social programs resulted in the rapid growth of street crime and increasing numbers of children on the street. Intrusive propaganda of private enterprise and individualism depreciated the value of intellectual labor and education. In short, Russian youth were thrust into the same media environment and macrosystem influences as their counterparts in the rest of the Western world at the same time as limited resources continued to wane.

During the 1990s in Russia, there was a negative change of the structure of macroenvironment and its influence on adolescents. A governmental-official system of ruling was penetrated by corruption and became indifferent to the fortunes of people. An abundance of dwarf political parties did not express the people's wishes and interests. A lack of actual youth organizations, on the one hand, and full deologisation of former values, empty inner development, lack of spirituality, and a venal SMC, on the other hand, have derogated the influence of the macroenvironment.

For the last 15 years there has been a harsh decrease in the quality of life and living conditions in many Russian families. This has contributed to increased family conflicts, leading to divorces and to adolescents' leaving their families. Street children are again an increasing population in Russia.

Research shows that the most serious life problem of modern Russian adolescents who find themselves living on the streets is their relations with parents. Regardless of interfamily conflicts that lead to leaving the family, these adolescents still remain attached. The most sincere and gentle words about their parents can be heard from children whose parents have been deprived of their rights for child abuse. The most cordial and full-of-hope words we've heard were in a colony for female delinquents. Among the 600 girls there, only 3 were from so-called "wealthy" families, illustrating the role that poverty plays in delinquency.

Unfortunately, since the 1990s, family violence, including violence toward children and women, has become a major problem in Russia. Research shows that Russian children are now one of the most unprotected categories of people of the world. As a result, they have often become victims of abuse, contempt, and exploitation.

In short, although evidence suggests that Russian street children maintain a strong attachment to abusive family members, many of them find themselves on the streets and the road to delinquency because of poverty, family violence, and sexual abuse.

The picture is not too different in large U.S. cities, where runaways and street children are more common than many of us would like to admit. Another factor in the United States—and perhaps in Brazil and Russia as well—that may increase the likelihood that adolescents will end up on the streets is maternal alcohol and substance abuse during pregnancy.

During the early 1980s, use of crack cocaine by expectant mothers introduced U.S. schools and social agencies to a large cohort of children with attachment problems, attention and learning difficulties, hyperactivity, and other abnormal behaviors. Research focused on the early characteristics and needs of so-called "crack kids," but little information about how these children fared as they entered adolescence has been published.

Crack baby is a term commonly used in the United States to describe infants born to mothers who ingested rock cocaine while pregnant. Early research, often exaggerated or misrepresented by the popular media, heightened social concern to epidemic proportions resulting in a moral crusade to "save" infants from the addicted caregivers. A public fervor to prosecute and jail mothers who abused drugs during pregnancy developed, along with a despair that public education would be destroyed when these babies entered school. Biogenics, class politics, and stereotypes of the "evil mother" shadowed the debates. The fervor has now faded, replaced by more thoughtful but often contradictory or confounded research on the developmental effects of in utero exposure to cocaine.

In 1987, it was estimated that as many as 375,000 infants born in the United States each year had been exposed to crack cocaine by maternal use. Although many consider this estimate to be high and there are probably no reliable national estimates of prenatal cocaine exposure, there are doubtless many adolescents and young adults today who were exposed to crack cocaine during gestation. Little information is available regarding how these maturing "crack kids" fare as they enter the passage to adulthood, but it is likely that many of them ended up on the streets or were arrested.

Women who abuse cocaine during pregnancy may experience a variety of complications, including spontaneous abortions, stillbirths, ruptured placentas, and premature delivery (Inciardi, Surrett, & Saum,

1997). Because cocaine crosses the blood-brain barrier after passing through the placenta during pregnancy, it also potentially affects the developing fetal brain, as well as other organs and tissues (Mayes, 1992). Because the fetal liver is not fully developed and cannot quickly eliminate the drug, it also has a far longer half-life in a fetus than in an adult. Documented consequences of exposure include impaired fetal growth, low birth weight, and small head circumference. Respiratory and urinary tract difficulties also appear more common among cocaine-exposed infants (Chasnoff, 1988). Some studies also report birth defects of the kidneys, arms, and heart; however, these studies may not have accounted for synergistic effects of other teratogens used during pregnancy, such as alcohol. Cocaine also appears to be linked to the likelihood of sudden infant death syndrome (SIDS) (Porat, Brodsky, Gianette, & Hurt, 1994), although this relationship is uncertain because of the difficulty of separating out the multiple effects of poverty, cigarette smoking, alcohol use, poor nutrition, and inadequate prenatal care from cocaine use (Zuckerman & Frank, 1992). Thus, studies do not agree regarding the increase of incidence of SIDS and other health problems among cocaine-exposed infants (Barton, Harrigan, & Tse,1995; Bauchner,1988; Fulroth, Duran, Nicjerson, & Espinoza, 1989) and are often difficult to interpret because of other risks present such as use of other teratogens and poor prenatal care. Regardless, there appears to be sufficient evidence to assume that crack babies are likely to be less healthy than other infants. Some researchers have claimed that difficulties seem to disappear as early as three years old (Griffith, 1994), and others have noted that nutrition and environment after birth may account for either continued poor health or improvement. If crack exposure during infancy does have long-term effects on physical health, however, crack kids may be less healthy, overall, than their nonexposed peers during adolescence, and early adulthood and may require more frequent medical care.

Because cocaine is a powerful central nervous system stimulant with lasting neurobehavioral effects, it can potentially retard social and emotional development. Mayes (1992) notes that potential manifestations include excessive crying, heightened reactivity to light and touch, delays in language development, and lower intelligence. It has been difficult to demonstrate long-term behavioral, cognitive, and language problems in children who were exposed prenatally to cocaine (Mentis & Lundgren, 1995). Because prenatal cocaine exposure was not widely recognized or researched until the mid-1980s, the study of neurological impairment related to use has a brief history and continued study is necessary to confirm or refute general clinical impressions (Inciardi et al., 1997). Documented clinical impressions of crack-exposed infants include sleep dysfunction, irregularities in response to stimuli, excessive crying, and fussiness (Dipietro, 1995). Most studies suggest that these infants are more easily aroused, but others have found cocaine-exposed infants to be more difficult to stimulate. Lester (1991) suggests this can be accounted for by the fact that the easily aroused infants are experiencing the effects of recent maternal cocaine use, and others are displaying the effect of chronic use on infant growth and development.

Studies using tools such as the Braselton Neonatal Behavioral Assessment Scale (NBAS) or the Bayley Scales of Infant Development (BSID) have mixed results. Dow-Edwards (1992) found that newborns exposed to crack had decreased interactive skills, short attention spans, comparatively depressed performance in psychomotor development, and oversensitivity to stimulation, coping with stimulus by either frantic wails or sleep. Bateman (1993) reported brief tremors for the first 24 hours after birth. Mayes, Bornstein, Chaworska, and Granger (1995) found evidence that visual information processing demonstrated increased arousal to stimuli that may exceed optimal levels for sustaining attention or processing information. Chasnoff, Griffith, Macgregor, Dirkes, and Burns (1989) found that cocaine-exposed infants demonstrated poorer state regulation, orientation, and motor performance than controls and presented more abnormal reflexes. In a carefully controlled study, Richardson, Hamel, Goldschmidt, and Day (1996) found maternal cocaine use to be significantly related to poorer autonomic stability, poorer motor maturity and tone, and increased abnormal reflexes two days after birth. They suggested that infants exposed to cocaine may be more vulnerable to the stress of birth and exhibit a delayed recovery from that stress. Mentis and Lundgren (1995) suggested that explicit conclusions are difficult to reach from this data because measures used may not be sufficiently sensitive to identify other potential problems, which may not manifest until later stages of development.

In a study of toddlers who had been exposed to crack cocaine while in utero, Howard, Beckwith, Rodning, and Kropenske (1989) found that, compared to controls, subjects were emotionally and socially underdeveloped and had difficulty learning. Drug-exposed children did not show strong feelings of pleasure, anger, or distress and appeared to be less purposeful and organized when playing. They also appeared unattached to their primary caregivers. During infancy, development of empathy is fostered by the affective relationship that develops between infant and caregiver (Barnett, 1987). Later, empathy develops when caregivers provide opportunities for children to experience a variety of emotions and encourage them to attend to the emotional experiences of others (Goldstein & Michaels, 1985).

Lack of attachment combined with poor attention span may make it difficult for "crack kids" to develop empathy. Similarly, avoidant or ambivalent attachment appears to foster an external locus of control (Guyot & Strehlow, 2000). Individuals with highly external loci of control assume that they have no control over their own actions or circumstances. From the perspective of these individuals, fate or destiny, those in power, or other criteria determine the outcome of events. They do not see their own behavior or effort as having any effect on the events in their lives.

Implications of this research for later development of crack kids suggests lack of empathy and a highly external locus of control as defined by Rotter (1966) may be common characteristics as they mature. The current profile for attention deficit hyperactivity disorder (ADHD), a condition that has been increasingly common in recent years, also sounds strikingly consistent with this early research on crack babies. Parent/child attachment, internal representation of the world, empathy, self-soothing, self-regulation, self-esteem, values and competencies, learning and organizational strategies, social skills, responsibility and problem-solving are all difficulties encountered in a child with ADHD personality development. Martinez and Bournival (1995) noted that ADHD children exhibit low cortical arousal as infants. Rapoport and Castellanos (1995) found evidence that children with ADHD had significantly smaller right frontal brain regions and right striatum than controls. These findings seem consistent with the physiological and neurological data gathered on crack-exposed newborns and suggest that attention deficit disorder (ADD) or ADHD may be yet another manifestation of in utero crack exposure as children mature. This is not to suggest that ADD or ADHD is indicative of maternal cocaine use, as a variety of other factors may also contribute to the condition. One precursor to the condition, however, may, indeed, be exposure to teratogens in utero, making it far more likely that crack kids will suffer from this condition than others.

An ADD or ADHD profile markedly affects learning, cognition, and educational success. Other cognitive developmental influences of cocaine exposure include delays in the acquisition of language skills, literacy, and memory. A study of 35 crack-exposed infants and 35 matched controls, van Baar and Graaf (1994) concluded that drug-exposed children tended to score lower on all general intelligence and language measures than controls and were functioning at a lower cognitive level as preschoolers. Similar studies by Mentis and Lundgren (1995) and Nulman (1994) provided similar results. Cognitive assessments using general cognitive, verbal performance, quantitative, and memory scales given by Hawley, Halle, Drasin, and Thomas (1995), however, did not reveal significant differences between drug-exposed and nondrug-exposed children. Barone (1994) studied 26 cocaine-exposed children from 1 to 7 years old who were placed in stable foster homes. She reported there were some noticeable delays, but, overall, literacy patterns were developing in a manner similar to nonexposed children. It appears that adverse cognitive effects may be mediated to some degree by a stable home environment and exacerbated by an unstable environment. Mayes (1992) suggested that a number of neurobehavioral differences between crack-exposed and nonexposed infants may disappear by six months of age, noting that the plasticity of the brain, combined with adequate care taking, may compensate for some or all of the neurological insult. Zuckerman (1993) concurs; however, it seems to be evident that prenatal cocaine exposure does effect neurological functioning and is manifested by inappropriate response to stimulus, attentional impairments, language difficulties, and learning problems. Such data suggest that difficulty in school, difficulty holding jobs, and relatively low verbal intelligence scores may be characteristic of crack kids during adolescence and early adulthood.

No comparative studies of adolescents and young adults who were exposed to crack cocaine in utero are presently available. Based on the data gathered on cocaine-exposed infants and children, however, several likely characteristics can be extrapolated. Adolescents and young adults exhibiting several of these characteristics may have difficulty completing their schooling, holding jobs, and functioning in society. Homelessness and incarceration may be likely potential outcomes for many members of this cohort unless intensive early intervention is continued throughout adolescence and early adulthood. Given the characteristics likely to present themselves during adolescence and early adulthood such as a strong desire to "fit in" with peers, low impulse control, low self-esteem and poor self-monitoring ability, aggression, and, eventually, prison are a likely future outcome for this group.

What can be done for this group? As noted in the Brazilian study, keeping street children in school is problematic. That is an important first step, though, assuming the schools are then willing to work with these adolescents. One example of a positive practice along these lines is the creation of a special school in the southwestern United States to work specifically with homeless children and adolescents. It was noted that many children could not attend public school because registering required an address, something not available to the homeless, so a special public school was created for children and adolescents with no address. Buses picked students up from wherever in the city they were. Social services and provision of food, clothing, and health care were integrated into the basic services. Curriculum was tailored to meet the needs of these students and offer vocational training. The effort was successful and resulted in keeping many street children in school and out of jail. Such programs should be developed in all communities where street children or homeless children exist.

Special educational strategies included providing a structured learning environment, breaking down assignments into small steps, using task analysis to sequence learning, and providing consistent reinforcement in the forms of praise and positive social recognition. All appear to be promising strategies. Encouraging positive peer interaction through cooperative group work was also beneficial. The use of school counselors, school psychologists, and other community resources to provide additional life skills training, with a cognitive-behavioral model, was also integrated.

There may be a strong underlying relationship between the current plethora of ADD- and ADHD-diagnosed students in U.S. public schools and maternal drug use that bears further investigation. Most crack kids portrayed in the U.S. media were African American or Hispanic, from high poverty areas. All crack kids were not necessarily from this environment, however, as a case study by McCarthy and Waters indicated. The subject was not born to a single, uneducated mother in the inner city, nor was he raised in poverty. Overall, despite obvious deficits, he experienced good parenting in a stable, structured home throughout most of his childhood. He had adequate nutrition, good medical care, and education.

This case supports the hypothesis that much of the early "crack data" was politically motivated, reflecting racial bias, gender bias, and classism. There are undoubtedly many other cases like this young man—crack kids born to white, middle and upper class homes who were missed in all of the early hype when data were collected primarily in treatment centers and public health facilities. A large cohort of "hidden" cases may exist, suggesting that estimates should be higher, rather than lower, for incidence of maternal drug use.

It is also worth noting that many characteristics noted in crack babies seemed to have lasting effects. Developmental delays, poor health and coordination, and cognitive deficits seemed lasting. On the other hand, the more labile emotional traits such as failure to attach, inability to bond, aggressiveness, and lack of control were lacking. Perhaps this suggests that a nurturing environment more easily ameliorates social outcomes than physical and cognitive outcomes. As Zuckerman and Frank (1994) noted, intervention focused on parenting is well worth pursuing and very effective.

Lasting physical and cognitive outcomes may be problematic for the social welfare system, especially as homelessness may be a particular problem for this group. Additional vocational counseling and jobs skills training may be needed to help this generation of crack babies as they enter adulthood. These services should perhaps also be coordinated with criminal justice organizations, where many of this group may find themselves.

An arbitrary, punitive criminal justice system may irrevocably damage the chances of recovery of many who otherwise seemed to be doing fairly well in delayed development toward a normal life. The behavioral tendencies predicted by in utero exposure to crack cocaine are probably more likely to lead to arrest of crack kids than of nonexposed adolescents and adults. We speculate that many of the current prison population in the United States under the age of 25 may indeed be "crack kids grown up." If this is the case, it would behoove society to find better ways of dealing with these individuals than incarceration. Cognitive-behavioral training programs, peer mentoring, appropriate social support, and education programs that lead to productive, albeit somewhat delayed, self-supporting lives would seem to be a wiser approach than supporting this group at taxpayer expense in a system that is likely to exacerbate rather than ameliorate problem behaviors when the focus is not on rehabilitation.

Additional research comparing crack-exposed and noncrack-exposed adolescents, though fraught with methodological problems and difficult to conduct, is warranted given the lasting nature and extensive impact of this problem. Also, research on young prison populations and incarcerated juveniles is an avenue worth pursuing. Adolescents and young adults who were exposed in utero to crack-cocaine, methamphetamine, and/or excessive alcohol are particularly at risk for homelessness, aggressive criminal behavior, and a lack of community support. This may result in incarceration for a substantial percentage of this group. A large-scale retrospective study of prison populations is warranted, and it may be important for psychologists who are evaluating probationers, parolees, and inmates to gather information on previous exposure to substances in utero and on behavioral risks associated with such exposure to better tailor treatment plans to the particular needs of "crack kids grown up." Focusing on strengths rather than weaknesses or deficits and providing highly structured environments with necessary training and support services seems warranted.

Several studies, including those recounted here, have described street children. There is little doubt that this group is more at risk, more likely to exhibit aggressive behavior, and more likely to be arrested. Still, as Grotberg (2002) pointed out, many adolescents who grow up in high-risk environments are successful in life; identifying factors that promote resilience for these youth in adverse circumstances is critical. Many children and adolescents are growing up in conditions of personal and social risk. Risk factors interfere with normal patterns of development. Poverty is one of these conditions and it has been considered a universal risk factor by many researchers (Hutz & Koller, 1997; Luthar & Ziegler, 1991).

More than 40 percent of children less than 14 years old in Brazil live in extreme poverty (IBGE, 1997). Juvenile delinquency is one of the developmental problems associated with poverty. Homes and neighborhoods marked by economic and social deprivation tend to produce the more visible forms of antisocial behavior (Kazdin, 1993; Masten & Garmezy, 1985; Sidman, 1995). The word delinquency is a legal rather than a psychological concept because it refers to observed and verified transgression of codified rules. Delinquents are those who have been convicted of committing infractions of these rules. Infractions are behaviors described as crimes, often including aggression, violence, or other antisocial behaviors.

In Brazil, adolescents who commit infractions are submitted to a special law, the Child and Adolescent Statute. This law considers protection of children and adolescents an absolute priority and obligation of the family, the society, and the state. When a child or adolescent is involved in a crime, the juvenile justice system can apply any one of the following measures: admonition, victim compensation, community service, freedom under supervision, restricted freedom, or deprivation of freedom for up to three years for educational purposes. Decisions as to which of the measures will be applied are considered on an individual, case-by-case basis. Those who are detained are generally those who have committed the most severe, violent crimes such as homicide and rape.

Delinquent adolescents do not all share the same history and behavioral characteristics (Loeber & Hay, 1997; Loeber & Stouthamer-Loeber, 1989). Many psychological, sociological, and even physiological factors and variables are associated with the development of delinquent behavior. Grusec and Lytton (1988) asserted that cognitive factors have been shown to be important determinants of aggressive behavior. Barash (1982) noted that aggression is a fundamental, adaptive response when resources are limited, pain is experienced, social systems are disrupted, or strangers appear. Durkin (1995) pointed out that level of frustration, social learning from family and peers, media influence, and physiological antecedents such as testosterone level all appear to be related to aggressive behavior based on empirical evidence.

Comparative studies among delinquents and nondelinquents have shown some differences in cognitive variables that could be related to the development of delinquency. Short and Simeonsson (1986), for example, reported significant differences between delinquents and nondelinquents in the ability to take others' perspectives. Díaz and Báguena (1989) also found significant differences in locus of control between delinquent and nondelinquent adolescents. Delinquents felt they had less internal control over environmental factors than nondelinquents. Tate, Reppucci, and Mulvey (1995) reported that delinquent adolescents appear to lack appropriate problem-solving skills. Wandersman and Nation (1998) noted the common use of aggression and violence as problem-solving strategies in poor families, contributing to delinquent behavior in their young. Regardless of the antecedents responsible for levels of aggression among delinquents and street children, rehabilitative measures for delinquent adolescents are likely to be effective, as there are no pathological or immutable differences between adolescents in this group and other adolescents. Anger management training is one viable option. McCarthy, Gold, and Garcia (1999) demonstrated that delinquents could be successfully treated through structured anger management training, as noted earlier in the book. Another promising strategy is to help delinquent adolescents develop a more internal sense of control over the environment. Although their previous experiences may not have established any clear connection between personal action and environmental outcomes, learning that personal effort and decisions do impact the environment in a predictable way may help this group in the future. Developing this internal sense of control is also related to critical thinking and problem solving, skills that many adolescents lack (McCarthy, 1998a). Developing critical thinking and problem-solving skills in adolescents, as described in the previous chapter, is another promising strategy for reducing violence (McCarthy, 1999), and some promising methods for accomplishing this have already been developed (McCarthy, 1995, 1998b). These strategies are also likely to reduce recidivism rates among delinquents. A prevalent myth that nothing can be done about delinquency seems to exist (Atwater, 1988). These results and this discussion suggest that it is possible to rehabilitate juvenile offenders. Adolescent violence is neither uncontrollable nor inevitable, and it is within our power to reduce its occurrence by identifying and promoting factors that promote resiliency such as effective parenting, modeling, mentoring, community cohesion, and thinking skills. When these factors are absent in the lives of delinquent adolescents, society should continue to invest in their rehabilitation by offering treatment programs that teach strategies to compensate such as anger management, critical thinking, and problem-solving skills. Developing community programs designed to help to slow down the migration to the streets, to keep children in school, and to return them to their families when possible is also an important strategy for reducing adolescent aggression.

It is our hope that the many ideas and strategies presented here, along with the data summarizing adolescent aggression, will be useful for those who work with teenagers throughout the world. As our world becomes more global and cultures become more similar and influenced by the same media, economic policies, and perceptions, it is our hope that the best rather than the worst practices, from the standpoint of appropriately channeling adolescent aggression, will be adopted by and adapted to each country. It takes not only a family or a village now, but a planet to accomplish the task of raising healthy, nonviolent children and adolescents. Let it be so for a better world of tomorrow.

CHAPTER 13

PHILOSOPHIES THAT FOSTER VIOLENCE: RELIGIOUS, CULTURAL, AND POLITICAL RISK FACTORS

Spare the rod and spoil the child. How many of us have heard that quote from the Bible used to justify use of corporal punishment with children from a religious standpoint? How many fundamental religions implicitly or explicitly encourage physical punishment of children and adolescents?

It should be noted, first, that the common understanding of that quotation is wrong. A rod, literally referring to the shepherd's cane, is a device for leading and pointing the way. Shepherds do not cane their sheep. The meaning is intended to stress the importance of leading, modeling, and providing direction to children. As we have suggested throughout this book, that is an essential task if we wish to prevent adolescent violence and appropriately channel aggression. It takes focused effort, time, and energy on the part of everyone to accomplish this. Parents, teachers, those in helping professions, entertainers, politicians, and society at large are all key players. Providing direction is a much more complicated enterprise than simply administering punishment; however, if we wish to curb the rising incidence of teen violence, it is necessary to do so, and to do so carefully.

Research over the decades has consistently demonstrated that children raised in authoritarian homes where violent punishment is common are more likely to have difficulties in their own lives. Behavior problems at school, delinquency, arrest for violent crimes, and a likelihood of abusing their own children are all likely outcomes (Pacheco,

McCarthy, & Hutz, 2005). The amount of unsupervised time watching television during childhood is also correlated with arrests for violent crimes, according to some studies. Modeling is powerful. Children who grow up with physical aggression as an accepted means of control will, in turn, use physical aggression toward others. This modeling does not apply just to parenting and experiences in the home, of course, although that is a powerful source. What children and adolescents observe and experience from their peer group, what they see in the media, and the cultural experiences they have also determine how they understand and use violence. The political climate is a factor (DeSouza & McCarthy, 2005). The philosophical underpinnings of the society in which they develop are also influential. This final chapter summarizes how these factors influence adolescent aggression and suggests ways to see that the appropriate messages are received.

Sociopolitical and Cultural Influences on Adolescent Aggression

Political socialization blends with cultural background to create a process through which children and adolescents acquire basic knowledge, values, and attitudes. Bronfenbrenner (1979) described clearly how interactions among various social structures, nested in each other like Russian dolls, influence social development. The microsystem, including the parent-child dyad and the immediate family with whom interactions occur on a daily basis, is nested within a mesosystem composed of other settings in which the individual participates, such as church or school. These are nested within an exosystem, which in turn affects what happens within the microsystems and mesosystems. This exosystem includes mass media, community resources, and similar influences. Finally, the most encompassing system, the macrosystem, permeates all of these other levels. It includes the beliefs and ideologies of society at large, the values that cement a particular culture. This societal blueprint is certainly influential in shaping the attitudes and behaviors of the members of a particular society. Attitudes and behaviors specifically related to aggression and violence are derived from these system influences. Although there is great diversity within many countries—certainly the larger ones such as Brazil, Russia, Canada, China, and the United States—in terms of attitudes and culture, there are also common ideologies that permeate the macrosystem of each country.

Brazil, China, the United States, and Russia all have had political revolutions, civil wars, and the use of force and violence by the government as a means of social control within their recent histories. The Civil and Revolutionary Wars in the United States set a tone of violence and aggression as a tool to further political and social ends, carried out now through slightly different means by use of force against other countries for specific economic and political ends. These messages within the macrosystem are not lost on adolescents. They are socialized to see aggression and violence as tools for survival, self-protection, and reaching desired ends. In addition to the historical use of systematic political violence within a culture, other factors are also influential. For example, Covell (1996) notes that the United States tends to be a far more individualistic culture than Canada. Durkin (1995) established that individualistic cultures tend to show more aggressive responses to conflict resolution at both individual and societal levels, from armed police forces to wars against other countries whose policies are not viewed as beneficial. This macrosystem influences individual behavior within society, tending to make it more violent. A concrete example is the number of murders with handguns in the United States compared to Canada in 1995; there were 8,915 in the United States and only 8 in Canada (Dorgan, 1995).

Nationalism, patriotism, and a common understanding of cultural symbols also influence this trend. Cooper (1965) suggested that patriotism allows the division of all people into "Us" and "Them"—"good guys" and "bad guys." For children who are socialized in a nationalistic, patriotic milieu, as our adolescents currently are experiencing, the world becomes organized as a series of rival gangs, and violent conflict is seen as the way to overcome conflict between these gangs and allow "good to prevail." Thus, teen violence should not be a great surprise to us. For some youth, violence and aggression even provide a sense of security. Research has indicated that Israeli adolescents frequently cite a strong military in their country as one of the major reasons they feel safe and secure (Raviv, Oppenheimer, & Bar-Tel, 1999).

Societies differ in the acceptance, expression, and control of aggression. Children growing up in high-conflict situations in Israel, Palestine, or Northern Ireland, for example, develop views concerning peace, war, and violence that differ from children in other situations. Researchers have described how a violent atmosphere and military aggression intrude into family relationships (Hobfell, 1991) and personality development (Punamaki, 1987) and how these things influence the development of moral reasoning (Fields, 1973; McCarthy et al., 2004).

In addition to cultural factors that provide social knowledge and form attitudes, situational factors also influence understanding. The concrete experience of violent conflict will influence how individuals conceptualize and respond to violence. Drawing on these ecological, cultural, and situational perspectives, it is logical to anticipate that adolescents' notions of violence would be based on practices in their immediate, close environments. If they see violence as acceptable, they will practice this behavior with peers and family members, just as they practice any other behavior they see as necessary for assuming an adult role. It is interesting to note that many adolescents in the United States see military service or going to war as a "rite of passage" into adulthood (McCarthy, Prandini, & Hollingsworth, 2001).

It should be no surprise that the cultural traditions, norms, values, and knowledge based in both immediate experience and history would influence the nature of peer relationships. The United States has a violent history, so violent youth are a natural result. And, as the United States takes an increasingly prominent role in other societies through globalization, this macrosystem is extended, with similar results being seen in other countries.

Maintaining Honor in a Confusing Milieu

"Don't you be dissing me!" Whether Hollywood originated the phrase or gang kids in the ghettos were responsible, it is commonly understood by all of us. Disrespect is an unpleasant condition for anyone to cope with. As human beings, we all are deserving of and desirous of the respect of others. Adolescents, because of the fragility of their developing identities, are especially desirous of obtaining the respect of their peers. Thus, disrespect, or any indication of this, are often grounds for violent conflict among adolescents.

It is worth noting that this same script—using violent conflict to demand respect—occurs on both a national level in terms of grounds for war and on a personal level in many authoritarian families. It is portrayed on television, in movies, and through popular songs. It also occurs in military training and in confrontations with police. Thus, the message is thoroughly integrated into the environment at all levels, including the microsystem, mesosystem, exosystem, and macrosystem for U.S. adolescents. The result is a lot of violent, aggressive behavior toward others who are perceived as being disrespectful. These behaviors range from fistfights with peers, to drive-by shootings, to firing on teachers and classmates, as occurred at Columbine.

Certainly all human beings are worthy of respect, and we hope that this message, rather than the message of demanding respect through violence, will eventually be what is portrayed to children and adolescents. The message has not been completely obliterated. It still survives in many family environments, school environments, philosophies, and religious teachings. But making this message paramount, rather than a message of earning respect through violence, is essential. It is a task we must all strive to accomplish if we wish to limit adolescent aggression. Instead, our current culture seems to make it all too likely that many adolescents will become violent criminals based on a gradual progression through what criminologist Lonnie Athens (1992, 1997) terms the "stages of the experiential process that creates violent criminals."

Athens's Stages of Violence

As Wolfgang and Ferracuti (1967) pointed out many years ago, when attempting to explain the development of violent subcultures, "we are led back to the external social environment as the area where the causative key to aggression must at present be found" (p. 143). Basing his research in symbolic interactionism, a profound theory that suggests that when social experiences are reduced to numbers and quantitative analysis, the meaning of the social experiences is lost, Athens interviewed more than 50 incarcerated violent criminals who had been convicted of aggravated assault, homicide, or rape, many in their mid or late teens or early twenties, searching for patterns and commonalties in their social experiences.

Richard Rhodes (1999) summarized his work in a nontechnical and engaging way in the book, *Why They Kill*, and we recommend this as further reading. Briefly, though, the stages Athens postulated based on careful research are:

1. Violent subjugation, personal horrification, and violent coaching
2. Belligerency
3. Violent performances
4. Virulency

An adolescent who eventually becomes a violent criminal would first, during childhood, be subjected to violence through physical punishment at home, bullying from peers and siblings, and witnessing violence. Next, the individual would reflect on this cruel treatment at the hands of others in search of meaning about how to interact with others. When a decision is reached to stop violent subjugation through violent self-defense and, eventually, offense, the belligerency stage is reached. The next result is a series of violent encounters in which the adolescent is now the aggressor rather than the victim. This is the third stage, violent performances. If these encounters are resolved with the adolescent as the "winner," perceived as earning respect in the eyes of self, peers, and models, then the final stage is reached and a dangerous violent criminal is likely the result.

Athens suggests several policy implications based on his conclusions and these stages, which are very much reminiscent of our suggestions. Parent training and attempts to reduce and stop domestic violence through school and social programs is an important starting point. Later, individual and group counseling and stress management techniques may be appropriate. At stage 3 and 4, intervening with structured programs that offer nonviolent coaching such as anger management training in detention facilities is recommended.

Religious and Philosophical Influences on Adolescent Aggression

The philosopher Spinoza noted in the seventeenth century that peace is not simply the absence of violence, but a virtue that comes from one's soul and one's mental understanding. Peace education, then, might certainly be a useful tool to integrate into schools and treatment centers to develop this mental understanding (Raviv et al., 1999). Information about historical figures who have actively refused to use violence such as Mahatma Gandhi and Martin Luther King can be integrated with training in a variety of strategies such as cooperation, mutual respect, interpersonal understanding, perspective-taking, mediation, and conflict resolution. Peace education should be approached as basic moral injunctions: Don't treat others unfairly and don't turn away from others in need.

Religious training, to varying degrees, may still impart these lessons, as well. The Christian ethic when based in the New Testament (love one another and turn the other cheek) as opposed to the Old Testament (an eye for an eye) includes socialization on these values. Buddhism and many other religions do, as well. Because of the diversity of religions in the world and the increasing trend in all countries to turn away from religion and become more secular, there is no guarantee that these messages will reach future generations in any systematic way through religious training, however. Because of the debate over, and resistance to, values education and moral education in public schools, there is also no other mechanism currently in place to instill these philosophies and values.

Families, Extended Families, and Mentoring Programs

Growth in the extent and forms of violence seems to be correlated with the increasing mobility of modern life. Some societies have maintained an extended family structure to a much greater degree than others, and this extended family structure can serve as a cushion and an additional means of building resilience in adolescents. When there are problems at home, either as part of normal identity development or because of dysfunctional relations within the immediate family, it is important to have another trusted family member with whom a longstanding and close relationship has been built to turn to.

In Brazilian families, it is common to have a special aunt or uncle with whom a relationship has been built to serve this function. Godparents may also fulfill this role. As mentioned previously, high mobility in the United States that tends to isolate nuclear families from their extended network of relatives may be part of the problem. Development is more difficult for adolescents when there is not a strong support network other than a parent to turn to. Building and nourishing relationships in the extended family is one way to assist troubled youth.

Formal mentoring programs and support networks within some church groups, as well as relationships with teachers, counselors, and other school staff—or even police and probation officers—may be less preferred but useful alternatives. When a strong extended family structure is not available, it is still important for youth to have a trusted adult to whom they can turn for advice. Finding ways to enhance the support structure, perhaps by assigning "foster aunts" and "foster uncles" within the neighborhood or community setting, rather than simply blaming parents for problems with their teens, is essential if we wish to remedy the problematic trend of teen violence we are currently witnessing.

It's Never Too Late To Change

It is our hope that the many ideas and strategies presented in this book, along with the data summarizing adolescent aggression, will be useful for those who work with teenagers throughout the world. As our world becomes more global, and cultures become more similar and influenced by the same media, economic policies, and perceptions, we hope that the best rather than the worst practices, from the standpoint of appropriately channeling adolescent aggression, will be adopted. It takes not only a family or a village now, but an entire planet to accomplish the task of raising healthy, nonviolent children and adolescents. Let it be so for a better world of tomorrow.

References and Sources Consulted

Aberastury, A., & Knobel, M. (1981). *Adolescência normal* [Normal Adolescence] (10th ed.). Porto Alegre: Artes Médicas.

Abrams, M. H., Donaldson, E. T., Smith, H., Adams, R. M., Monk, S. H., Lipking, L., Ford, G. H. & Daiches, D. (1974). *The Norton anthology of English literature, Vols. 1 & 2.* New York: W. W. Norton & Company.

Andrade, J. (1979). *Epidemiologia da tentativa de suicídio em Ribeirão Preto.* [Epidemiology of Suicide Attempts in Ribeirão Preto]. Dissertation, Universidade de São Paulo, Ribeirão Preto, SP.

Aptekar, L. (1988a). Street children of Colombia. *Journal of Early Adolescence, 83,* 225–241.

Aptekar, L. (1988b). Colombian street children, their mental health and how they can be served. *International Journal of Mental Health, 173,* 81–104.

Aptekar, L. (1989). Colombian street children: Gamines or Chupagruesos. *Adolescence, 24,* 783–794.

Arnett, J. J. (2000). Emerging adulthood: A conception of development from the late teens through the twenties. *American Psychologist, 55,* 469–480.

Arons, A. B. (1982). Phenomenology and logical reasoning in introductory physics courses. *American Journal of Physics, 50,* 1. 13–20.

Arons, A. B. (1984). Education through science. *Journal of College Science Teaching, 13,* 4, 210–220.

Arons, A. B. (1985). Critical thinking in the baccalaureate curriculum. *Liberal Education, 71,* 141–158

Aronson, E. (2001). Educational strategies to reduce school violence: The jigsaw classroom and other cooperative learning techniques. Paper presented at the 2001 Annual Convention of the Rocky Mountain Psychological Association, Reno, NV, April 18, 2001.

Aronson, E., Stephan, C., Sikes, J., Blaney, N., & Snapp, M. (1978). *The jigsaw classroom*. Beverly Hills, CA: Sage.

Athens, L. (1992). *The creation of dangerous violent criminal*. Urbana, IL: University of Illinois Press.

Athens, L. (1997). *Violent criminal acts and actors revisited*. Urbana, IL: University of Illinois Press.

Atwater, E. (1988). *Adolescence*. Englewood Cliffs, NJ: Prentice Hall.

Baar, A. van., & Graaf, F. (1994). Cognitive development of preschool age infants of drug-dependent mothers. *Developmental Medical Child Neurology, 36*, 1036–1075.

Báguena, M. J., & Díaz, A. (1991). Personality, sexual differences and juvenile delinquency: Structural analysis. *Análisis y Modificacion de Conduta, 17*, 427–437.

Bailey, S. (2001). Breaking the cycle: Challenge and opportunities, *British Journal of Psychiatry, 179*, 496–497.

Bandura, A. (1962). Social learning through imitation. In M. R. Jones (Ed.). *Nebraska symposium on motivation*. Lincoln: University of Nebraska Press.

Bandura, A. (1965). Influence of models' reinforcement contingencies on the acquisition of imitative responses. *Journal of Personality and Social Psychology, 16*, 589–595.

Bandura, A. (1968). What TV violence can do to your child. In O.N. Larsen (Ed.). *Violence and the media*. New York: Harper and Row.

Bandura, A. (1969). Social learning theory of identificatory processes. In D. A. Goslin (Ed.), *Handbook of socialization theory and research*. Chicago: Rand McNally.

Bandura, A. (1971). *Social learning theory*. New York: General Learning Press.

Bandura, A., Ross, D., & Ross, S. (1963). Imitation of film mediated aggressive models. *Journal of Abnormal and Social Psychology, 67*, 601–607.

Bandura, A., & Walters, R. H. (1963). *Social Learning and Personality Development*. New Jersey: Holt, Rhinehart & Winston.

Banks, S. (1971). Testimony presented before the Federal Trade Commission on behalf of the Joint Committee of the Association of National Advertisers and the American Association of Advertising Agencies, Washington, D.C., October 28, 1971.

Barash, D. P. (1982). *Sociobiology and behavior*. London: Heinemann.

Barfield, C. K., & Hutchinson, M. A. (1989). Observations on adolescent anger and anger control group in residential and day treatment. *Residential Treatment for Children and Youth, 7*, 45–53.

Barker, G., & Knaul, F. (1991). Exploited entrepreneurs: Street and working children in developing countries. *Childhope USA*, Working Paper 1.

Barnes, C. A. (1992). Critical thinking: An educational imperative. *New Directions for Community Colleges, 20*, 1.

Barnett, M. A. (1987). Empathy and related responses in children. In N. Eisenberg & J. Strayer (Eds.), *Empathy and its development*, (pp.146–162). Washington, D.C.: American Psychological Association.

Baron, J. B. & Sternberg, R. J. (Eds.) (1990). *Teaching thinking skills: Theory and practice.* New York: Freeman.

Barone, D. (1994). Myths about crack babies. *Educational Leadership, 52,* 67–68.

Barros, M. (1991). As mortes por suicídio no Brasil. [Death by suicides in Brazil]. In R. Cassorola, (Ed.), *Do suicídio: Estudos brasileiros.* [About suicide: Brazilian studies]. Campinas: Papirus.

Barton, S. J., Harrington, N. & Tse, J. (1995). Prenatal cocaine exposure: Implications for practice, policy development and needs for future research. *Journal of Prenatal Nursing, 15,* 10–22.

Bass, G. M. & Perkins, H. V. (1984). Teaching critical thinking skills with CAI: A design by two researchers shows computers can make a difference. *Electronic Learning, 4,* 2, 32–34.

Bastos, O. (1974). Comportamentos suicidas em uma unidade psiquiátrica de hospital universitário. [Suicidal behavior at a university psychiatric hospital]. Recife, PE, Brazil: Faculty of Medicine, Federal University at Pernambuco.

Bateman, D. A. (1993). The effects of intrauterine cocaine exposure in newborns. *American Journal of Public Health, 83,* 190–193.

Bathia, S. Kahn, M., Mediratta, R., & Sharma, A. (1987). High risk suicide factors across cultures. *International Journal of Social Psychiatry, 33,* 226–236.

Bauchner, H. (1988). Cocaine use during pregnancy: prevalence and correlates. *Pediatrics, 82,* 888–895.

Baxandall, P. R. (1978). *Proof in mathematics: If, then and perhaps.* ERIC/IRC Information Reference Center. Columbus, OH: Ohio State University.

Beardslee, W. R., Wright, E. J., Salt, P., Rothberg, P. C., Drezner, K., & Gladstone, T. R. G. (1997). Examination of preventive interventions for families with depression: Evidence of change. *Development and Psychopathology, 9,* 109–130.

Beck, R., & Fernandez, E. (1998). Cognitive-behavioral therapy in the treatment of anger: A meta-analytic approach. *Cognitive Therapy and Research, 22,* 63–74.

Becker, J. (1998a). What we know about the characteristics and treatment of adolescents who have committed sexual offences, *Journal of the American Professional Society on the Abuse of Children, 3,* 317–329.

Becker, J. (1998b). The assessment of adolescent perpetrators of childhood sexual abuse. *Irish Journal of Psychology, 19,* 68–81.

Bee, H. (1996). *A criança em desenvolvimento* [The developing child]. Porto Alegre: Artes Médicas.

Belenko, S. (1996). *Comparative models of treatment delivery in drug courts.* Washington, D.C.: The Sentencing Project.

Belenko, S. (1998). Research on drug courts: A critical review. *National Drug Court Institute Review, 1,* 1–42.

Bender, D. L. & Leone, B. (1988). *Opposing viewpoints: Poverty.* St. Paul, MN: Greenhaven.

Bender, S. L., Word, C. O., Diclemente, R. J., Crittendon, M. R., Persuad, N. A., & Ponton, L. E. (1995). The developmental implications of prenatal and/or postnatal crack cocaine exposure in preschool children: A preliminary report. *Developmental and Behavioral Pediatrics, 16,* 418–424.

Bennett, L., & Fineran, S. (1998). Sexual and severe physical violence among high school students: Power beliefs, gender and relationship, *American Journal of Orthopsychiatry, 68,* 645–652.

Bentovim, A. (2002). Preventing sexually abused young people from becoming abusers, and treating the victimisation experiences of young people who offend sexually, *Child Abuse and Neglect, 26,* 661–678.

Berger, K. S. (1992). *The developing person through the lifespan.* New York: Worth.

Best, J.B. (Ed.) (1994). *Troubling children: Studies of children and social problems.* New York: Aldine de Grayter.

Beyersdorfer, J. M., & Schauer, D. K. (1992). Writing personality profiles: Conversations across the generation gap. *Journal of Reading, 35,* 612–616

Bezenilla, J. J. & Ogden, J. (1992). Logical sentences and searches. *Journal of Computer Assisted Learning, 6,* 1. 37–44.

Bistline, J. L. & Frederick, F. P. (1984). Anger control: A case study of a stress inoculation treatment for a chronic aggressive patient. *Cognitive Therapy and Research, 8,* 551–556.

Bitner, B. L. (1989, March). *Developmental patterns of logical reasoning of students in grades six through ten: Increments and plateaus.* Paper presented at the Annual Meeting of the National Association for Research in Science Teaching. San Francisco, CA.

Bitner, B. L. (1990, April). *Thinking processes model: Effect on logical reasoning abilities of students in grades six through twelve.* Paper presented at the Annual Meeting of the National Association for Research in Science Teaching, Atlanta, GA.

Blosser, P. E. & Helgeson, S. L. (Eds.) (1984). Investigations in science education. *Investigations in Science Education, 10,* 1.

Bobo, L. (1988). Group conflict, prejudice and the paradox of contemporary racial attitudes. In P. A. Katz & D. A. Taylor (Eds.), *Eliminating racism: Profiles in controversy.* New York: Plenum Press.

Bonilla, D. M. (Ed.) (2000). *School violence.* New York: The Reference Shelf.

Bonner, B., Marx, B., Thompson, J.,& Michaelson, P. (1998). Assessment of adolescent sexual offenders. *Journal of the American Professional Society on the Abuse of Children, 3,* 374–383.

Boroughs, R. (1990). Amputating assets. *U.S. News and World Report,* May 4, 1990.

Boswell, G., & Wedge, P. (2003). A pilot evaluation of a therapeutic community for adolescent male sexual abusers. *International Journal for Therapeutic and Supportive Organizations, 24,* 259–276.

Bosworth, K., Espelage, D., & DuBay, T. (1998). A computer-based violence prevention intervention for young adolescents: Pilot study. *Adolescence, 33*, 785–795.

Botega, N., Cano, F., Kohn, S., Knoll, A., Pereira, A., & Bonardi, C. (1995). Tentativa de suicídio e adesão ao tratamento: Um estudo descritivo em hospital geral. [Descriptive study of those who attempt suicide and are brought to a general hospital]. *Jornal Brasileiro de Psiquiatria, 44*, 19–25.

Bouhmama, D. (1984). Assessment of Kohlberg's stages of moral development in two cultures. *Journal of Moral Education, 13*, 124–132.

Branscombe, N. R., & Wann, D. L. (1994). Collective self-esteem consequences of outgroup derogation when valid social identity is on trial. *European Journal of Social Psychology, 24*, 641–657.

Brent, D. (1989). Suicide and suicidal behavior in children and adolescents. *Pediatrics in Review, 10*, 269.

Brewer, M. B., & Brown, R. J. (1997). Intergroup relations. In D. T. Gilbert, S. T. Fiske & G. Lindzey (Eds.), *The handbook of social psychology*. (Vol. 2). Boston: McGraw-Hill.

Bright, G. W. (1983). Use of a game to instruct logical reasoning. *School Science and Mathematics, 83, 5*, 395–405.

Briones, M. (2000). When your child is molested by a youth: Fighting denial, In R. Moser, & C. Frantz, (Eds.), *Shocking violence: Youth perpetrators and victims—A multi-disciplinary perspective*. London: Charles C. Thomas Publishing.

Bronfenbrenner, U. (1979). *The ecology of human development: Experiments by nature and design*. Cambridge, MA: Harvard University Press.

Bronfenbrenner, U. (1994). Ecological models of human development. In T. Husen & T. N. Posthelwaite (Eds.), *International encyclopedia of education* (2nd ed.). New York: Elsevier.

Brown, A. (1999). Working with young people: Linking policy and practice. In M. Book-Erooga & H. Masson (Eds.), *Children and young people who sexually abuse others: Challenges and responses*. New York: Routledge.

Brown, A. J. & Campione, J. C. (1990). Communities of learning and thinking, or a context by any other name. *Contributions to Human Development, 21*, 108–125. New York: Karger.

Brown, E., & Kolko, D. (1998). Treatment efficacy and program evaluation with juvenile sexual abusers: A critique with directions for service delivery and research. *Journal of the American Professional Society on the Abuse of Children, 3*, 362–373.

Brown, G. L., Goodwin, F. K., Ballenger, J. C., Goyen, P. F., and Major, L. I. (1979). Aggression in humans correlates with cerebrospinal fluid amine metabolites. *Psychiatry Research, 1*, 131–139.

Buehner, L. J. & Lucas, V. H. (1986). MAP: A model for teaching problem solving. *British Columbia Journal of Special Education, 10, 3*, 251–259.

Bull, R. (2001) *Children and the law*. New York: Springer-Verlag.

Bull, R., & Rumsey, N. (1988). *The social psychology of facial appearance.* New York: Springer-Verlag.

Burns, S. (1983). *From student to banker: Observations from the Chase Bank.* Washington, D.C.: Office of National Affairs, Association of American Colleges.

Burton, D. (2000). Were adolescent sexual offenders children with sexual behaviour problems? *Sex Abuse: Journal of Research and Treatment, 12,* 37–48.

Bykov, S. V. (2004). Diagnostics of personality locus of control in asocial adolescent groups. *Psychology Journal, 25,* 3.

Campbell, D. (2000). Breaking the shame shield: Thoughts on the assessment of adolescent child sexual abusers. *Richard e Piggle, 8,* 25–41.

Camus, A. (1952). *Le mythe de Sisphe.* [Myth of Sisyphus]. Paris: Gallimard.

Canter, A. (1998). Sources for school psychologists. *Communique, 27,* 3.

Cassorla, R. (1984a). Jovens que tentam suicídio. Características demográficas e sociais: Um estudo comparativo com jovens normais e com problemas mentais (I). [Youth who attempt suicide. Social and demographic characteristics: A study comparing normal youth to youth with psychiatric problems (I).] *Jornal Brasileiro de Psiquiatria, 33,* 3–12.

Cassorla, R. (1984b). Jovens que tentam suicídio. Antecedentes mórbidos e de condutas auto destrutivas: Um estudo comparativo com jovens normais e com problemas mentais (II). [Youth who attempt suicide: Morbid and self-destructive behavior antecedents (II).] *Jornal Brasileiro de Psiquiatria, 33,* 93–98.

Cassorla, R. (1985). Jovens que tentam suicídio: Relacionamento social, gravidez e abortamentos: Um estudo comparativo com jovens normais e jovens com problemas mentais (III). [Youth who attempt suicide. Social relationships, pregnancy, and abortion: A study comparing normal youth to youth with psychiatric problems (III).] *Jornal Brasileiro de Psiquiatria, 34,* 151–156.

Cassorla, R. (1987). Comportamentos suicidas na infância e adolescência. [Suicidal behavior among children and adolescents.] *Jornal Brasileiro de Psiquiatria, 36,* 137–144.

Cassorla, R. (1991a). *Do suicidio: Estudos brasileiros.* [About suicide: Brazilian studies]. Campinas: Papirus.

Cassorla, R. (1991b). *Da morte: Estudos brasileiros.* [About death: Brazilian studies]. Campinas: Papirus.

Chabrol, H. (1990). *A depressão do adolescente.* [Adolescent's depression]. Campinas: Papirus.

Chasnoff, I. J. (1984). Prenatal drug exposure: Effects on neonatal and infant growth and development. *Neurobehavioral Toxicology and Teratolology, 8,* 357–362.

Chasnoff, I. J. (1988). Drug use and women: Establishing a standard of care in Prenatal abuse of licit and illicit drugs. *Annals of the New York Academy of Sciences, 5,* 208–210.

Chasnoff, I., Griffith, D. Macgregor, S., Dirkes, L., & Burns, K. (1989). Temporal patterns of cocaine use in pregnancy: Perinatal outcomes. *Journal of the American Medical Association, 261*, 1741–1744.

Cocorro, E. F. (1987). Cortical serotonin and impulsive aggression. *British Journal of Psychiatry, 155*, 52–62.

Cohen, C. E. (1981). Person categories and social perception: Testing some boundaries of the processing effects of prior knowledge. *Journal of Personality and Social Psychology, 40*, 441–452.

Colby, A., & Damon, W. (1992). *Some do care: Contemporary lives of moral commitment.* New York: Free Press.

Colby, A., & Kohlberg, L. (1987). *The measurement of moral judgment:* Vol. I & II. Cambridge: Cambridge University Press

Cole, M. (1979). Culture, cognition & IQ testing. *National Elementary Principal, 54*, 4, 49–52.

Cole, M. & Scribner, S. (1977). Literacy without schooling: Testing for intellectual effects. *Harvard Educational Review, 48*, 4, 448–461.

Cole, M., Sharp, K. & Lave, L. (1976). The cognitive consequences of education: Some empirical evidence and theoretical misgivings. *Urban Review, 9*, 4, 218–233.

Cook, M. (1989). Ideas. *Arithmetic Teacher, 36*, 7.

Cook, G. & Martinello, M. (1993, April). *Implementing interdisciplinary theme studies in the urban middle school: Problems and possibilities.* Paper presented at the American Educational Research Association Annual Meeting, Atlanta, GA.

Cooper, C. (1997). *Drug court survey report: Executive summary.* Washington, D.C.: American University.

Cooper, P. (1965). The development of the concept of war. *Journal of Peace Research, 2*, 1–17.

Cosgrove, J. G. (1990). Towards a working definition of street children. *International Social Work, 33*, 185–192.

Covell, K. (1996). Adolescents' attitudes toward international conflict: A cross-national comparison. *International Journal of Behavioral Development, 19* (4), 871–883.

Crocker, J., & Luhtanen, R. (1990). Collective self-esteem and ingroup bias. *Journal of Personality and Social Psychology, 58*, 60–67.

Crow, L. & Hawes, S. (1985, April). *The effects of teaching logical reasoning upon student critical thinking and science achievement.* Paper presented at the Annual Meeting of the National Association for Research in Science Teaching, French Licks, IN.

Csikszentmihalyi, M., & Larson, R. (1984). *Being adolescent.* New York: Basic Books.

Curcio, J. L., & First, P. (1993). *Violence in the schools: How to proactively prevent and defuse it.* San Francisco, CA: Corwin Press, Inc.

Curwen, T. (2003). The importance of offense characteristics, victimization history, hostility and social desirability in assessing empathy of male adolescent sex offenders. *Sex Abuse: Journal of Research and Treatment, 15*, 347–364.

Damon, W. (1990). Social relations and children's thinking skills. *Contributions to Human Development, 21*, 95–106.

Dangel, R., Deschner, J., & Rasp, R. (1989). Anger control training for adolescents in residential treatment. *Behavior Modification, 13*, 447–458.

Darcy, J. & Travers, J. (1993). *Human development across the lifespan.* Dubuque, IA: William Brown, Pub.

Davis, L. D., & Boster, L. H. (1993). Cognitive-behavioral-expressive interventions with aggressive and resistant youth. *Residential Treatment for Children & Youth, 10*, 55–68.

DeAngelis, T. (2001). Substance abuse treatment: An untapped opportunity. *Monitor on Psychology, 32*, 24–25.

DeBerry, S. (1991). *The externalization of consciousness and the psychopathology of everyday life.* Westport, CT: Greenwood.

DeBerry, S. (1993). *Quantum psychology.* New York: Praeger.

DeHart, F. E. & Bleaker, G. W. (1988). Young adult realistic novels: Models for information transfer? *Journal of Youth Services in Libraries, 2*, 1, 64–70.

Deschenes, E. P., Turner, S., & Greenwood, P. W. (1995). Drug court or probation? An experimental evaluation of Maricopa County's drug court. *Justice System Journal, 18*, 55–73.

DeSouza, L., & McCarthy, S. (2005). *Elaborations of peace and war among children in Southern Brazil.* Paper presented in the Forensic Psychology Symposia chaired by E. Bishop at the 65th Annual Convention of the International Council of Psychologists, Foz do Iguacu, Brazil.

DeSouza, L., Spern, T, McCarthy, S., & Biaggio, A. (2005). Understanding of peace, war and violence among children in southern Brazil. *Journal of Peace Psychology.*

Devine, P. G. (1989). Stereotypes and prejudice: Their automatic and controlled components. *Journal of Personality and Social Psychology, 56*, 5–18.

Díaz, A., & Báguena, M. J. (1989). Factores personales. Analisis estructural en adolescentes delincuentes y no delincuentes. [Personal factors: Structural analysis with delinquent and non delinquent adolescents]. *Delincuencia, 1*, 277–306.

Dien, D. (1982). A Chinese perspective on Kohlberg's theory of moral development. *Developmental Review, 2*, 331–341.

Dipietro, J. (1995). Reactivity and regulation in cocaine exposed neonates. *Infant Behavior and Development, 18*, 407–414.

Dorgan, C. (1995). *Gale country and world rankings reporter.* New York: Thompson International.

Dovidio, J. F. (2002). *Why can't we just get along? Aversive racism and interracial distrust.* Paper presented at the 24th Annual National Institute on the Teaching of Psychology, St. Petersburg, FL, January 5, 2002.

Dovidio, J. F., & Gaertner, S. L. (1998). On the nature of contemporary prejudice: The causes, consequences and challenges of aversive racism. In

J. Eberhardt & S. T. Fiske (Eds.), *Confronting racism: The problem and the response* (pp. 1–32). Newbury Park, CA: Sage.

Dow-Edwards, D. (1992). *Perinatal substance abuse: Research findings and clinical implications.* Baltimore: Johns Hopkins University Press.

Durkheim, E. (1992). *O suicidio: Estudo sociologico* (5th ed.). [Suicide: A sociological study. (5th ed.)] Lisboa: Presença.

Durkin, K. (1995). *Developmental social psychology: From infancy to old age.* Oxford, UK: Blackwell.

Dutra, E. M. (1997). *Estudo epidemiológico do suicídio no RN no período 1985–1996.* [An epidemiological study of suicides in RN between 1985–1996.] Trabalho apresentado na 50th Reunião da SBPC, Natal, RN. [Paper presented at the 50th reunion of SBPC, Natal, RN.]

Dutra, E. M. (1998a). *Caraterísticas epidemiológicas do suicídio de jovens de 10 a 24 anos no RN.* Trabalho apresentado na XXVII Reunião Anual da Sociedade Brasileira de Psicologia. Ribeirão Preto, SP. [*Epidemiological characteristics of youth between 10 and 24 years of age who commit suicide.* Paper presented at the 27th Annual Reunion of the Brazilian Psychological Society, Ribeirão Preto, SP.]

Dutra, E. M. (1998b). Reflexões existenciais e psicossociais do suicídio de adolescentes. [Psychosocial and existential considerations about adolescents' suicide] *Psicologia em Estudo, 3,* 81–91.

Dutra, E. M. (2000). *Compreensão de tentativas de suicídio de jovens sob o enfoque da Abordagem Centrada na Pessoa.* [Understanding suicidal tendencies in youth within the framework of the Person Centered Approach]. Tese de Doutorado não publicada. [Unpublished doctoral dissertation.] Instituto de Psicologia, USP, São Paulo.

Eagly, A.H., Ashmore, R.D., Makhijani, M.G., & Longo, L.C. (1991). What is beautiful is good but …: A meta-analytic review of research on the physical attractiveness stereotype. *Psychological Bulletin, 110,* 107–128.

ECA—Estatuto da Criança e do Adolescente. Lei Federal n°8069/1990. [The Child and Adolescent Statute—(Brazilian) Federal law]. (1990)

Eccles, J. S., Midgeley, C., Wigfield, A., Buchanan, C. M., Reuman, D., Flanagan, C., & MacIver, D. (1993). Development during adolescence: The impact of stage-environment fit on young adolescents' experiences in schools and families. *American Psychologist, 48,* 90–101.

Eckert, S. (1998). Counseling of sexual abusers, In L. Palmatier, (Ed.), *Crisis counseling for a quality school community: Applying WM Glasser's choice theory* (pp. 227–268). New York: Accelerated Development Inc.

Edwards, C. (1994). Cross-cultural research on Kohlberg's stages: The basis for consensus. In W. Puka (Ed.), *Moral development. A compendium.* Vol. 5. New York: Garland.

Elkind, D. (1985). Egocentrism redux. *Developmental Review, 5,* 218–226.

Elliot, D. S., Hamburg, B. A., & Williams, K. R. (1998). *Violence in American schools.* New York: Cambridge University Press.

Ennis, R. H. (1989). Critical thinking and subject specificity: clarification and needed research. *Educational Researcher, 18, 3,* 4–10.

Erickson, E. H. (1968). *Identity, youth and crisis.* New York: Norton.

Erickson, E. H. (1985). *Childhood and society.* New York: Norton.

Erooga, M., & Masson, H. (1999). *Children and young people who sexually abuse others: Challenges and responses* (p. 278). New York: Routledge.

Fagan, T. K., & Wise, P. S. (2000). *School psychology: Past, present, and future* (2nd ed.). Bethesda, MD: NASP Publications.

Fanselow, M. S. (1991). The midbrain pereaqueductal gray as coordinator of action in response to fear and anxiety. In A. Depaulis & R. Bandler (Eds.), *The midbrain periaqueductal graymatter: Functional, anatomical and neurochemical organization.* New York: Plenum Press.

Feijo, M. (1998). *Suicidio: Entre a razão e a loucura.* [Suicide: Between madness and reason.] São Paulo: Lemos Editorial.

Feindler, E. L. (1995). *Anger disorders: Ideal treatment package for children and adolescents with anger disorders.* New York: Taylor and Francis.

Feindler, E. L., Marriott, A. S., & Iwata, M. (1984). Group anger control training for junior high school delinquents. *Cognitive Therapy and Research, 8,* 299–311.

Feiring, B. (1996). Concepts of romance in 15-year-old adolescents. *Journal of Research on Adolescence, 6,* 181–200.

Fenn, K., McCarthy, S., Trent, D., & Hutz, C. (2004, August). *International collaboration to improve suicide prevention programs in adolescent detention facilities.* Paper presented as part of a symposia on Adolescence at the 2004 Meeting of the International Union of Psychological Sciences, Beijing, China.

Fenson, L. & Fenson, J. (Eds.) (1992). *Annual editions in human development.* Guilford, CT: Dushkin.

Feuerstein, R. (1980). *Instrumental enrichment: An intervention program for cognitive modifiability.* Baltimore, MD: University Park Press.

Fields, R. (1973). *Society on the run: A psychology for Northern Ireland.* Harmondsworth, England: Penguin Books.

Figueiredo, L. C. (1998). Adolescência e violência: Considerações sobre o caso brasileiro. [Adolescents and violence: Considerations about the Brazilian case.] In D. L. Levisky (Ed.), *Adolescência: Pelos caminhos da violência* [Adolescence: Paths to violence]. São Paulo: Casa do Psicólogo.

Fiske, S. T. (1993). Social cognition and social perception. *Annual Review of Psychology, 44,* 155–194.

Fiske, S. T., & Taylor, S. E. (1991). *Social cognition.* New York: McGraw-Hill.

Flanagan, K., & Hayman-White, K. (2000). An Australian adolescent sex offender treatment program: program and client description. *Journal of Sexual Aggression, 5,* 59–77.

Flannelly, K. J., Murroka, M., Blanchard, D., & Blanchard, R. (1985). Specific anti-aggressive effects of fluprozine hydrochloride. *Psychopharmacology, 87,* 86–89.

Fleming, M. (Ed.) (1982). Challenges in the future for teachers and students of English. *Arizona English Bulletin, 24*, 3.

Foreman, K. H. (1988). Cognitive style, cognitive ability and acquisition of initial programming competence. *Proceedings of selected research papers presented at the annual meeting of the association for educational communications and technology.* New Orleans: AECT.

Forster, L. M. K., Barros, H. M. T., Tannhauser, S. L., & Tannhauser, M. (1992). Meninos de rua: Relação entre abuso de drogas e atividades ilícitas. [Street children: The relationship between drug use and illicit activities.] *ABP-APAL, 14*, 115–120.

Foxhall, K. (2001). Preventing relapse. *Monitor on Psychology, 32*, 46–47.

Frank, D., Bresnahan, K., & Zuckerman, B. (1993). Maternal cocaine use: Impact on child health & development. *Advances in Pediatrics, 40*, 65–99.

Freire, P. (1973). *Educating for critical consciousness.* New York: Seabury Press.

Freire, P. & Macedo D. (1987). *Literacy: Reading the word and the world.* South Hadley, MA: Bergin & Garvey.

Freud, A. (1958). Adolescence. *Psychoanalytic Society of the Child, 15*, 255–278.

Freud, A. (1969). Adolescence as a developmental disturbance. In G. Caplan, & S. Lebovici (Eds.), *Adolescence: Psychological perspectives* (pp. 5–10). New York: Basic Books.

Freud, A. & Burlingham, D. (1943). *War and children.* Madison, CT: International Universities Press.

Fulroth, R., Duran, D. Nicjerson, A. & Espinoza, J. (1989). Perinatal outcome of infants exposed to cocaine and/or heroin in utero. *American Journal of Disabilities in Children, 143*, 8, 905–910.

Fyson, R., Eadie, T., & Cooke, P. (2003). Adolescents with learning disabilities who show sexually inappropriate or abusive behaviours: Development of a research study. *Child Abuse Review, 12*, 305–314.

Galotti, K. & Komatsu, L. K. (1989). Correlations of syllogistic reasoning skills in middle childhood and early adolescence. *Journal of Youth and Adolescence, 18*, 1, 85–96.

Garbarino, J. (1992). Developmental consequences of living in dangerous and unstable environments: The situation of refugees children. In M. McCallin (Ed.), *The psychological well-being of refugee children: Research, practice and policy issues.* Geneva: International Catholic Child Bureau.

Garber, J. A., Lewinsohn, P. M., Seeley, J. R., & Brooks-Gunn, J. (1997). Is psychopathology associated with the timing of pubertal development? *Journal of the American Academy of Child and Adolescent Psychiatry, 31*, 1768–1776.

Garmezy, N. (1974). The study of competence in children at risk for severe psychopathology. In E. J. Anthony & C. Koupernick (Eds.), *The child in his family: Children at psychiatric risk* (Vol. 3, pp. 77–97). New York: Wiley.

Gauvin, R. (1989, April). *Influence of knowledge of a post-test and child age on adult-child planning.* Paper presented at the biennial meeting of the Society for Research in Child Development. Kansas City, MO.

Gauvin, R. & Rogoff, T. (1989). Collaborative problem solving and children's planning skills. *Developmental Psychology, 25,* 1, 139–151.

Gibbon, E. (1960). *The decline and fall of the roman empire.* New York: Harcourt, Brace & Javanovich.

Gielen, U., & Kelly, D. (1983). Buddhist Ladakh: Psychological portrait of a non-violent culture. Presented at the Annual Conference of the Society for Cross-Cultural Research, Washington DC.

Gilligan, C. (1977). In a different voice: Women's conceptions of self and morality. *Harvard Educational Review, 47.*

Gilligan, C. (1979). Women's place in a man's life cycle. *Harvard Educational Review, 49.*

Gilligan, C. (1982). *In a different voice: Psychological theory and women's development.* Cambridge, MA: Harvard University Press.

Gold, A. & McCarthy, S. (1998). Anger Management Training. Poster presented at the Annual Convention of the American Psychological Society, Washington, D.C.

Gold, A. & McCarthy, S. (2003). Anger Management Training Workshop, International Council of Psychologists Convention, Toronto, August 12, 2003.

Gold, A. & McCarthy, S. (2005) Anger Management Training: Training the Trainers. Continuing Education Workshop presented at the International Council of Psychologists Convention in Foz do Iguacu, Brazil, July 15, 2005.

Goldman, S., & Beardsless, W. (1999). Suicide in children and adolescents. In D. Jacobs, (Ed.), *The Harvard Medical School guide to suicide assessment and intervention.* San Francisco: Jossey-Bass Publishers.

Goldstein, A. P. (1996). *Violence in America: Lessons on understanding the aggression in our lives.* San Francisco: Davies-Black Publishing.

Goldstein, A. P., & Glick, B. (1987). *Aggression replacement training: A comprehensive intervention for aggressive youth.* Champaign, IL: Research Press.

Goldstein, A. P., & Michaels, G. Y. (1985). *Empathy: Development, training and consequences.* Englewood Cliffs, NJ: Erlbaum.

Goleman, D. (1995). *Emotional intelligence.* New York: Bantam

Gomes, W., De Souza, M., & McCarthy, S. (2005). Reversible relationship between quantitative and qualitative data in self-consciousness research: A normative semiotic model for the phenomenological dialogue between data and capta. *Quality and Quantity.* Manuscript accepted for publication.

Gomide, P. (1998). *Menor infrator: A caminho de um novo tempo.* [Delinquent minor: On the way to a new time.] Curitiba: Juruá.

Gorsuch, R. L., & Barnes, M. L. (1973). Stages of ethical reasoning and moral norms of Carib youths. *Journal of Cross-Cultural Psychology, 4,* 283–301.

Gratton, F. (1996). Youth suicide: A rational act. *Canadian Mental Health, 43,* 32–55.

Green, L. & Masson, H. (2002). Adolescents who sexually abuse and residential accommodation: Issues of risk and vulnerability. *British Journal of Social Work, 32,* 149–168.

Green, R. (1989). At-risk youth can succeed. *School Administrator, 46,* 1, 13–16.

Griffith, D. (1994). Three year outcome of children exposed prenatally to drugs. *Journal of the Academy of Child and Adolescent Psychiatry, 33,* 20–27.

Grinder, R. E. (1985). The gifted in our midst: By their divine deeds, neuroses and mental test scores we have known them. In F. D. Horowitz & M. O'Brien (Eds.), *The gifted and talented: Developmental perspectives.* Washington, D. C.: American Psychological Association

Grotberg, E. H. (1995). *A guide to promoting resilience in children.* The Hague, Netherlands: Bernard van Leer Foundation.

Grotberg, E. H. (1999a). Countering depression with the five building blocks of resilience. *Reaching Today's Youth, 4,* 66–72.

Grotberg, E. H. (1999b). *Tapping your inner strength.* Oakland, CA: New Harbinger Publications.

Grotberg, E. H. (2000). International resilience research project. In A. L. Comunian & U. Gielen (Eds.), *International perspectives on human development.* Vienna, Austria: Pabst Science Publishers.

Grotberg, E. H. (2001a). Introduccion: nuevas tendencia en resiliencia. [Introduction: New trends in resilience.] In A. Melillo & N. Suarez-Ojeda (Eds.), *Resiliencia., Discububriendo las proprias fortalezas* [Resilience: Discovering your inner strengths.] Buenos Aires, Argentina: Paidos.

Grotberg, E. H. (2001b). Resilience programs for children in disaster. *Ambulatory Child Health, 7,* 75–83.

Grotberg, E. H. (2002).From terror to triumph: The path to resilience. In C. Stout (Ed.), *The psychology of terrorism* (pp. 285–207). Westport, CT: Praeger Publishers.

Grusec, J. E., & Lytton, H. (1988). *Social development: History, theory and research.* New York: Springer Verlag.

Guernsey, J. (1993). *Youth violence.* New York: Random House.

Guyot, G., & Strehlow, A. (2000, April). *Parent attachment, adult attachment style and locus of control.* Paper presented at the 2000 Annual Meeting of the Southwestern Psychological Association, Dallas, TX.

Hagan, M., & Cho, M. (1996). A comparison of treatment outcomes between adolescent rapists and child sexual offenders. *International Journal of Offender Therapy and Comparative Criminology, 40,* 113–122.

Hagan, M., Gust-Brey, K., Cho, M., & Dow, E. (2001). Eight year comparative analyses of adolescent rapists, adolescent child molesters, other adolescent delinquents, and the general population. *International Journal of Offender Therapy and Comparative Criminology, 45,* 314–324.

Hains. A. A., & Miller, D. J. (1980). Moral and cognitive development in delinquent and non-delinquent children and adolescents. *Journal of Genetic Psychology, 137,* 21–35.

Hall, G. S. (1904). *Adolescence: Its psychology and its relation to physiology, anthropology, sociology, sex, crime, religion and education.* Vol. 2. Englewood Cliffs, NJ: Prentice Hall.

Hall, G. S. (1921). *The message of the zeitgeist: Educational psychologist.* Washington, D.C.: American Psychological Association.

Hallpike, C.R. (2004). *The evolution of moral understanding.* London: Prometheus Research Group.

Halpern, D. (1984). *Thought and knowledge: An introduction to critical thinking skill.* Hillsdale, NJ: Erlbaum.

Hamilton, S. F. (1990, April). *Linking school learning with learning on the job.* Paper presented at the Annual Meeting of the American Educational Research Association, Boston, MA.

Hamzah, S., Madsen, J., & Sin, G. T. (1989). *Managing plural society.* Singapore: Longman.

Harkness, S., Edwards, C. P., & Super, C. M. (1981). Social roles and moral reasoning: A case study in a rural African community. *Developmental Psychology, 17,* 595–603.

Harrison, T. R. (1984, November). *Application of popular adolescent literature to adolescent development and to adolescent psychology.* Paper presented at the annual meeting of the Mid-south Educational Research Association, New Orleans, LA.

Hartley, N. K. (1990). *An analysis of the professional development needs of Colorado vocational educators.* Denver: Colorado State Community College and Occupational Education System.

Harvey, A. L. (1985, March). *The validity of six beliefs about factors related to statistics achievement.* Paper presented at the annual meeting of the American Educational Research Association, Chicago, IL.

Hathurn, M. (1993). Personal communication between author and curriculum specialist for Phoenix Union High School District, Phoenix, AZ, March 8, 1993.

Hawley, T., Halle, L., Drasin, A., & Thomas, S. (1995). Children of addicted mothers: Effects of the crack epidemic on the caregiving environment and the development of preschoolers. *American Journal of Orthopsychiatry, 65,* 364–379.

Heidegger, M. (1927). *Ser e Tempo* [Being and time]. (8th ed.). Petrópolis: Vozes.

Heiman, M. & Slomianko, J. (1992a). *Critical thinking skills.* Washington, D.C.: NEA.

Heiman, M. & Slomianko, J. (1992b). *Thinking skills instruction: Concepts and techniques.* Washington, D.C.: NEA.

Heiman, M., Narode, R., Slomianko, J. & Lochhead, J. (1992). *Teaching thinking skills: Mathematics.* Washington, D.C.: NEA.

Hernstein, R., Nickerson, R., Sanchez, M. & Swets, J. (1986). Psychology in action: Teaching thinking skills. *American Psychologist, 41*, 11, 1279–1289.

Hershkowitz, I., Horowitz, D., Lamb, M., Orbach, Y., & Sternberg K. (2004). Interviewing youthful suspects in alleged sex crimes: A descriptive analysis. *Child Abuse and Neglect, 28*, 423–438.

Hetherton, T. F. (2002). *The social mind: Neuroscience in personality, social and developmental psychology.* Paper presented at the 24th Annual National Institute on the Teaching of Psychology, St. Petersburg, FL, January 4, 2002.

Heubner, A. M., & Garrod, A. C. (1993). Moral reasoning among Tibetan monks: A study of Buddhist adolescents and young adults in Nepal. *Journal of Cross-Cultural Psychology, 24*, 167–185.

Heyman, G. & Daly, E. (1992). Teaching critical thinking in vocational-technical and occupational classes. *New Directions for Community Colleges, 20*, 1, 103–108.

Hilton, Z., Harris, G., & Rice, M. (2003). Adolescents perceptions of the seriousness of sexual aggression: Influence of gender, traditional attitudes, and self reported experience. *Sex Abuse: Journal of Research and Treatment, 15*, 201–214.

Hirschberg, D. (1992). Source and information: Critical thinking skills instruction in the community college. *New Directions for Community Colleges, 20*, 1, 109–116.

Hobfell, S. (1991). War-related stress: Addressing the stress of war and other traumatic events. *American Psychologist, 46*, 848–855.

Holm, J., & Bowler, J. (1994) (Eds.). *Making moral decisions.* London: Pinter Pub.

Hora, P. F., Schma, W. G., and Rosenthal, T. A. (1999). Therapeutic jurisprudence and the drug court movement: Revolutionizing the criminal justice system's response to drug abuse and crime in America. *Notre Dame Law Review, 74*, 7–14.

Howard, J. Beckworth, L., Rodning, C., & Kropenske, V. (1989). The development of young children of substance-abusing parents: Insights from seven years of intervention and research. *Bulletin of the National Center for Clinical Infant Programs, 9*, 8–12.

Hunt, M. (1982). *The story of psychology.* New York: Doubleday.

Hunter, C. B. & Wold, A. L. (1982). Computer games in the classroom. *Curriculum Review, 21*, 3, 273–275.

Hunter, J., & Lexier, L. (1998). Ethical and legal issues in the assessment and treatment of juvenile sex offenders. *Journal of the American Professional Society on the Abuse of Children, 3*, 339–348.

Hunter, J., Hazelwood, R., & Slesinger, D. (2000). Juvenile perpetrated sex crimes: Patterns of offending and predictors of violence. *Journal of Family Violence, 15*, 81–93.

Hutz, C. (Ed). (2002). *Children and adolescents at risk: Theoretical aspects and strategies for intervention.* Sao Paulo, Brazil: Casa do Psicologa.

Hutz, C., Koller, S., & Bandeira, D. (1996). Resiliência e vulnerabilidade em criancas em situação de risco. [Resilience and vulnerability among children at risk.] *Coletâneas da ANPEPP, 1,* 79–86.

Hutz, C., da Silva, D., & McCarthy, S. (2004). Brazil's street children: Who are they? Proceedings of the 62nd Annual Convention of the International Council of Psychologists. Padua, Italy: University Press.

Hutz, C. S., & Koller, S. H. (1997). Questões sobre o desenvolvimento de crianças em situação de rua. [Issues about the development of street children.] *Estudos de Psicologia, 2,* 175–197.

Hutz, C. S., & Koller, S. H. (1999). Methodological and ethical issues in research with street children. In M. Raffaelli & R. W. Larson (Eds.). Homeless and working youth around the world: Exploring developmental issues. *New Directions for Child and Adolescent Development, 85,* 59–70.

Hutz, C. S., Conti, L., & Vargas, S. (1994). Rules used by Brazilian students in systematic and nonsystematic reward allocation. *Journal of Social Psychology, 134,* 331–338.

Hutz, C. S., Koller, S. H., Ruschel, D. B., & Forster, L. M. K. (1995). *Researching street children: Methodological and ethical issues.* Paper presented at the meeting of the Society for Research in Child Development, Indianapolis, IN: ERIC Document Reproduction Service No. PS 023 280.

Hylton, B. J. (1996). *Safe schools: A security and loss prevention plan.* Boston: Buttersworth-Heinnemann.

IBGE-UNICEF. (1997). *Indicadores sobre crianças e adolescentes—Brasil, 1991–1997.* [Indicators about children and adolescents—Brazil, 1991–1997].

Inciardi, J. A., Surrett, H. L., & Saum, C. A. (1997). *Cocaine-exposed infants: Social, legal and public policy issues. Drugs, health and public policy series,* Vol. 5. London: Sage Publications.

Inhelder, B. & Piaget, J. (1958). *The growth of logical thinking from childhood to adolescence: An essay on the construction of formal operational structures.* New York: Basic Books.

Iozzi, L. A. (1987). *Science, technology and society: Preparing for tomorrow's world. A multidisciplinary approach to problem solving and critical thinking.* Longmont, CO: Sopris West, Inc.

Iran-Nejad, A. (1990). Active and dynamic self-regulation of learning processes. *Review of Educational Research, 60,* 4, 573–602.

Iwasa, N. (1992). Postconventional reasoning and moral education in Japan. *Journal of Moral Education, 21,* 3–16.

Jafar, J., McCarthy, S., Kolodinsky, W., Schroeder, V. (2003). The impact of cultural norms and values on moral judgement of Malay and American Adolescents. *Proceeds of the International Conference of Cross-cultural Psychology.* London: International Association of Cross-Cultural Psychology.

Jones, B. F. (1982). *Chicago mastery learning: Reading (2nd ed).* Watertown, MA: Mastery Education Corporation.

Jones, M. K. & Norman, J. T. (1989). *The effect of a preservice elementary science methods course emphasizing the mastery of science process skills on the development of integrated process skills and logical thinking.* Paper presented at the Annual Meeting of the National Association for Research in Science Teaching, March 30–April 1, 1989, San Francisco, CA.

Karandashav, V. (2002). ICOPE: International Conference on Psychology Education. Retrieved from http://www.ibapnet.org.br/foz.

Karolides, N. J. (Ed.) (1987). Beyond the two Rs. *Wisconsin English Journal,* 29, 2, 1–26.

Kaufman, K., Hilliker, D., & Daleiden, E. (1997). Subgroup differences in the modus operandi of adolescent sexual offenders. *Journal of the American Professional Society on the Abuse of Children, 1,* 17–24.

Kaufman, K., Holmberg, J., Orts, K., McCrady F., & Rotzien, A. (1998). Factors influencing sexual offenders' modus operandi: An examination of victim-offender relatedness and age. *Journal of the American Professional Society on the Abuse of Children, 3,* 349–361.

Kazdin, A. (1993). Adolescent mental health. *American Psychologist, 48,* 127–141.

Keating, D. (1988). *Adolescents' ability to engage in critical thinking.* Madison, WI: National Center on Effective Secondary Schools.

Keller, M., Edelstein, W., Fang, F-X., & Fang, G. (1998). Reasoning about responsibilities and obligations in close relationships: A comparison across two cultures. *Developmental Psychology, 34,* 731–741.

Kellner, M. H., & Tutin, J. (1995). A school-based anger management program for developmentally and emotionally disabled high school students. *Adolescence, 30,* 813–825.

Kettle, P. (2001). *Biological and social causes of school violence.* New York: Macmillan.

King, N., Lancaster, N., Wynne, G., Nettleton, N., & Davis, R. (1999). Cognitive-behavioral anger management training for adults with mild intellectual disability. *Scandinavian Journal of Behavioral Therapy, 28,* 19–22.

Knobel, M. (1981). *A sindrome da adolescência normal.* [The syndrome of normal adolescence.] In M. Aberastury & M. Knobel, (Eds.), *Adolescência normal* [Normal adolescence]. Porto Alegre: Artes Medicas.

Kohlberg, L. (1963). The development of children's orientation toward a moral order. *Vita Humana, 6,* 11–32.

Kohlberg, L. (1964). Development of moral character and moral ideology. In M. L. Hoffman & L. W. Hoffman (Eds.), *Review of child development research,* Vol. 1. New York: Russell Sage.

Kohlberg, L. (1967). Moral and religious education and the public schools: A developmental view. In T. R. Sizer (Ed.), *Religion and public education.* Boston: Houghton-Mifflin.

Kohlberg, L. (1969). Stage and sequence: The cognitive-developmental approach to socialization. In D. A. Goslin (Ed.), *Handbook of socialization theory and research* (pp. 347–380). Chicago: Rand McNally.

Kohlberg, L. (1970). Moral development and the education of adolescents. In R. F. Purnell (Ed.), *Adolescents and the American high school.* New York: Holt, Rhinehart & Winston.

Kohlberg, L. (1971). From is to ought: How to commit the naturalistic fallacy and get away with it in the study of moral development. In T. Mischel (Ed.), *Cognitive development and epistemology.* New York: Academic.

Kohlberg, L. (1982). *The psychology of moral development.* San Francisco: Harper & Row.

Kohlberg, L., & Blatt, M. (1972). The effects of classroom discussion on moral development. In L. Kohlberg & E. Turiel, (Eds.), *Recent research in moral development.* New York: Holt, Rhinehart & Winston.

Kohlberg, L., & Eifenbein, D. (1981). Capital punishment, moral development, and the constitution. In L. Kohlberg (Ed.), *The philosophy of moral development.* San Francisco: Harper & Row.

Koller, S. H., & Hutz, C. S. (2001). Street children: Psychological perspectives. In N. J. Smelser & P. B. Baltes (Eds.), *International Encyclopedia of the Social & Behavioral Sciences* (pp. 15157–15160). Oxford: Pergamon.

Kotila, L., & Lonnequist, J. (1987). Adolescents who make suicide attempts repeatedly. *Acta Psiquiatrica Scandinavia, 76,* 386–393.

Koviacs, M. (1992). *Morte e desenvolvimento humano* [Death and human development]. Sao Paulo: Casa do Psicologo.

Krahe, B., Scheinberger-Olwig, R., & Waisenhoefer, E. (1999). Sexual aggression amongst adolescents: A prevalence study including an East-West comparison. *Zeitschrift fuer Sozialpsychologie, 30,* 165–178.

Kristiansen, C. M., & Giuletti, R. (1990). Perception of wife abuse: Effects of gender, attitudes toward women and just-world beliefs among college students. *Psychology of Women Quarterly, 14,* 177–189.

Kubik, E., Hecker, J., & Righthand, S. (2002). Adolescent females who have sexually offended: Comparisons with delinquent adolescent female offenders and adolescent males who sexually offend. *Journal of Child Sexual Abuse, 11,* 63–83.

Kuhn, D. (1999). A developmental model of critical thinking. *Educational Researcher, 28,* 2, 16–26.

Langer, E., Bashner, R., & Chanowitz, B. (1985). Decreasing prejudice by increasing discrimination. *Journal of Personality and Social Psychology, 49,* 113–120.

Laycock, J. (1979). *Gifted children.* Glenview, IL: Scott, Foresman & Co.

Leary, R. (1993). "A qualitative study of the effects of anger management training." Unpublished doctoral dissertation. Arizona State University.

LeBlanc, M., & Lapointe, C. (1999). Sexual aggression in boys: Comparison of aggressors, victims, and aggressors who are victims with other adolescents with problem behaviours. *Canadian Journal of Criminology, 41,* 479–511.

LeCroy, C. W. (1988). Anger management or anger expression: Which is most effective? *Residential Treatment for Children and Youth, 5,* 29–39.

Lei, T., & Cheng, S. (1987). A little but special light on the universality of moral judgment development. In L. Kohlberg, D. Candee, & A. Colby (Eds.), *Rethinking moral development.* Cambridge: Harvard University Press.

Lerner, M. J., & Miller, D. T. (1978). Just world research and the attribution process: Looking back and ahead. *Psychological Bulletin, 85,* 1030–1051.

Lester, B. (1991). Neurobehavioral syndromes in cocaine-exposed newborn infants. *Child Development, 62,* 694–705.

Letourneau, E. (2004). A comment on the first report. *Sexual abuse: Journal of Research and Treatment, 16,* 77–81.

Levisky, D. (1998). *Adolescência: Pelos caminhos da violência.* [Adolescence: Paths to violence]. Sao Paulo: Casa do Psicólogo.

Lewis, D. C. (1998). New studies find drug courts and drug treatment of prisoners, paroles and teens cut crime and drug use. *Physician Leadership on National Drug Policy, 10.*

Lewis, M. (1990). Self-knowledge and social development in early life. In L. A. Pervin (Ed.), *Handbook of personality: Theory and research* (pp. 277–300). New York: Guilford Press.

Lewis, M., Sullivan, M. W., Stanger, C., & Weiss, M. (1989). Self-development and self-conscious emotions. *Child Development, 60,* 146–156.

Lewis, R. (1981). *The philosophical roots of lifelong learning.* Toledo, OH: Center for the Study of HigheEducation.

Leyba, T. (1993). Personal communication. South Mountain High School, Phoenix, AZ.

Linn, M. C. (1989) Scientific reasoning during adolescence: The influence of instruction in science knowledge and reasoning strategies. *Journal of Research in Science Teaching, 26,* 2, 171–187.

Lipman, M. & Sharp, A. (1980). *Social inquiry: Instructional manual to accompany MARK. Institute for the Advancement of Philosophy in Children.* Montclair, NJ: First Mountain Foundation, Montclair State College.

Lipman, M., Sharp, A. M. & Oscanyan, F. S. (1980). *Philosophy in the classroom* (2nd ed.). Philadelphia, PA: Temple University Press.

Little, A. L., & Little, S. F. (2001). *How to become an exemplary middle school principal: A three-step professional growth handbook.* Westerville, OH: National Middle School Association.

Loeber, R., & Hay, D. (1997). Key issues in the development of aggression and violence from childhood to early adulthood. *Annual Review of Psychology, 48,* 371–410.

Loeber, R., & Stouthamer-Loeber, M. (1989). Development of juvenile aggression and violence. *American Psychologist, 53,* 242–259.

Lowenstein, L. (1998). *Paedophilia—The sexual abuse of children, its occurrence, diagnosis and treatment.* London: Able Publishing Limited.

Luthar, S. S., & Ziegler, E. (1991). Vulnerability and competence: A review of research on resilience in childhood. *American Orthopsychiatric Association, 6,* 6–22.

Lykken, D. T. (1988). *The antisocial personalities.* Englewood Cliffs, NJ: LEA.

Ma, H. K. (1989). Moral orientation and moral judgments in adolescents in Hong Kong, Mainland China, and England. *Journal of Cross-Cultural Psychology, 20,* 152–177.

Maciel, W., Schmidt, B. J., Santoro, M., Azevedo, M. A., & Guerra, V. N. A. (1991). Street children in Brazil. *International Child Health, 1,* 19–20.

Manocha, K., & Mezey, G. (1999). British adolescents who sexually abuse: A descriptive study. *Journal of Forensic Psychiatry, 9,* 588–608.

Maqsud, M. (1977). Moral reasoning of Nigerian and Pakistani Muslim adolescents. *Journal of Moral Education, 7,* 40–49.

Marcia, J. E. (1992). Identity and self-development. In R. M. Lerner, A. C. Petersen, & J. Brooks-Gunn (Eds.), *Encyclopedia of adolescence* (Vol. 1). New York: Garland.

Markus, H., & Nurius, P. (1986). Possible selves. *American Psychologist, 41,* 954–969.

Marriott, S. A.. & Iwata, M. (1984). Group anger control training for junior high school delinquents. *Cognitive Therapy and Research, 8,* 299–311.

Marshall, R., Yorks, L. & Pitera, J. (1993). Redeployment: An organizational transformation strategy which activates and uses individual ego energy to enhance corporate performance in the globally competitive market of the 90's. *Model Practices: Proceedings of the 1992 Conference on Ego Energy in Business.* San Francisco, CA: Jossey-Bass.

Martin, D. S. (1983a, November). *Can teachers become better thinkers?* Paper presented at the Annual Conference of the National Staff Development Center, Tulsa, OK.

Martin, D. S. (1983b, February). *Thinking skills: A critical new role in teacher education.* Paper presented at the Annual Meeting of the American Association of Colleges for Teacher Education, Detroit, MI.

Martinez, A. & Bournival, B. (1995). ADHD: The tip of the iceberg. *ADHD Report, 3,* 6.

Maslow, A. (1968). *Toward a psychology of being.* New York: Van Nostrand.

Massachusetts State Department of Education. (1987). *Moving geometry from the back of the schoolroom: A report on geometry and measurement in the 1986 assessment.* Boston, MA: Education Assessment Program.

Masten, A. S., & Garmezy, N. (1985). Risk, vulnerability, and protective factors in developmental psychopathology. In B. B. Lahey. & A. E. Kazdin (Eds.), *Advances in clinical child psychology, 8,* 1–53.

Mat Saat, B. (1993). *Tingkahlaku tak normal.* [Normal adolescent development]. In Abdul Halim (Ed.), *Psikologi Melayu.* [Malaysian Psychology]. Kuala Lumpur: Dewan Bahasa dan Pustaka.

Matthews, R., Hunter, J., & Vuz, J. (1997). Juvenile female sexual offenders: Clinical characteristics and treatment issues. *Sexual abuse: Journal of Research and Treatment, 9,* 187–199.

Mayes, L. C. (1992). The problem of prenatal cocaine exposure: A rush to judgment. *Journal of the American Medical Association, 267,* 406–408.

Mayes, L.C., Bornstein, B., Chaworska, C., & Granger, G. (1995). Information processing and developmental assessments in 3-month-old infants exposed prenatally to cocaine. *Pediatrics, 95,* 539–545.

McCarthy, S. (1995). *Teaching reality-based logic to improve adolescents' critical thinking skills.* Doctoral dissertation. Tempe, AZ: Arizona State University.

McCarthy, S. (1998a). The need for logic instruction in public schools. *The Korean Journal of Thinking and Problem Solving, 8, 2.*

McCarthy, S. (1998b). Teaching logic to adolescents to improve thinking skills. *Korean Journal of Thinking and Problem-Solving, 8, 1.*

McCarthy, S. (March, 1999a). *U.S. perspectives on challenges for teaching psychology in the 21st century. Pratiques Psychologique.* Paris: French Psychological Society.

McCarthy, S. (1999b). Student preferences for electronic instructional options in a community college introductory psychology class. *Community College Journal of Research and Practice, 23, 3.*

McCarthy, S. (2000). Teaching style, philosophical orientation and the transmission of critical thinking skills in U.S. public schools. *The Korean Journal of Thinking and Problem Solving, 10, 1.*

McCarthy, S. (2001). *International perspectives on teaching critical thinking and problem solving. Teaching of Psychology.* Englewood Cliffs, NJ: Lawrence Erlbaum Associates.

McCarthy, S. (2002). Preventing terrorism among adolescents through global psychology. In C. Stout (Ed.), *The psychology of terrorism.* (pp. 285–207). Westport, CT: Praeger Publishers.

McCarthy, S., & Gold, A. (2002). *Using anger management training to reduce violence in public schools.* Paper presented at the 8th National Conference on Alternatives to Suspension, Expulsion and Dropping out of School, Orlando, FL, January 24, 2002.

McCarthy, S., & Gold, A. (2003). *Anger management training: A strategy to work with troubled adolescents.* Paper presented at the Northern Russia Psychological Society Conference, Vologda, Russia, November 1, 2003.

McCarthy, S., Gold, A., & Garcia, E. (1999). Effects of anger management training on aggressive behavior in adolescent boys. *Journal of Offender Rehabilitation.* Doylestown, PA: Taylor & Francis.

McCarthy, S., Jafar, J., & Artemeyeva, V. (2004). *Comparative Moral Development of Malaysian, Russian and American Adolescents.* Paper presented as part of a symposia on adolescent issues at the 2004 conference of the International Union of Psychological Sciences in Beijing, China, August, 2004.

McCarthy, S., Prandini, C., & Hollingsworth, F. (2001). Rites of passage: A comparison of perceptions of American and Italian adolescents. *Proceedings of the 2001 Conference of the Arizona Educational Research Association.* Tempe: Arizona State University.

McCarthy-Tucker, S. (1995). *Teaching logic to improve adolescents' critical thinking skills.* Paper presented at the 15th International Conference on Critical Thinking, Sonoma, CA.

McGarvey, J., & Lenaghan, M. (1996). A structured group approach with adolescent perpetrators. *Child Abuse Review, 5,* 203–213.

Mead, M. (1928). *Coming of age in Samoa.* New York: Morrow.

Meichenbaum, D. (1977). *Cognitive Behavioral Modification: An Integrated Approach.* New York: Plenum.

Meindl, J. R., & Lerner, M. J. (1984). Exacerbation of extreme responses to an outgroup. *Journal of Personality and Social Psychology, 47,* 71–84.

Mello, M. & Abreu, A. (1990). Tentativas de suicídio no pronto socorro: Avaliação de uma experiência e propostas. [Attempted suicides in an emergency room: Assessment of an experience and further proposals.] *Temas: Teoria e Practica do Psiquiatria, 20,* 192–201.

Menninger, K. (1970). *Eros & Thanatos: Opposing conditions of mankind.* São Paulo: IBRASA.

Mentis, M., & Lundgren, N. (1995). Effects of prenatal exposure to cocaine and associated risk factors on language development. *Journal of Speech and Hearing Research, 38,* 1303–1318.

Metropolitan Life Insurance. (1993). *Metropolitan Life Survey of the American Teacher: Violence in America's Public Schools.* Metropolitan Life Insurance Company by Louis Harris and Associates, Inc.

Miccio-Fonseca, L. (2000). Adult and adolescent female sex offenders: Experiences compared to other female and male sex offenders. *Journal of Psychology and Human Sexuality, 11,* 75–88.

Michigan State Board of Education. (1988). *Michigan essential goals and objectives for mathematics education.* Lansing, MI : Author

Mill, J. S. (1862). *System of logic, ratiocinative and inductive, being a connected view of the principles of evidence and the methods of scientific investigation.* London: Parker, Son and Bourn.

Miller, I. (1986). Techniques for teaching word problems. *Lifelong Learning, 9,* 4, 29–31.

Miller, J. (2001). *Culture and moral development.* In D. Matsumoto, Handbook of culture and psychology. New York: Oxford University Press.

Miller, K. (1993). Personal communication with author at South Mountain High School, Phoenix, AZ. April 12, 1993.

Miller, J. & Bersoff, A. (1992). Differences between justice and interpersonal responsibilities resolved? *Journal of Personality and Social Psychology, 62,* 541–554.

Mioto, R. (1994). *Familias de jovens que tentam suicidio.* [Families of youth who attempt suicide]. Tese de Doutorado. [doctoral dissertation]. UNICAMP, Campinas, SP.

Miranda, P., & Queiroz, E. (1991). *Pensamento suicida e tentativa de suicídio entre estudantes de Medicina.* [Suicidal thoughts and suicide attempts among medical students.] *Revista ABP-APAL,13,* 157–160.

Mitchell, K. (2000). School safety resources. *The ERIC Review, 71,* 35–39.

Mizuno, S. (1999). Psychosocial development and moral development: An exploratory comparison of adolescents in Japan and America. *Psychological Reports, 84,* 51–62.

Morris, P. (1984). Where's the logic in the introductory economics curriculum? *Economics, 20,* 87, 109–111.

Murphy, W., DiLillo, D., Haynes, M., & Steere, E. (2001). An exploration of factors related to deviant sexual arousal among juvenile sex offenders. *Sexual Abuse: Journal of Research and Treatment, 13,* 91–103.

Murray, J. P. (1980). *Television and youth: Twenty-five years of research and controversy.* Stanford, WA: Boys Town Center for the Study of Youth Development.

Muss, R. E. (1996). *Theories of adolescence.* (6th ed.). New York: McGraw-Hill.

Narode, R., Heiman, M., Lochhead, J. & Slomianko, J. (1992). *Teaching thinking skills: Science.* Washington, D.C.: NEA.

Neubert, G. & Binko, J. (1992). *Inductive reasoning in the secondary classroom.* Washington, D.C.: NEA.

Norazit, S. (1995). *The Malay family and urban adaptation: A case study.* Paper presented at the conference on The Malay Cosmology, University of Malaya, Kuala Lumpur.

Norris, V. P. (1990). *Developing positive attitudes toward school in middle school dropout prevention program using multidisciplinary units.* Practicum Report: Nova University.

Novaco, R. W. (1975). *Anger Control: The Development and Evaluation of an Experimental Treatment.* Lexington, MA: Lexington Books.

Nulman, I. (1994). Neurodevelopment of adopted children exposed in utero to cocaine. *Canadian Medical Association Journal, 151,* 1591–1597.

Nunes, S. (1988). *Atendimento de tentativas de suicídio em um hospital geral.* [Attending to suicide attempts in a general hospital.] *Jornal Brasileiro de Psiquiatria, 37,* 39–41.

O'Banion, J. D. (1989, March). *Bridging the gap between literature and composition: Rediscovering the synthesis of logical and narrative argumentation.* Paper presented at the Annual Meeting of the Conference on College Composition and Communications, Seattle, WA.

Okagaki, L., & Sternberg, R. J. (1990). Teaching thinking skills: We're getting the context wrong. *Contributions to Human Development, 21,* 61–77.

Okagaki, L., & Sternberg, R. J. (1993). Parental beliefs and children's school performance. *Child Development, 64,* 36–56.

Okonkwo, R. (1997). Moral development and culture in Kohlberg's theory: A Nigerian (Igbo) evidence. *IFE Psychologia: An International Journal, 5,* 117–128.

Oliveira, M., Nishiyama, P., Steinmacher, D., Ramos, B., Salmazo, J., Itinose, A., Silva, A., & Machinski, Jr., M. (1997). Análise epidemiológica das tentativas de suicídio atendidas pelo Centro de Controle de Intoxicacoes de Maringá

(PR), no período de 1991–1994. [Epidemiological analysis of attempted suicides at the Center for the Control of Intoxications in Maringá (PR) from 1991–1994]. *Psicologia em Estudo*, *2*, 75–87.

Oliver, P. (1985, August). *How well are we meeting the goals of high school debate?* Paper presented at the National Forensic League Conference, Kansas City, MO.

Ooi, Y. P. & Ang, R. P. (2004). A social problem-solving skills training program for aggressive children. *Korean Journal of Thinking and Problem-Solving*, *14*, 61–73.

O'Reilly, G., Sheridan, A., Carr, A., Cherry, J., Donahoe, E., McGrath, K., Phelan, S., Tallon, M., & O'Reilly, K. (1998). A descriptive study of adolescent sexual offenders in an Irish community based treatment programme. *Irish Journal of Psychology*, *19*, 152–167.

Organizacao Mundial de Saude (OMS). (1993). *Violence and health*. Geneva, Switzerland: World Health Statistics Quarterly of the World Health Organization.

Organização Panamericana de Saúde. (1994). *Promocion de la Salud en las Americas*. [Promoting health in the Americas]. Consejo directivo OPAS XXXVII Reunion-OMS XLV Reunion, Washington, DC. [Address at the 37th Annual Convention in Washington, DC].

Otto, R. (1986). Logical reasoning patterns in students and social studies instruction. (ED27460).

Pacheco, J. (2004). *A construção do comportamento anti-social em adolescentes autores de atos infracionais: Uma análise a partir das práticas educativas e dos estilos parentais*. [The development of anti-social behavior in adolescents who commit crimes: An analysis of parental styles and educational practices]. Doctoral dissertation. Porto Alegre: Universidade Federal do Rio Grande do Sul.

Pacheco, J., McCarthy, S., & Hutz, C. (2005). *Parenting style as a predictor of juvenile delinquency*. Paper presented in the Forensic Psychology Symposia chaired by E. Bishop at the 65th Annual Convention of the International Council of Psychologists, Brazil

Pallone, N. (2003). *Treating substance abusers in correctional contexts*. New York: Haworth Press.

Parker, W. (1989). Critical reasoning on civic issues. *Theory and Research in Social Education*, *27*, 1, 7–32.

Paul, R. (1992). *Critical thinking: What every person needs to survive in a rapidly changing world*. Santa Rosa, CA: Foundation for Critical Thinking.

Perkins, D. (1985, March). *Knowledge as design: Teaching thinking through content*. Paper presented at the Connecticut Thinking Skills Conference, Wallingford, CT.

Peters, R. (1996). Evaluating drug court programs: An overview of issues and alternative strategies. http://gurukul.ucc.american.edu/justice/justb6.htm.

Peters, R. (1999). *Current drug court evaluation results.* Paper presented at the National Association of Drug Court Professionals 5th Annual Training Conference. Miami Beach, FL.

Peterson, R. (1986, September). *Toward the advancement of teaching logical thinking: A mental processing model for proportional reasoning.* Paper presented at the United States-Japan Seminar on Science Education, Honolulu, HI.

Pettigrew, T. F. (1978). The ultimate attribution error: Extending Allport's cognitive analysis of prejudice. *Personality and Social Psychology Bulletin, 5,* 461–476.

Phelps, E. A., O'Connor, K. J., Cunningham, W. A., Funayama, E. S., Gatenby, J. C., & Banaji, M. R. (2000). Performance on indirect measures of race evaluation predicts amygdala activation. *Journal of Cognitive Neuroscience, 12,* 729–738.

Piaget, J. (1932). *The moral judgment of the child.* London: Routledge & Kegan Paul.

Piaget, J. (1950). *The child's conception of the world.* New York: Harcourt, Brace & Javonovich.

Piburn, M. & Baker, D. (1988). *Reasoning about logical propositions and success in science.* Paper presented at the Annual Meeting of the American Educational Research Association, April 5–9, 1988, New Orleans, LA.

Pithers, W. & Gray, A. (1998). The other half of the story: Children with sexual behaviour problems. *Psychology, Public Policy and Law, 4,* 200–217.

Pokorny, A. (1969). Myths about suicide. In H. Resnick (Ed.), *Suicidal behaviors.* Boston: Little Brown.

Pontes, C. (1986). *Suicídio em Fortaleza: Estudo de 28 anos.* [Suicide in Fortaleza: A 28-year longitudinal study]. Fortaleza: Imprensa Universitária da Universidade Federal do Ceará.

Porat, R., Brodsky, D., Gianette, J., & Hurt, H. (1994). Prenatally exposed to cocaine: Does the label matter? *Journal of Early Intervention, 182,* 119–130.

Presseisen, B. (1992). *Thinking skills: Research and practice.* Washington, D.C.: NEA.

Punamaki, R. (1987). Childhood under conflict: The attitudes and emotional life of Israeli and Palestinian children. (Research Report No. 32). Tampere, Finland: Tampere Peace Research Institute.

Quellmalz, E. (1990). Developing criteria for performance assessments: The missing link. *Applied Measurement in Education, 4,* 4, 319–331.

Rapoport, J. & Castellanos, J. (1995, Nov.). *Neurological profiles of children with ADD.* Paper presented at the C.H.A.D.D. Conference, Washington, D.C.

Raviv, A., Oppenheimer, L., & Bar-Tel, D. (1999). *How children understand war and peace.* San Francisco: Jossey-Bass.

Rhodes, R. (1999) *Why they kill.* New York: Random House.

Richardson, G. A., Hamel, S. Goldschmidt, L., & Day, N. (1996). The effects of prenatal cocaine use on neonatal neurobehavioral status. *Neurotoxicology & Teretotology, 18*, 519–528.

Richardson, G., Kelly, T., & Graham, F. (1997). Group differences in abuser and abuse characteristics in a British sample of sexually abusive adolescents. *Sexual Abuse: Journal of Research and Treatment, 9*, 239–257.

Robinson, J. H. (1921). *The mind in the making.* New York: Harper.

Robinson, K. (2001). Research update: Reports on recent drug court research. *National Drug Court Institute Review, 3*, 121–134.

Rogers, C. (1959). A theory of therapy, personality and interpersonal relationship as developed in the Client-Centered Framework. In S. Koch, (Ed.), *Psychology: A study of a science.* New York: McGraw-Hill.

Rogers, C. (1974). *Tornar-se pessoa.* [Becoming a person]. Lisboa: Moraes.

Rogers, C. & Kinger, M. (1975). *Psicoterapia e relações humanas.* [Psychotherapy and human relations]. Belo Horizonte: Interlivros.

Rogoff, B. (1990). *Apprentices in thinking.* New York: Oxford University Press.

Rosa, J. (1996). *Sintomas depressivos em adolescentes e em seus pais.* [Depression symptoms in adolescents and their parents.] *Pediatra Moderna, 32*, 2, 136–145.

Rosenbaum-Cale, K. (1992). *Teaching thinking skills: Social studies.* Washington, D.C.: NEA.

Rosemberg, F. (1990). *A concepção de família subjacente a programas para crianças e adolescentes em situação de rua.* [Implicit family conceptualizations in programs for children and adolescents on the streets.] In E. A. Carlini (Ed.), *Abuso de drogas entre meninos e meninas de rua do Brasil.* [Drug abuse among boys and girls on the streets in Brazil.] UNFDAC-CEBRID, São Paulo: Editora Ave Maria.

Rosemberg, F. (1994). *Contagem de crianças e adolescentes em situação de rua na cidade de São Paulo.* [Counting children and adolescents on the streets in São Paulo]. Relatório técnico, Secretaria da criança, família e bem-estar social.

Rosenthal, R. (1985). From unconscious experimenter bias to teacher expectancy effects. In J. B. Dusek, V. C. Hall, & W. Meyer (Eds.), *Teacher expectancies.* Hillsdale, NJ: Erlbaum.

Ross, L. D. (1977). The intuitive psychologist and his shortcomings: Distortions in the attribution process. In L. Berkowitz (Ed.), *Advances in experimental social psychology* (Vol. 10). New York: Academic Press.

Rotter, J. B. (1966). Generalized expectation for internal versus external control of reinforcement. *Psychological Monographs, 80*, 609–618.

Rubin, K. H. & Schneider, F. W. (1973). The relationship between moral judgment, egocentrism and altruistic behavior. *Child Development, 44*, 661–665.

Runkle, S. & Tansey, P. (1980). *Logic: A unit for 4-8 graders especially for gifted and talented.* Area Agency 7, Cedar Falls, IA. (ED2444433).

Rutter, M. (1979). Protective factors in children's responses to stress and disadvantage. *Annals of the Academy of Medicine, Singapore, 8*, 324–338.

Rutter, M., Izard, C., & Read, P. (1987). Psychosocial resilience and protective mechanisms. *American Journal of Orthopsychiatry, 57*, 316–331.

Ryan, G. (1997). Consequences for the youth who has been abusive. In G. Ryan & S. Lane (Eds.), *Juvenile sexual offending: Causes, consequences and correction*. Oxford, London.

Ryan, G. (1998). The relevance of early life experience to the behaviour of sexually abusive youth. *Irish Journal of Psychology, 19*, 32–48.

Ryan, G. (1999). Treatment of sexually abusive youth: The evolving consensus. *Journal of Interpersonal Violence, 14*, 422–436.

Ryan, G., Miyoshi, T., Metzner, J., Krugman, R., & Fryer, G. (1996). Trends in a national sample of sexually abused youths. *Journal of the American Academy of Child and Adolescent Psychiatry, 35*, 17–25.

Salminen, S. (1992). Defensive attribution hypothesis and serious occupational accidents. *Psychological Reports, 70*, 1195–1199.

Satel, S. (2001). Drug treatment: The case for coercion. *National Drug Court Institute Review, 3*, 1–58.

Savin-Williams, R. C. & Berndht, T. J. (1990). Friendship and peer relations. In S. S. Feldman & G. R. Elliott (Eds.), *At the threshold: The developing adolescent*. Cambridge, MA: Harvard University Press.

Schatz, A. & Eddington, M. (1995). What can we do about violence? A Bill Moyers special, part 1: Juveniles locked up. [Videocassette]. Available from Films for Humanities and Sciences, Box 2053, Princeton, NJ 08543–2053.

Schlegel, A. & Barry, H., III (1991). *Adolescence: An anthropological inquiry*. New York: Free Press.

Schlichter, K. J. & Horan, J. J. (1981). Effects of stress inoculation on the anger and aggression management skills of institutionalized juvenile delinquents. *Cognitive Therapy and Research, 5*, 359–365.

Scribner, S. (1977). Developmental theories applied to cross-cultural cognitive research. *Annals of the New York Academy of Sciences, 285, 3*, 366–373.

Seidman, R. (1990). Computer programming and logical reasoning: Unintended cognitive effects. *Journal of Educational Technology Systems, 18, 2*, 123–141.

Seto, M., Lalumiere, M., & Blanchard R. (2000). The discriminative validity of a phallometric test for pedophilic interests among adolescent sex offenders against children. *Psychological Assessment, 12*, 319–327.

Seymour, D. (1992). *Materials for classroom use*. Palo Alto, CA: Dale Seymour Publications.

Shakespeare, W. (1982). A Winter's Tale. In *Collected Works of William Shakespeare*. London: Oxford University Press.

Shaw, E. (1985, April). *Effects of microcomputer simulations on achievement and attitudes of middle school students*. Paper presented at the Annual Meeting of the National Association for Research in Science Teaching, French Lick Springs, IN.

Shaw, J., Lewis, J., Loeb, A., Rosado, J., & Rodriguez, R. (2001). Child on child sexual abuse: Psychological perspectives. *Child Abuse and Neglect, 24,* 1591–1600.

Sheerin, D. (1998).Legal options in Ireland for getting adolescent sex offenders into treatment programmes and keeping them there. *Irish Journal of Psychology, 19,* 181–189.

Sheridan, A., McKeown, K., Cherry, J., Donohoe E., McGrath, K., O'Reilly K., Phelan, S., & Tallon, M. (1998). Perspectives on treatment outcome in adolescent sexual offending: A study of a community-based treatment programme. *Irish Journal of Psychology, 19,* 168–180.

Sherif, M., Harvey, L. J., White, B. J., Hood, W., & Sherif, C. W. (1988). *The robber's cave experiment: Intergroup conflict and cooperation.* Middletown, CT: Weslayan University Press.

Shoemaker, B. & Lewin, L. (1993). Curriculum and assessment: Two sides of the same coin. *Educational Leadership, 50,* 8, 56–58.

Short, R. J. & Simeonsson, R. J. (1986). Social cognition and aggression in delinquent adolescent males. *Adolescence, 8,* 159–176.

Shweder, R. A. (1990). Cultural psychology—What is it? In J. W. Stigler, R. A. Shweder, & G. Herdt (Eds.), *Cultural psychology: Essays on comparative human development* (pp. 1–43). Cambridge: Cambridge University Press.

Shweder, R. A. & Much, N. C. (1987). Determinants of meaning: Discourse and moral socialization. In W. M. Kurtines & J. L. Gewirtz (Eds.), *Moral development through social interaction* (pp. 197–244). New York: Wiley.

Shweder, R. A., Mahapatra, M., & Miller, J. (1987). Culture and moral development. In J. Kagan & S. Lamb (Eds.), *The emergence of morality in young children* (pp. 1–90). Chicago: University of Chicago Press.

Sidman, M. (1995). *A coerção e suas implicações.* [Coercion and its implications.] Campinas: Editorial Psychology.

Siegler, R. S. (1991). *Children's thinking* (2nd ed.). Englewood Cliffs, NJ: Prentice Hall.

Silva, G. (1999). *Resiliencia y violencia politica en ninos.* [Children resilience and political violence.] Lanus, Argentina: Universidad Nacional de Lanus.

Silverman, L. K. (1989). It all began with Leta Hollingworth: The story of giftedness in women. *Journal of the education of the gifted, 12,* 2, 86–98.

Simmons, C. & Simmons, C. (1994). Personal and moral adolescent values in England and Saudi Arabia. *Journal of Moral Education, 23,* 3–16.

Sitnikov, V. & Parnyuk, N. (2004, August). *Social perceptions of friend and foe for Russian street children.* Paper presented at the 2004 Meeting of the International Union of Psychological Sciences as part of symposium chaired by C. Hutz. Beijing, China.

Smith, C. A. & Lazarus, R. S. (1990). Emotion and adaptation. In L. A. Pervin (Ed.), *Handbook of personality: Theory and research* (pp. 609–637). New York: Guilford Press.

Smith, G. & Fischer, L. (1999). Assessment of juvenile sexual offenders: Reliability and validity of the Abel Assessment for Interest in Paraphilias. *Sexual Abuse: Journal of Research and Treatment, 11*, 207–216.

Snarey, J. (1985). Cross-cultural universality of social-moral development: A critical review of Kohlbergian research. *Psychological Bulletin, 97,* 202–232.

Snyder, M. Tanke, E. D., & Berscheid, E. (1977). Social perception and interpersonal behavior. On the self-fulfilling nature of social stereotypes. *Journal of Personality and Social Psychology, 35,* 655–666.

Spicer, K. (1991, October). *The application of critical thinking in the public relations curriculum.* Paper presented at the Annual Meeting of the Speech Communication Association, Atlanta, GA.

Spratlan-Mitchell, P. (1993). Personal communication between author and English instructor at South Mountain High School, May 24, 1993, Phoenix, AZ.

Spurgeon, A., McCarthy, S., & Waters, T. (1999). Developing a substance abuse relapse indicator questionnaire for adults on intensive probation: A pilot study. *Journal of Offender Rehabilitation.*

Stahl, R. (1988). Materials and resources review. *Social Studies Teacher, 9,* 4, 9–10.

Steinberg, I. & Levine, A. (1997). *You and your adolescent: A parents guide for ages 10 to 20.* New York: Harper Perenniel.

Stephan, W. G. (1989). A cognitive approach to stereotyping. In D. Bartal, C. F. Graumann, A. W. Kruglanski, & W. Stroebe (Eds.), *Stereotyping and prejudice: Changing conceptions.* New York: Springer-Verlag.

Stern, S. B. (1999). Anger management in parent-adolescent conflict. *The American Journal of Family Therapy, 27,* 181–193.

Sternberg, R. (1985). Criteria for intellectual skills training. *Educational Researcher, 12,* 6–26.

Sternberg, R. (1998).Abilities are forms of developing expertise. *Educational Researcher, 27,* 3, 1120.

Stigler, J. W., Shweder, R. A., & Herdt, G. (1990). *Cultural psychology: Essays on comparative human development* (pp. 1–43). Cambridge: Cambridge University Press.

Suarez-Ojeda, N. (2001). Una concepcion latinoamericana: La resiliencia communitaria. [A Latin American concept: The resilient community.] In A. Mililo & N. Suarez-Ojeda (Eds.), *Resiliencia: Discubriendo las proprias fortalezas.* [Resilience: Discovering your inner strengths.] (pp. 67–82). Buenos Aires, Argentina, Paidos.

Swaffer, T. & Hollin, C. R. (1997). Adolescents' experiences of anger in a residential setting. *Journal of Adolescence, 20,* 567–575.

Swann, W. B. & Ely, R. J. (1984). A battle of wills: Self-verification versus behavioral confirmation. *Journal of Personality and Social Psychology, 46,* 1287–1302.

Swenson, C., Henggeler, S., Schoenwald, S., Kaufman, K., & Randall, J. (1998). Changing the social ecologies of adolescent sexual offenders: Implications of the success of multi-systemic therapy in treating serious anti-social behaviour in adolescents. *Child Maltreatment:- Journal of the American Professional Society on the Abuse of Children, 3,* 330–338.

Tagney, J. P., Hill-Barlow, D., Wagner, P. E. Marschall, D. E., Borenstein, J. P., Saftner, J., Mohr, T., & Gramzow, R. (1995). Assessing individual differences in constructive versus destructive responses to anger across the lifespan. *Journal of Personality and Social Psychology, 70,* 780–796.

Tajfel, H. (1982). *Social identity and intergroup relations.* London: Cambridge University Press.

Tappan, M. B. & Packer, M. J. (1991). Narrative and storytelling: Implications for understanding moral development. *New Directions for Child Development, 54,* 345–372.

Tardif, M. (2001). Sexual abuse perpetrated by women and female adolescents: The ultimate taboo. *Revue Quebecoise de Psychologie, 22,* 111–135.

Tate, D. C., Reppucci, N. D., & Mulvey, E. P. (1995). Violent juvenile delinquents. *American Psychologist, 50,* 777–781.

Teixeira, E. (1997). *Ocorrência de suicídio na região sudoeste do Paraná.* [Incidents of suicide in southeast Paraná.] Contato. CPR-08, Ano 17, 87.

Thorndike, E. (1917). Reading and reasoning: A study of mistakes in paragraph reading. *Journal of Educational Psychology, 8,* 323–332.

Thornton, B. (1992). Repression and its mediating influence on the defensive attribution of responsibility. *Journal of Research in Personality, 26,* 44–57.

Tietjen, A. M. & Walker, L. (1985). Moral reasoning and leadership among men in a Papua New Guinea society. *Developmental Psychology, 21,* 982–992.

Tillich, P. (1976). *A coragem de ser* (3rd ed.) [Courage to be.] Rio de Janeiro: Paz e Terra.

Tjas, K., Nelsen, E., & Taylor, M. (1993). Successful alumni as role models for high school youth. *High School Journal, 80,* 103–110.

Toch, T., Gest, T., & Guttman, M. (1993) Violence in schools, *U.S. News & World Report, 115,* (18), p. 30, citing data from Congressional Quarterly Researcher.

Trindade, J. (1996). *Delinqüência juvenil.* [Juvenile delinquency.] Porto Alegre: Artes Médicas.

Troyat, V. (1987). *Peter the great.* New York: Scribner.

Turner, J. C. (1987). *Rediscovering the social group: A self-categorization theory.* Oxford, England: Basil Blackwell.

Tyler, F. B., Tyler, S. L., Echeverry, J. J., & Zea, M. C. (1991). Making it on the streets in Bogota: A psychosocial study of street youth. *Genetic, Social and General Psychology Monographs, 117,* 395–417.

Tyler, K. & Cauce, A. (2002). Perpetrators of early physical and sexual abuse among homeless and runaway adolescents. *Child Abuse and Neglect, 26,* 1261–1274.

Tyson, P. D. (1998). Physiological arousal, reactive aggression, and the induction of an incompatible relaxation response. *Aggression and Violent Behavior, 3,* 143–158.

UNICEF United Nations Children's Fund. (1991). *The state of the world's children.* Oxford: Oxford University Press.

UNICEF United Nations Children's Fund. (1993). *The state of the world's children.* Oxford: Oxford University Press.

Vaillant, G. & Davis, T. (2000). Social/emotional intelligence in mid-life resilience in school boys with low-testing intelligence. *American Journal of Orthopsychiatry, 70,* 215–222.

Van Slyck, M., Stern, M., & Eldedour, S. (1999). Adolescent's beliefs about their conflict behaviors: Correlates, consequences and cross-cultural issues. In A. Raviv, L. Oppenheimer, & D. Bar-Tel (Eds.), *How children understand war and peace.* San Francisco: Jossey-Bass.References

Vasudev, J. (1994). Ahimsa, justice, and the unity of life: Postconventional morality from an Indian perspective. In M. E. Miller & S. R. Cook-Greuter (Eds.), *Transcendence and mature thought in adulthood: The further reaches of adult development* (pp. 237–255). Lanham, MD: Rowman & Littlefield.

Veneziano, C. & Veneziano, L. (2002). Adolescent sex offenders: A review of the literature. *Trauma, Violence, and Abuse, 3,* 247–260.

Veneziano, C., Veneziano, L., & Legrand, S. (2000). The relationship between adolescent sex offender behaviours and victim characteristics with prior victimisation. *Journal of Interpersonal Violence, 15,* 363–374.

Vergnes, M., Depaulo, A., & Boehrer, A. (1986). Parachlorophenylalinine-induced serotonin depletion increases offensive but not defensive aggression in male rats. *Physiological Behavior, 36,* 653–658.

Vizard, E. & Usiskin, J. (1999). Providing individual psychotherapy for young sexual abusers of children, In M. Book-Erooga & H. Masson (Eds.), *Children and young people who sexually abuse others: Challenges and responses.* New York: Taylor & Francis/Routledge Publishing.

Vizard, E., Monck, E., & Misch, P. (2001). Child and adolescent sex abuse perpetrators: A review of the research literature, In R. Book-Bull (Ed.), *Children and the law: The essential readings in developmental psychology.* London: Blackwell Publishers.

Von Baar, A. & Graaf, F. (1994). Cognitive development of preschool age infants of drug-dependent mothers. *Developmental Medical Child Neurology, 36,* 12, 1036–1075.

Wandersman, A. & Nation, M. (1998). Urban neighborhoods and mental health. *American Psychologist, 53,* 647–656.

Werner, E. & Smith, R.S. (1972). *Vulnerable but invincible: A study of resilient children.* New York: McGraw-Hill.

Werner, H. & Kaplan, B. (1963). *Symbol formation: An organismic-developmental approacht to language and expression of thought.* New York: Wiley, 1963.

Wertsch, J. (1987). *Vygotsky and the social formation of the mind.* Cambridge, MA: Harvard University Press.

Wheeler, E. D. & Baron, S. A. (1994). *Violence: In Our Schools, Hospitals, and Public Places.* Los Angeles: Pathfinder Publishing.

Wilcox, D. & Dowrick, P.W. (1992). Anger management with adolescents. *Residential Treatment for Children and Youth, 9,* 29–39.

Wolfgang, M., & Ferracuti, F. (1967). *The subculture of violence.* London: Tavistock.

Wood, C., Welman, M., & Netto, L. (2000). A profile of young sex offenders in South Africa. *Southern African Journal of Child and Adolescent Mental Health, 12,* 45–58.

Woods, J. (1997). Breaking the cycle of abuse and abusing: Individual psychotherapy for juvenile sex offenders. *Clinical Child Psychology and Psychiatry, 2,* 379–392.

Zainal, & Kling (1995). The Malay family—Beliefs and realities. *Journal of Comparative Family Studies, 26,* 43–66.

Zechmeister, E. & Johnson, J. (1992). *Critical thinking: A functional approach.* Pacific Grove, CA: Brooks/Cole Publishing.

Zeidler, D. (1984). Hierarchical relationships among formal cognitive structures and their relationship to principalled moral reasoning. *Journal of Research in Science Teaching, 22,* 5, 461–472.

Zhao-Xiong, H. & Lester, D. (1998). Methods for suicide in Mainland China. *Death Studies, 22,* 571–579.

Zimbardo, P. G. (2002, January). President's column: Going forward with commitment. *Monitor on Psychology, 33,* 5.

Zuckerman, B. (1993). Children exposed to cocaine prenatally: Pieces of the puzzle. *Neurotoxicology & Teratology, 15,* 281–312.

Zuckerman, B. & Frank, D. A. (1992). Crack kids: Not broken. *Pediatrics, 82,* 337–339.

Zuckerman, B. & Frank, D. A. (1994). Prenatal cocaine & marijuana exposure: Research and clinical implications. In I. Zaigon & T. Slotkin (Eds.), *Maternal substance abuse and neurodevelopment.* New York: Academic Press.

INDEX

ABOUT THE SERIES

As this new millennium dawns, humankind has evolved—some would argue has devolved—exhibiting new and old behaviors that fascinate, infuriate, delight, or fully perplex those of us seeking answers to the question, "Why?" In this series, experts from various disciplines peer through the lens of psychology telling us answers they see for questions of human behavior. Their topics may range from humanity's psychological ills—addictions, abuse, suicide, murder, and terrorism among them—to works focused on positive subjects including intelligence, creativity, athleticism, and resilience. Regardless of the topic, the goal of this series remains constant—to offer innovative ideas, provocative considerations, and useful beginnings to better understand human behavior.

Chris E. Stout
Series Editor

ABOUT THE SERIES EDITOR AND ADVISORY BOARD

CHRIS E. STOUT, Psy.D., MBA, is a licensed clinical psychologist and is a clinical full professor at the University of Illinois College of Medicine's Department of Psychiatry. He served as a nongovernmental organization special representative to the United Nations. He was appointed to the World Economic Forum's Global Leaders of Tomorrow, and he has served as an invited faculty at the annual meeting in Davos, Switzerland. He is the founding director of the Center for Global Initiatives. Stout is a fellow of the American Psychological Association, past president of the Illinois Psychological Association, and is a distinguished practitioner in the National Academies of Practice. Stout has published or presented over 300 papers and 30 books and manuals on various topics in psychology. His works have been translated into six languages. He has lectured across the nation and internationally in 19 countries and has visited six continents and almost 70 countries. He was noted as being "one of the most frequently cited psychologists in the scientific literature" in a study by Hartwick College. He is the recipient of the American Psychological Association's International Humanitarian Award.

BRUCE BONECUTTER, Ph.D., is Director of Behavioral Services at the Elgin Community Mental Health Center, the Illinois Department of Human Services state hospital serving adults in greater Chicago. He is also a clinical assistant professor of psychology at the University of

Illinois at Chicago. A clinical psychologist specializing in health, consulting, and forensic psychology, Bonecutter is a longtime member of the American Psychological Association Task Force on Children and the Family. He is a member of the Association for the Treatment of Sexual Abusers, International, the Alliance for the Mentally Ill, and the Mental Health Association of Illinois.

JOSEPH FLAHERTY, M.D., is chief of psychiatry at the University of Illinois Hospital, a professor of psychiatry at the University of Illinois College of Medicine, and a professor of community health science at the UIC College of Public Health. He is a founding member of the Society for the Study of Culture and Psychiatry. Flaherty has been a consultant to the World Health Organization, the National Institute of Mental Health, and the Falk Institute in Jerusalem. He's been director of undergraduate education and graduate education in the Department of Psychiatry at the University of Illinois. Flaherty has also been staff psychiatrist and chief of psychiatry at Veterans Administration West Side Hospital in Chicago.

MICHAEL HOROWITZ, Ph.D., is president and professor of clinical psychology at the Chicago School of Professional Psychology, one of the nation's leading not-for-profit graduate schools of psychology. Earlier, he served as dean and professor of the Arizona School of Professional Psychology. A clinical psychologist practicing independently since 1987, his work has focused on psychoanalysis, intensive individual therapy, and couples therapy. He has provided disaster mental health services to the American Red Cross. Horowitz's special interests include the study of fatherhood.

SHELDON I. MILLER, M.D., is a professor of psychiatry at Northwestern University, and director of the Stone Institute of Psychiatry at Northwestern Memorial Hospital. He is also director of the American Board of Psychiatry and Neurology, director of the American Board of Emergency Medicine, and director of the Accreditation Council for Graduate Medical Education. Miller is also an examiner for the American Board of Psychiatry and Neurology. He is founding editor of the *American Journal of Addictions* and founding chairman of the American Psychiatric Association's Committee on Alcoholism. Miller has also been a lieutenant commander in the military, serving as psychiatric consultant to the Navajo Area Indian Health Service at Window Rock, Arizona. He is a member and past president of the Executive Committee for the American Academy of Psychiatrists in Alcoholism and Addictions.

DENNIS P. MORRISON, Ph.D., is chief executive officer at the Center for Behavioral Health in Indiana, the first behavioral health company ever to win the Joint Commission on Accreditation of Health Care Organizations Codman Award for excellence in the use of outcomes management to achieve health care quality improvement. He is president of the board of directors for the Community Healthcare Foundation in Bloomington and has been a member of the board of directors for the American College of Sports Psychology. He has served as a consultant to agencies including the Ohio Department of Mental Health, Tennessee Association of Mental Health Organizations, Oklahoma Psychological Association, North Carolina Council of Community Mental Health Centers, and the National Center for Health Promotion in Michigan.

WILLIAM H. REID, M.D., is a clinical and forensic psychiatrist and a consultant to attorneys and courts throughout the United States. He is a clinical professor of psychiatry at the University of Texas Health Science Center. Reid is also an adjunct professor of psychiatry at Texas A&M College of Medicine and Texas Tech University School of Medicine, as well as a clinical faculty member at the Austin Psychiatry Residency Program. He is chairman of the Scientific Advisory Board and medical advisor to the Texas Depressive & Manic Depressive Association as well as an examiner for the American Board of Psychiatry and Neurology. He has served as president of the American Academy of Psychiatry and the Law, chairman of the research section for an International Conference on the Psychiatric Aspects of Terrorism, and medical director for the Texas Department of Mental Health and Mental Retardation. Reid earned an Exemplary Psychiatrist Award from the National Alliance for the Mentally Ill. He has been cited on the Best Doctors in America listing since 1998.

About the Authors

SHERRI N. MCCARTHY is Associate Professor of Educational Psychology, Northern Arizona University. She was a contributor to *The Psychology of Terrorism* (Praeger, 2002).

CLAUDIO SIMON HUTZ is Professor of Developmental Psychology, Universidade Federal do Rio Grande do Sul, Brazil.